KW-356-574

BUSINESS MERGERS
AND TAKE-OVER BIDS

WITHDRAWN
FROM
UNIVERSITY OF PLYMOUTH
LIBRARY SERVICES

90 0771985 4

BUSINESS MERGERS
AND TAKE-OVER BIDS

by

RONALD W. MOON
B.Litt.(Oxon.), F.C.A.

*A study of the post-war pattern of
amalgamations and reconstructions
of companies*

GEE & CO (PUBLISHERS) LIMITED
151 STRAND, LONDON WC2R 1JJ

FIRST PUBLISHED 1959
SECOND EDITION 1960
THIRD EDITION 1968
FOURTH EDITION 1971
FIFTH EDITION 1976

© GEE & CO (PUBLISHERS) LIMITED

SBN 85258 153 X

PLYMOUTH POLYTECHNIC
LEARNING RESOURCES CENTRE

ACCN.
No.   50666 - X

CLASS 338.83
No.   MOO

Cntrl. No. 085258 153 X
-0. SEP. 1977

Made and printed in Great Britain by
GEE & CO (PUBLISHERS) LIMITED, LONDON AND ST ALBANS

CONTENTS

PREFACE TO FIRST EDITION

Business mergers and take-over bids have been very much in the news in recent years. The formal merger might be described as amalgamation by consent of all the parties involved but brought to fruition, as a rule only after protracted negotiations. On the other hand, the take-over bid – largely a product of the inflationary conditions of the post-war period – is initiated by one of the parties and frequently put through without any preliminary discussion. Although gaining the consent of the members, it often takes effect with the grudging approval (and sometimes outright disapproval) of the directors of the company or companies being acquired.

Both are, therefore, symptomatic of the society in which we live, For an economic system such as ours, where free enterprise still holds sway, is necessarily in a perpetual state of flux, functioning by a process of increasing adaptation to an environment which is constantly dissolving and reforming. In this way, the individual branches of industry are always growing or shrinking, to the accompaniment of some social upheaval and distress. Even so, long-term trends in industry cannot be arrested except by frustrating or denying altogether the benefits to be obtained from economic progress.

In the long run, therefore, there is no real solution to the take-over bid, dividend-stripping, the 'loss' company and the 'shell'. They are all the inevitable consequences of various restraints imposed upon the normal workings of the economic system from time to time. If recent events have accomplished nothing more than show politicians and the public alike just how economic forces will ultimately overrule physical and legal controls, they will have served a useful purpose.

R. W. M.

LONDON, *October 1958.*

PREFACE TO SECOND EDITION

Mergers and take-over bids have remained firmly in the forefront of public discussion ever since the publication of the first edition. Recent legislative and other changes, however, call for some revision of the text. In particular, the Capital Issues Committee has been put into cold storage so far as domestic new issues are concerned; the bid for British Aluminium – that *cause célèbre* among take-overs – brought several important issues to a head; publication of the 'City's' code of procedure for bids created quite a stir in financial circles; non-voting shares have been the subject of much critical discussion; shares of no par value have come up for another airing; finally, the coincidence of the Jasper affair and a General Election brought the promise of an official inquiry into the working of the Companies Act 1948 (with take-over bids singled out for special attention).

In deference to many requests, an index has been included with this edition.

R. W. M.

November 1959.

PREFACE TO THIRD EDITION

The text has been revised so as to reflect those changes in law and practice which have come into effect since 1959. In particular, attention is drawn to the terms of the Monopolies and Mergers Act 1965, and the text of 'The City Code on Take-overs and Mergers' published in 1968.

In addition, consideration of the defensive measures that can be mounted against a bid and the economic and political issues posed by foreign bids are now dealt with in separate chapters.

R. W. M.

March 1968.

PREFACE TO FOURTH EDITION

The opportunity has arisen for dealing with the revised text of the 'City Code' and the Department of Trade and Industry's (previously the Board of Trade) policy guidelines on mergers, both published in 1969.

The dissolution of the Industrial Reorganization Corporation and the Prices and Incomes Board following the change of Government in June 1970, also calls for comment.

The growth of multinational companies is bound to excite more and more interest now that Britain appears to be on the brink of joining the Common Market, and the issues involved here are fully explored.

Finally, due attention is given to the A.S.S.C.'s controversial exposure draft on *Accounting for Acquisitions and Mergers* which was published early in 1971.

R. W. M.

July 1971.

PREFACE TO FIFTH EDITION

Take-over bids first made their bow on the financial scene as long ago as 1951. This new edition, therefore, faithfully mirrors the changes in merger motives, the law and the voluntary regulations which have taken place over the past twenty-five years and includes the latest version of the 'City Code' published in April 1976.

In order to amplify certain matters, common to all take-overs, the opportunity has been taken to introduce a separate chapter dealing specifically with the contents of the offer document and, additionally, a selection of typical examination questions has been included in an Appendix.

R. W. M.

April 1976.

CHAPTER I

INTRODUCTION

Take-over bids first erupted upon the financial scene in 1951/52. Prior to that time, the formal amalgamation, generally known as a scheme of arrangement under S.206, Companies Act, 1948, had long held sway. The latter could perhaps be described as a 'marriage by consent' in the sense that the scheme evolved as a result of lengthy – and friendly – negotiations between the two parties, separate class meetings were required at which three-quarters of the shareholders by value needed to signify their approval to the scheme and finally the scheme had to be sanctioned by the Court.

The take-over bid, by contrast, could be best described as a 'shot-gun marriage'. Very often, there has been no previous contact between the two parties, the offer is put to the general body of ordinary, and sometimes preference, shareholders as well, despite vocal and written opposition to the bid made by the directors, and in the final analysis a simple 50·1 per cent of acceptances is enough to change the legal control of the company, although most offers are conditional upon acceptance by a much higher percentage of shareholders. For instance, 90 per cent acceptance level would enable the bidder to acquire the remaining 10 per cent by compulsory acquisition.

What then gave impetus to the take-over technique and why did the method of acquisition first come into prominence in 1951/52?

There are a number of reasons which, in a collective sense, help to explain the birth of the take-over phenomenon. First, a long period of voluntary dividend restraint came to an end with a change of government in 1951. During and after the war, therefore, dividend payments had failed to keep pace with the growth in profits. Thus profits in 1952 were 3·2 times their 1938 level, whereas dividends were only 1·2 times the pre-war figure.

Secondly, some assets, particularly freehold and leasehold property and quoted investments, all included at original cost in the Balance Sheet were grossly undervalued as a result of 12 years of wartime and post-war inflation.

Thirdly, most companies were more than well supplied with cash. In fact cash was, in a sense, being hoarded, because of shortages of new plant and equipment (much of which was being exported) and as result of the rationing of raw materials – through official rationing schemes during the war years and unofficial rationing procedures in the immediate post-war years.

All these factors together tended to depress the market price of quoted ordinary shares or to put it another way round, the market price did not respond to the intrinsic or concealed value of company assets. The very special circumstances, therefore, provided almost unprecedented opportunities for a few shrewd, far-sighted and aggressive businessmen to embark upon a series of deals which transformed the whole merger milieu almost overnight.

Indeed, the 1952–55 stock market boom and the so-called 'boardroom revolution' of those days was often blamed upon the dramatic series of take-over bids which captured the newspaper headlines during that period. The original select band of bidders, Charles Clore, Hugh Fraser, Harold Samuel and Isaac Wolfson[1] were much in the public eye in those early days when take-over techniques were being devised and refined. Hugh Fraser, for example, was credited with the financing of cash offers by the so-called 'leapfrog' method or sale/leaseback property transaction as it is better known today. Charles Clore was also adept at using this particular procedure. Moreover Clore, Fraser and Wolfson all made frequent use of non-voting ordinary shares when presenting the content and terms of an offer for approval, thereby giving credence to the cult of the 'voteless equity' as it was known at the time.

Meanwhile, the original exponents of the take-over technique, or in Lord Fraser's case his son, are still active today on the take-over front but in the 1960's and 1970's they were joined by a new generation of bidders, prominent among whom were such redoubtable characters as Jim Slater, James Hanson, Oliver Jessel, Nigel Broackes, Jimmy Goldsmith, Maxwell Joseph and Pat Matthews.

When companies coalesce or firms unite in some form, the result is variously described as an 'absorption', 'amalgamation', 'fusion', 'merger' or 'take-over'. While all these terms are used from time to time in business and financial circles, they are all, unfortunately, terms of art without any clear or precise legal meaning. Indeed, the word 'takeover' according to one respected financial journalist was originally coined by a hard-pressed sub-editor who was desperately searching for a synonym for 'amalgamation'[2]. Nevertheless, Halsbury defines amalgamation as 'a blending of two or more existing undertakings into one undertaking, the shareholders of each blending company becoming substantially the shareholders in the company which is to carry on the blended undertakings. There may be amalgamation either by the transfer of two or more undertakings to a new company, or by the transfer of one or more undertakings

---

[1] Sir Charles Clore (Sears Holdings); Lord Samuel (Land Securities); Sir Isaac Wolfson (Great Universal Stores) and the late Lord Fraser (the House of Fraser and Scottish and Universal Investments Ltd).
[2] *Financial Advertising & Public Relations* by P. Biddlesombe. Business Books Ltd, page 197.

to an existing company'.[1] Although, therefore, the word 'amalgamation' is probably the one most commonly used by the business community when referring to a unification of interests, the word 'merger' has been preferred here because it seems better suited to embrace the wide range of ways and means by which that union may be achieved.

At this point, however, it is not inappropriate to mention the Accounting Standards Steering Committee's exposure draft on 'Accounting for Acquisitions and Mergers', published in January 1971 (but later withdrawn when it ran into a conflict of opinion over the accounting treatment of goodwill as well as doubts about the legal implications under the then current company law). The Committee made a valiant attempt to draw a subtle distinction between a merger and an acquisition. In this context, a merger is said to represent a continuation of the former ownership of the business of the amalgamating companies, while an acquisition involves substantial changes in the ownership and business of at least one of the companies. The definition also includes a size test which caused a good deal of disquiet among industrial accountants.

Perhaps the truth of the matter is that one cannot hope for more than a pragmatic rule at this moment of time so long as accounting concepts themselves are in a state of flux, particularly with regard to the changing purchasing power value of money.

Economists have, for long, studied the implications of amalgamations and mergers within the setting of monopoly, or, to be more exact, imperfect competition. They allude to 'combines', 'cartels', 'trusts' in the same context, but again these terms are merely indicative of the formation of groups within national boundaries or on an international scale, hence the forign terms sometimes used, cartel (German – kartel), trust (United States).

Furthermore, three broad types of integration are distinguished – the 'vertical integration' and 'horizontal integration' and diversified or 'conglomerate' mergers.

The former denotes a merger between business at different stages of production or distribution, i.e., a manufacturing concern may merge with another firm producing, say, its main raw material, so as to assure itself of uninterrupted supplies, of the right quality in the required quantities. Or moving the other way, a manufacturing firm may decide to invade the wholesale or retail trades, either selling its products in bulk to middlemen or actually selling direct to the public. In either case, the firm aims to secure a foothold in the marketing of its product, and often the right to determine the eventual selling price. In short, 'vertical integration' means the

[1] Halsbury's *Laws of England*, Third edition, Volume 6, Part 3, section 20, paragraph 1547, page 764.

linking of a series of processes in manufacture from the raw material to the finished product.

'Horizontal integration', on the other hand, indicates that firms doing the same kind of work are linked together. Thus, the combination is generally one between businesses of the same type, i.e., between two or more manufacturing firms in the same trade or between several retailers.

'Conglomerate' or diversified mergers though not exactly a new phenomenon represent a relatively new field of interest, and policy in regard to them is still unclear. Indeed, there is no generally accepted definition by which a conglomerate merger can be distinguished from certain kinds of horizontal or vertical mergers. A pure conglomerate may be said to occur when one company takes over another in a totally different industry, with no important common factors between them in production, marketing, research and development or technology. Such mergers result in no reduction in competition and it might, therefore, seem to follow that they could be disregarded or, perhaps, be left to the regulating powers of the market, the commercial judgment of the firms concerned and the attitude of the shareholders.

However, conglomerate mergers have certain additional features. The first is that there are no obvious natural limits to the size which conglomerates can attain or – relying here upon American experience – to the speed with which they can develop. Rapid growth and giant size companies are not in themselves undesirable attributes; but they attract attention (often adverse) and may force other firms to take defensive measures of an undesirable nature. The 'General Observations on Mergers' which the Monopolies Commission submitted in 1969 with its reports on the Unilever/Allied Breweries and Rank/De la Rue mergers are relevant here. In particular the Commission drew attention to the need for more financial information so as to assist in the proper assessment of past performance and merger prospects. The Commission went on to suggest that companies might be called upon to provide separate accounting information for distinct types of business contained in one group.

At present, published financial information is almost wholly confined to the quoted public company sector and quarterly analyses are given in the *Board of Trade Journal*[1] – carrying on the initial spadework undertaken by the National Institute of Economic and Social Research between 1949 and 1953.

Horizontal mergers are by far the largest type of market structure but it is interesting to observe that diversified or conglomerate mergers have made some headway since 1965.

But looking beyond this static information, one wonders whether

[1] Now called *Trade and Industry* after the new department of that name.

Analysis by Type of Integration

	1965 %	1966 %	1967 %	1968 %
Horizontal	73	83	89	83
Vertical	17	9	—	3
Diversified	10	8	11	14
Total	100	100	100	100
(Of which acquisitions by foreign owned companies)	9	9	2	8

Source: *Board of Trade Guide to Mergers*, 1969.

the giants are strengthening their position or whether the trend is going the opposite way. From their own observations, most people would, no doubt, be inclined to hazard a guess that industrial concentration is increasing rather than decreasing. And that view is borne out in another investigation made by N.I.E.S.R.[1] Using a very different measuring rod – market valuations of companies, rather than balance sheet values – this study suggests that in the sector of the economy operated by public companies (which, incidentally, has shown a striking growth in the last half-century) the market valuation of the shares of the larger companies tended to increase, in comparison with that of the smaller companies, from 1885 to 1939. Thereafter there was a small decline between 1939 and 1950 due, doubtless, to war-time restrictions in rationing and post-war shortages, which may have given a fillip to the smaller business at the expense of the big firm.

The authors of this paper, in discussing the influence of amalgamations, however, suggest that in studying changes in business concentration over time more attention should be paid to the internal growth of firms than to the possibility of combination among firms.[2] They reach this conclusion by examining the distribution of a sample number of amalgamations as shown in the following table (which gives the number of firms, the mean and variance of the logarithms of their sizes at the beginning of the period in which the amalgamation took place, and the corresponding values after amalgamation):

TABLE I
Statistics of firms involved in amalgamation
Units: $\log^2$

	1885–96 Before	After	1896–1907 Before	After	1907–24 Before	After
Number	Nil		11	5	40	13
Mean	Nil		1·18	2·20	1·15	3·54
Variance	Nil		5·47	6·56	5·18	3·01

	1924–39 Before	After	1939–50 Before	After
Number	58	25	109	50
Mean	1·59	3·24	1·93	4·00
Variance	6·30	5·06	6·93	4·52

[1] *The Analysis of Business Concentration: A Statistical Approach*, by P. E. Hart and S. J. Prais. Read before the Royal Statistical Society on February 15th, 1956.
[2] Results which conform with a more detailed examination of mergers in the United States by Lintner and Butlers (1950). *Review of Economics and Statistics*.

The data showed that the firms involved in amalgamations were of larger than average size even before amalgamation; and, further, that the rate of amalgamation hardly changed throughout, about 7 per cent of quoted firms being involved in a fifteen-year period. In their view, while the level of business concentration certainly tends to increase in consequence of amalgamations, the amount of change is quite small in comparison with changes due to internal growth.

Another study also conducted at the N.I.E.S.R. was based on an analysis of the concentration-ratios indicating the shares of Census of Production Trades controlled by the largest business units in 1951
As the authors point out:[1]

'The degree of concentration in a particular trade depends, to some extent, on the way in which it is defined. In general, the more broadly an industry is defined (that is, the greater the number and range of the principal products that comprise it) the higher will be the number of business units included and the lower will be its concentration-ratio. Thus concentration-ratios for individual products are frequently higher than the concentration-ratio for the trade of which they form part.

'Furthermore, the choice of categories of concentration to which trades may be classified must be somewhat arbitrary. There is no established definition of 'high' or 'low' concentration which can be used. For our purposes, however, it is convenient to distinguish three categories of employment and/or net output concentration by which trades can be classified:
(a) high concentration (67 per cent and over);
(b) medium concentration (34–66 per cent);
(c) low concentration (33 per cent and under).
'In the table below, the 220 trades which have been selected for the 1951 analysis are arranged according to these three categories of concentration, and the relative importance of the trades in the three categories is shown by their aggregated employment. Thus, it can be seen that the fifty high concentration trades (or more than one-fifth of the total number of trades) account for only 10 per cent of the total employment in the 220 trades, while the sixty-nine medium concentration trades (or just under one-third of the total number) account for another 24 per cent of the total employment. The largest concentration category, both in terms of the number of trades and total employment, comprises 101 low-concentration trades, representing 46 per cent of all trades and 66 per cent of total employment.'

TABLE II
DISTRIBUTION OF 220 TRADES BY CONCENTRATION CATEGORY, 1951

Concentration category (employment or net output)			Trades No.	% of total	Employment 000s	% of total
High (67 per cent and over)	..	..	50	23	636	10
Medium (34–66 per cent) ..	..	..	69	31	1,545	24
Low (33 per cent and under)	..	..	101	46	4,188	66
TOTAL	..	..	220	100	6,369	100

[1] *Concentration in British Industry*, by R. Evely and I. M. D. Little, Cambridge University Press, 1960.

Commenting on the high-concentration trades, the authors make three points.

First, the number of business units in the great majority of these high-concentration trades is relatively small. Thus, only thirteen of the fifty high-concentration trades have more than thirty units, and among the others are eight where the units are ten or under (including three for which the Board of Trade concentration-ratios are 100 per cent), and twenty-nine with eleven to thirty units.

Secondly, the size of the trades in terms of employment varies considerably, for the smallest has an employment of 800 persons and the largest 46,000.

Thirdly, the high-concentration trades are very varied in their type of activity. They include producer goods trades, such as transmission chains, cement, and wrought-iron and steel tubes, as well as such consumer trades as razors, wallpaper, margarine and bicycles.

In attempting to explain this phenomenon, the authors suggest that there is a variety of obstacles to new entry and to growth which appear to be significant in the case of high-concentration trades. Nevertheless, firms do enter many of the high-concentration trades, and firms do grow despite the obstacles and difficulties. 'But', they observe, 'it may be easier to enter the trade by purchasing a going concern than by starting from scratch, though it may still need considerable financial resources to grow after that.' As they point out, the firm that has grown in the soap trade to the extent of reducing the share controlled by Unilever was Thomas Hedley, after it had been acquired by one of the leading American soap concerns Procter & Gamble. As an example of the maintenance of concentration, one may point to the situation now where the battle is still being waged on the detergent front.

More recent research undertaken by Dr S. Aaronovitch and Malcolm C. Sawyer carries the story a stage further,[1] but, as they point out, regrettably the publication of the 1968 Census of Production results took place only in the summer of 1974, so with a few exceptions the statistical story has to end in 1968.

It seems that each census of production has reported the data in a somewhat different way, which means that the precise number of firms and the measuring rod for size (sales, employment or output) has varied from period to period. As a result, it is virtually impossible to make direct and precise comparisons between the position in 1935 and that in 1968. Nevertheless, the authors tried to give some indication of the trend over the period in question. The measure of concentration which they used in their article is the *concentration ratio*, i.e. the percentage of an industry's sales, em-

[1] The Concentration of British Manufacturing, Lloyd's Bank Review, October, 1974, No. 114.

16   BUSINESS MERGERS AND TAKE-OVER BIDS

ployment or output accounted for by a number of large firms. Thus, a four-firm concentration ratio of 70 per cent means that the four largest firms account for 70 per cent of the industry's sales or employment or output. Using this basis, the rates of change in concentration 1935–1968 were presented in the following table.

RATES OF CHANGE IN CONCENTRATION 1935–1968

	1935–51 %	1951–58 %	1958–63 %	1963–68 %
Annual change-over period	+7·22	+5·21	+8·27	+8·66
Annual rate of change	0·44	0·73	1·60	1·67

This indicates that the annual rate of change has nearly quadrupled between the first and the last periods. As they point out, if the same rate of increase of concentration shown in 1958–68 has continued up to 1974 then the average level of *five-firm* concentration would stand at 76 per cent compared with an estimated 52 per cent in 1935. Separately published information regarding acquisitions tends to confirm the figure of 76 per cent and supports the impression that acquisitions have played a very important part in increasing concentration, particularly since 1958. One fact is quite clear, however, the 1950's marked the beginning of a prolonged period of acceleration in concentration in manufacturing industry.

During 1958–63, larger than average increases in concentration were to be found in food, drink, paper, printing and publishing. In the next period, 1963–68, metal manufacturing, electrical engineering, textiles, bricks, pottery, glass and cement exhibited above average increases.

As the authors observe: 'It is likely that these above average increases in concentration were associated with the merger booms of these years.'

The first statistical series on the subject of mergers and acquisitions specifically dealt with the period 1954–68, where the data was obtained as a by-product of the annual analysis of some 2,000 quoted company accounts, undertaken by the Board of Trade. The analysis specifically excluded companies mainly operating abroad and agricultural, shipping, insurance, banking, finance and property companies[1].

The second statistical series began in 1969 and covered the analysis of acquisitions and mergers of industrial and commercial companies in the United Kingdom based upon reports in the financial press supplemented by special inquiries to determine the form, value and timing of particular acquisitions.

Moreover, acquisitions and mergers involving financial com-

[1] A discussion of the information available under the first series was contained in an article *Acquisitions and Mergers of Companies in Trade and Industry*, 26th August, 1971.

panies (insurance, banking, etc) are the subject of a separate analysis prepared by the Bank of England and published in the Bank of England Quarterly Bulletin and Financial Statistics.

TABLE III

EXPENDITURE ON ACQUISITIONS AND MERGERS OF
INDUSTRIAL AND COMMERCIAL COMPANIES, 1969–1975

Year				No. of companies acquired	Total consideration £m	Average consideration £m
1969	..	..	..	..	846	1,069	1·3
1970	..	..	..	..	793	1,122	1·5
1971	..	..	..	..	884	911	1·0
1972	..	..	..	..	1,210	2,532	2·1
1973	..	..	..	..	1,205	1,304	1·0
1974	..	..	..	..	504	508	1·0
1975	..	..	..	..	315	291	0·9

(Source: Business Monitor, M.7, H.M.S.O.)

Altogether, nearly 15,000 companies (of which perhaps as many as 1,500 were themselves quoted companies) were acquired by quoted public companies for a total consideration of just under £14,000m during the twenty-two year span 1954–75, which witnessed the birth and subsequent adoption of the take-over technique on an ever-increasing scale.

Up until 1966, the average consideration was well under £0·5m, but from then on, the average consideration more than doubled, reaching a peak of £2·8m in the 1968 'merger boom' before falling back again to around the £1·0m average until the next record year for mergers, 1972 (a record year whether judged on the basis of absolute numbers or on the value of the total consideration), when, once again, average consideration crossed the £2·0m mark. Since then, merger activity has declined in the wake of the deep economic recession at home and abroad and at a time when the Financial Times ordinary share index plummeted from a point above 500 to a low point of 146 at the beginning of 1975.

Whether the absorption of one company by another represents an increase in business concentration or the diversification of the acquiring company's interests depends to some extent on the degree of refinement of the statistical classifications used.

Some light is thrown on the situation in the latest survey of mergers prepared by the staff of the Monopolies Commission[1] which deals with the period 1958–68.

In the period of eleven years to the end of 1968 the number of 'large' companies decreased from 2,024 to 1,253 – a reduction of 771 or 38 per cent. The largest reductions in numbers occurred in the textiles, drink, non-electrical engineering and wholesale distribution classifications. The largest reductions expressed as percentages of

[1] Department of Trade and Industry, H.M.S.O., 1970

numbers at the end of 1957 were in drink (63 per cent) and food (54 per cent).

However, after making adjustments for 'natural' growth, there appears to be little change in the pattern of acquired companies judged by their size and number.

The complete table is given below:

TABLE IV

NET ASSETS AND NUMBER OF COMPANIES IN POPULATION

	Net Assets end 1967 £m	Reduction 1957–68 No.	Reduction as % of 1957
Textiles	1,214	88	41
Drink	1,825	85	63
Non-electrical manufacturing ..	1,246	82	36
Wholesale distribution ..	702	71	38
Electrical engineering	1,567	47	42
Retail distribution	1,447	47	33
Food	1,014	46	54
Chemicals and allied	2,883	39	45
Paper, printing and publishing	1,257	36	33
Bricks, pottery, glass, etc. ..	686	36	43
Miscellaneous services	592	34	38
Metal n.e.s.	712	32	29
Vehicles	1,012	28	44
Clothing and footwear	362	25	37
Metal manufacture	692	21	27
Other manufacturing	459	16	29
Construction	278	11	20
Shipbuilding	162	10	37
Transport	382	8	23
Timber, furniture	129	7	17
Tobacco	620	1	12
Leather and fur	18	1	8
Total	£19,203	771	38

Professor J. K. Galbraith alluded to the new industrial state in the course of the 1966 Reith Lectures.[1]

'The last seventy years, and especially those since Hitler's war, have been a time of great change in the basic arrangement of economic life. Merely to list these changes will assure you that I have a firm grasp of the commonplace. Machines have extensively replaced crude man-power, and one machine increasingly instructs other machines in the process we call automation. Industrial companies or corporations have become very large. They are no longer directed by great entrepreneurs as a right of ownership. They deploy large amounts of capital much of which they derive from their own earnings. This is now the important modern source of savings. We do not allow income needed for industrial expansion to get into the hot and eager hands of those who might use it for personal consumption.'

He was even more forthright in his views about the modern corporation:

[1] *The Listener*, November 17th, 1966.

'Economists have anciently quarrelled over the reasons for the great size of the modern corporation. Is it because size is essential in order to reap the economies of modern large-scale production? Is it, more insidiously, because the big firm wishes to exercise monopoly power in its markets? There is little truth in both these shop-worn answers. The firm must be large enough to carry the large capital commitments of modern technology. It must also be large enough to control its markets. But the modern firm is larger than these purposes require. Why is this? And why, although it is large enough to have the market power associated with monopoly, is it that consumers do not complain excessively about exploitation? We have here the answer. The great size of General Motors, though it allows the economies of scale and the control of markets, is primarily in the service of planning. And for this planning – control of supply, control of demand, control of capital supply, absorption or minimization of risk where it cannot be avoided – there is no clear upper limit to the desirable size. It could be that the bigger the better.

'A prime requirement of the planning authority is control over its own decisions. Decisions come not from individuals but from groups. The groups are numerous, as often informal as formal, and subject to constant change in composition.'[1]

One cannot escape the awesome conclusion that, given good management, the modern corporation to a large extent controls its own destiny, though it cannot altogether escape the slings and arrows of economic fortune. However, Professor G. C. Allen, holder of the chair of political economy at London University, takes issue with some of Professor Galbraith's conclusions.[2] He produces a table of United Kingdom companies' earnings on capital employed over the last ten years which goes a long way to demolish the argument that bigness in any one industry is a sure sign of a steady or increasing return on capital employed, regardless of management ability and consumer preference.

'How', asks Professor Allen, 'can you reconcile this with the Galbraith idea that big business can virtually plan to make what profits it chooses to a point where profit-making is no longer the major preoccupation of the board?'

Professor Allen insists that there is competition – either actual or potential – and any business that thinks otherwise is in for a rude awakening. Although the consumer may not be king any more, it seems that he still commands unbounded respect!

---

[1] *The Listener*, November 24th, 1966.
[2] *Economic Fact and Fantasy*, Institute of Economic Affairs, March 1967.

CHAPTER II

MERGERS – THE PROS AND CONS

A number of benefits or advantages are said to stem from mergers, some of them real enough, and others, perhaps, rather more ephemeral in their effect. In many ways, the precise advantages claimed for mergers depend so much on the timing of the event. For instance, some advantages may be identified directly with adverse conditions of trade, viz. concentration of production and the closing down of excess capacity during a trade depression. While, in other and more prosperous times, the advantages may lie in the additional spare capacity brought into use immediately, during a period of expanding trade or the opportunity of buying out an established firm at a price which is considerably below that entailed in erecting new buildings and installing new plant and machinery at current prices. In short, the benefits to be gained from mergers may vary according to the economic climate in which they are born. Thus a merger which was negotiated pre-war during a period which witnessed the sharp ups and downs of the trade cycle coupled with a persistently high level of unemployment might well rest upon certain advantages which would appear to conflict with those attributable, say, to post-war mergers brought to fruition during a period when full, and sometimes over-full, employment existed together with excessive demand on resources caused by inflation. Even so, there are many advantages and disadvantages to be found which are common to both sets of circumstances.

Before discussing the relative advantages and disadvantages, however, something must first be said about the background – the history of industry – which so often provides the *raison d'etre* for mergers.

At the beginning of the Industrial Revolution, industry and commerce in this country consisted largely of one-man businesses, or possibly a partnership of two or three men, with ten or a dozen craftsmen or journeymen working for them. With the advent of the Industrial Revolution the unit became larger, and this tendency was given further impetus by the creation of the joint-stock company. Seen in this light, the subsequent era of business integration when firms grew out of their restricted local connections seeking national, and even international markets, is not difficult to understand.[1]

[1] For an interesting historical study of the trend towards mergers during the past hundred years or so in the cement, calico printing, soap, flat-glass, motor and brewing industries, readers are referred to *Effects of Mergers*, by P. Lesley Cook. Allen & Unwin, 1958.

Confronted over the years with a succession of booms and slumps, wars, bad harvests and good harvests, shortages and a surfeit of raw materials, almost all established firms have experienced a somewhat chequered history. Sometimes drastic measures have been imposed like capital reduction, reconstruction or at worst a liquidation. On the other hand, some firms have emerged, not only unscathed, but immeasurably strengthened by merger with weaker competitors. These changes have, in their turn, set in motion parallel mergers in other branches of industry and trade. Nowhere is this more in evidence than in the banking world where the process of concentration saw the number of banks in England reduced from some 400 in 1857 to about 40 by 1918.

'By the end of the nineteenth century the great changes which were to culminate in the formation of the Big Five had begun. In 1860 there were still about forty-six private banks in London, but a movement towards amalgamation had already set in. The size of business firms was in many cases outpacing the growth in size of the banks, and this factor, no doubt, hastened the bank amalgamations which were beginning to take place. The First World War resulted in many more industrial amalgamations of firms into very large capitalized units, and in order to meet the situation further bank amalgamations and absorptions took place. A Treasury Committee reported in 1918 that while it saw no objection to further absorptions of local banks, no further amalgamations between the big banks ought to take place.'[1]

Evidently, the process of amalgamation is not yet completely exhausted in the banking field for back in 1957 a merger was arranged between the National Bank of Scotland and the Commercial Bank of Scotland Ltd. The boards of the two banks and of Lloyds Bank (which is the principal shareholder of the National Bank) were all agreed that a merger of shareholders' interests would be beneficial 'having in mind the general banking position in Scotland'.[2] It was felt that in spite of the other amalgamations that had taken place in Scotland in recent years, further rationalization of that banking system was desirable to meet the challenge of modern conditions, and this came about early in 1968 with the merger of Scotland's two largest banks – the Royal Bank of Scotland and the National Commercial Bank of Scotland. In England, too the process has some way to go as the National Provincial Bank took over the District Bank in 1962 only to be merged itself with the Westminster Bank in 1968. The latter went on to acquire Lombard Banking in 1969. Meanwhile, Barclays merged with Martins and Lloyds linked up with the Bank of London and South America.

Then in 1971, Barclays Bank bid £80 million – in a mixture of shares and unsecured loan stock – for the 43·5 per cent of Barclays D.C.O. which it did not already hold.

[1] *The City*, by E. C. Ellinger, page 115.
[2] *The Times*, October 29th, 1957.

One might also hazard a guess that growing competition from foreign – particularly American – banks, economizing in staff and premises, preparing for expensive computer installations and having the resources to cater for the industrial giants of today, may have prompted this and other bank mergers.

Meantime, the Bank of England has placed a ban on any further mergers involving clearing banks or Scottish banks.

The birth of the joint-stock liability company was also a major factor in the development of large-scale capitalist industry. More than a century has passed since that prime instrument of economic growth, the Limited Liability Act of 1855, reached the Statute Book. As from that date, the limitation of the shareholder's liability to the amount of his subscription was first made a general right instead of a rare privilege. Before 1855, limited liability was still available only by private Acts of Parliament or by letters patent granted in practice by the Board of Trade, which could limit the liability of members at its discretion. Even so, the idea of limited liability was repugnant to many and the Act of 1855 was vehemently opposed at the time, the main argument being that general limited liability was not needed because capital in the United Kingdom was plentiful and freely available. They were, however, hopelessly wrong in their views, for the need was subsequently proved by the use made of it.

'Registrations of limited liability companies grew from 276 in 1858, to 691 in 1863, 1,034 in 1879, and over 1,600 a year in 1881–83. From 1885 onwards full returns were made by the Registrar of Companies. In that year the capital of the railway companies incorporated by Act of Parliament was £816 million, and that of the other companies – on the Registrar's list – £495 million. By 1912, while the railway capital had been less than doubled, the capital of the companies on the Registrar's list had increased nearly fivefold to £2,335 million.'[1]

Since then, the nominal capital of limited liability companies has risen sharply in spite of the nationalization of other industries besides the railways. By the end of 1965, the number of public companies with a share capital was 10,867 having a total issued capital of £12,057 million. Moreover, the total number of companies on the register has more than doubled since 1950, passing the half-million mark during 1965. In 1964 alone, 48,315 new companies were registered in Great Britain – the highest number in any year since records were started over one hundred years ago. It is, perhaps, significant that over 80 per cent of all companies registered in the United Kingdom were then classified as 'exempt' private companies, so their trading results and financial position remained very much a closed book as far as the general public were concerned.

[1] *A Hundred Years of 'Ltd'. The Times*, December 9th, 1965.

The abolition of exempt private company status under the Companies Act 1967, therefore, represented a complete break with the past. Henceforth private limited companies fell into line with public companies as regards filing a copy of their annual report and accounts and the disclosure of information therein (unless, of course, they choose the escape route provided of re-registering as unlimited companies).

Meanwhile, it is significant that the rate of creation of new companies has slowed down since the Finance Act 1965 removed many of the previous tax advantages of limited company status.[1]

In most countries the amount of any individual's private capital has diminished and simultaneously the optimum size of industrial units has greatly increased. The ability to raise huge capitals in relatively small individual sums has been indispensable to this end. In this country, at any rate, the long chain of committees and Companies Acts have severly curtailed – if not entirely eliminated – the opportunities for fraud and irresponsibility. Although many companies have fallen by the wayside during the course of time, the ones that have managed to stay the course have often expanded and developed as much through mergers on the way along as through internal growth from retained profits. The First World War and its aftermath gave some impetus to the merger movement, particularly among the basic industries. In the tin-plate industry, for instance, we learn that in the nineteen-twenties, the concentration of ownership reduced the number of independent tin-plate producers.

'The movement, a limited one which ceased in 1926, was a consequence not of technical requirements but of the expansion of steel production in South Wales during the war and of the economic climate of the post-war years. It was one phase of the movement which was visible throughout the British steel industry once the reconstruction boom had passed: the acquisition by steel producers of increased and assured outlets for their expanded steel capacity. Combination was vertical, there being no instances of horizontal integration, of mergers which involved tin-plate makers alone. So far as the tin-plate industry was concerned the pre-war position was reversed. Then there had been investment by tin-plate firms in steel production to secure supplies of tin-plate bar; after 1918 steel firms integrated forward to secure outlets for their steel.'[2]

Later on, in 1945, the claims of modernization led to the merger of two leading firms in the industry, Richard Thomas, which had itself grown through a series of mergers, and Baldwins Ltd.

Much the same story of mergers and reconstructions can be recounted by almost every other industry since they all experienced,

---

[1] The total number of registered companies is now over 600,000 of which 583,000 of them are private.
[2] *The British Tinplate Industry*, by W. E. Minchinton, page 152.

to a greater or lesser degree, a period of rapid war-time expansion followed by an equally sharp post-war decline in trade. The weak disappeared from the scene: the strong, resilient enough to weather the storm, emerged severely battered. Nevertheless there were many casualties. The period of the great trade depression was at hand, and once again the basic industries faced a critical time. The remedy was rationalization. The late Sir Henry Clay tells us that:

'The policy of segregating the armament interests and concentrating them with those of Vickers in a new company, while closing down plant redundant to any probable demand, was called "rationalization". The same principles were to be applied to other depressed industries, which brought their troubles to the Governor.'[1]

We are told that the latter:

'used the term *rationalization* as a convenient label for the policy he wished to further. It was a current catchword, which, strictly applied, indicated what was aimed at. Industry is continually in process of re-adjustment to changes in its technical or commercial conditions. It is liable to cling to traditional and existing methods, which change has made obsolete or inept. War and the post-war boom had checked the normal piecemeal process of adjustment, while at the same time they created new commercial conditions vastly different from those of industry before 1914. After the war low profits or losses in the industries most in need of readjustment – the older export industries – and high taxation had further handicapped and delayed necessary changes; while Government policy had been directed rather to relieving the resultant unemployment than to creating conditions in which employment would expand. For some industries markets had suffered a permanent contraction, with excessive competition for what was left; in others technical advance had rendered much existing equipment obsolete or inefficient.

'Popular usage identified rationalization with amalgamation; amalgamation was only an incident or means. If an industry suffered, like shipbuilding or coal or cotton, from capacity excessive in relation to any probable demand for its product and an organized contraction was necessary, some merging of existing units, and still more some united action by the industry as a whole (as distinct from efforts by isolated firms) would be essential. Again, if an industry were in need of expensive re-equipment, as the steel industry was, joint action might be needed to secure an economic volume of output, and the acquisition and employment of the new equipment might be facilitated by a merger of existing firms. But in every case the first need was a rational criticism of the existing organization of the industry (as distinct from a single firm), some measures to assure a market and then finance for such technical improvement as the scientists could suggest.'[2]

Acting through Securities Management Trust and its brain-child the Bankers' Industrial Development Co, the Bank of England was able to give first aid to many important firms. Indeed, the main purpose in forming the Bankers' Industrial Development Co was:

[1] *Lord Norman*, by Sir Henry Clay, page 321.
[2] *Lord Norman*, by Sir Henry Clay, pages 356–357.

'to examine, assist and finance the amalgamation, reconstruction and reorganization on an economic and rationalized basis of groups of British companies engaged in important industries'.[1]

Firms in the armament, iron and steel, cotton and shipbuilding industries came under its wing, while firms in many other industries propounded schemes which, however, did not lead to concrete proposals. Lord Norman was, however, fully aware of the limits of what could be done, and distrustful of sweeping measures of amalgamation for amalgamation's sake.

'He insisted that an amalgamation might be too large, especially if it aimed at covering a whole trade; that it was dangerous unless there were in sight men capable of managing the new concern; and that it could not be considered except on the basis of an expert examination of the firms to be absorbed and the plants they would contribute. Again and again he insisted at interviews that the process was troublesome and technical, involving questions of methods, materials, markets and persons.'[2]

The upsurge in world trade, however, soon brought more profitable times and the need for further rationalization gradually faded away. The next event was the rearmament programme which went some way to restore the fortunes of industry in general. Not long afterwards, the Second World War was upon us. Few mergers took place during the 1939–45 period, the impact of controls, rationing and concentration of industry causing a virtual standstill or freezing of the existing pattern of industry. And it wasn't until some time after the war, when rationing and most of the more rigid controls could be dispensed with, that industry resumed the trend towards larger units. Unlike the inter-war period, of course, expansion of trade was now the motive force.

Almost all industries shared in this regrouping process either as a result of orthodox mergers or more often as a consequence of the new technique of take-over bids imposed upon firms – frequently without the consent of the directorate. The post-war years have, for example, seen a steady stream of amalgamations in the motor-car and commercial motor vehicle industries. leading to greater opportunities for simplification in components and parts. The same process was at work in the engineering, food, paper, paint, brewery, electrical engineering, textiles,[3] chemicals and plastics industry.

[1] *Lord Norman*, page 329.
[2] *Lord Norman*, page 357.
[3] Underlining the fact that, unlike most industries, many branches of textiles may still face further shrinkage in volume, if not in value, of output, and further adaptation, and must still contemplate the effect of 'surplus capacity'. The strength of the industry may, therefore, be increased by more vertical integration, the practice whereby the successive processes – spinning, weaving, finishing, merchanting – are carried on by one firm, not by different firms working as specialists. The large spinning combines, for example, continue to extend their weaving activities by amalgamations.

Latterly, a number of hotels, property companies, insurance companies, investment trusts, merchant banks and discount houses have been caught in the toils of take-over bids, events which have lent an air of respectability to the whole procedure. Greater mechanization has also played its part. We learn, for instance, that:

'since flour was decontrolled in 1953 the plant bakeries, which are now estimated to be producing about 65 per cent of the country's bread, have been the prize for which Allied Bakers and the milling groups, Ranks and Spillers, have been fighting.'[1]

Manufacturing methods are changing too. Over the next decade or so the growing use of nuclear energy, radio-active isotopes and the like, together with the raising of the dignity of labour by the increasing use of automation, is bound to accelerate the trend towards the bigger unit. Lowering unit costs by increasing output may be achieved more easily through a process of mergers and take-overs, in addition to the linking up of business throughout the world through royalty and licensing arrangements.

The application of the Restrictive Trade Practices Act also seems predestined to stimulate mergers. 'One reaction to the Restrictive Trade Practices Act is to amalgamate', says a writer in the *Manchester Guardian Review of Industry*.[2]

'The merger movement, stimulated by high taxation and financial stringency, is being intensified by the attack on price agreements. Both horizontal and vertical groupings are going on; firms are trying to buy each other up either on the same level or by acquiring suppliers and outlets. The survivors are likely to face a period of intense competition.'

The intense struggle for markets and the succession of mergers and bids which ensued in the electrical cable industry after the price agreement was abandoned (A.E.I. – W.T. Henleys Telegraph Works; A.E.I. – London Electric Wire Co; British Insulated Callender's Cables – Telegraph Construction and Maintenance Co; B.I.C.C. – Scottish Cables; Enfield Rolling Mills – Enfield Cables), shows how an industry reacts to the problem of excess capacity and the novelty of price competition. Already, this legislation has caused an alteration in the form of at least one merger, because it would have involved the registration of certain proposals with the Registrar of Restrictive Trading Agreements. For this reason, the original proposal to amalgamate British Waxed Wrappings (a subsidiary of Spicers) with the two waxed paper subsidiarys of Wiggins, Teape (Griffith & Diggens and Waxed Papers) was abandoned. Instead, Spicers arranged to sell British Waxed Wrappings outright to Wiggins, Teape for the sum of £3 million.[3]

[1] 'Britain's Bread', *The Financial Times*, October 29th, 1957.
[2] March 1958.
[3] *The Investors' Chronicle*, October 30th, 1959.

Since then the law has developed considerably. Parliament has given us the Resale Prices Act 1964, and the Monopolies and Mergers Act 1965. This latter Act came into force in August 1965. The 1965 Monopolies and Mergers Act gave power to the Board of Trade, and hence to its successor the Department of Trade and Industry, to scrutinize and, if thought fit, refer to the Monopolies Commission (later renamed the Monopolies and Mergers Commission) for further investigation and report all mergers where (a) the gross assets to be acquired exceeded £5 million, calculated to be the sum of current assets before deduction of liabilities plus fixed assets plus goodwill if any or (b) where the acquisition would create or intensify a monopoly. In short, (a) is the size test, while (b) is the market penetration test. The latter was defined in the Monopolies and Restrictive Practices Act, 1948, as being one-third share of the market, and was applicable until reduced to one-quarter of the market share by the Fair Trading Act 1973, which became operative on November 1st, 1973.

To implement the 1965 Act, the Board of Trade formed an internal and inter-departmental mergers panel whose function is to consider the facts as known and make a recommendation to ministers whether a particular merger should be referred. The following constitutes a brief review of the work of the mergers panel since its inception in August, 1965 up to the end of 1975.

Approximately 8,000 mergers and take-overs have been recorded during the period, of which about 900 came under the scrutiny of the Board of Trade under either test (a) or (b) or, in some cases, both tests. The vast majority were cleared within a matter of two to three weeks, leaving a hard core of 29 merger cases (excluding two specific newspaper references) which were referred to the Monopolies Commission for investigation and report. A number of proposed mergers were subsequently abandoned before the Commission's Report (10 such cases were noted), leaving 19 'live' references which are listed in the table below, of which 10 were cleared, i.e. were not considered to be against the public interest (but two such mergers were not proceeded with at the time – Deutal Mftg bid for Amalgamated Deutal and Unilever's bid for Allied Breweries, 8 were held to be against the public interest and one report is still pending).

While any conclusions based on such a small number of mergers must be tentative, the data does suggest that there has been a greater tendency to refer those mergers which met both criteria; size or monopoly by themselves have only been judged to raise questions of possible detriment to the public interest in a very few cases.[1]

[1] *The Operation of the Mergers Panel Since 1965*, by J. D. Gribbin. Trade and Industry, Vol. 14, No. 3, page 70.

TABLE V

	Year	Proposed or Actual Merger	Dat of M. Comm. Report	Outcome
1	1965	British Motor Corpn/Pressed Steel	25.1.66	Took place
2	1966	Ross Group/Ass Fisheries	24.5.66	Did not take place
3	1966	Dental Manfg or Dentists Supply Co of New York/Amalgamated Dental Co	11.8.66	Did not take place
4	1966	Guest, Keen & Nettlefolds/Birfield	19.1.67	Took place
5	1966	B.I.C.C./Pyrotenax	2.6.67	Took place
6	1967	United Drapery/Montague Burton	15.9.67	Did not take place
7	1968	Barclays/Lloyd's/Martins Banks	10.7.68	Did not take place
8	1968	Thorn Electric/Radio Rentals	22.6.68	Took place
9	1969	Unilever/Allied Breweries	3.6.69	Did not take place
10	1969	Rank Orgn/De la Rue	3.6.69	Did not take place
11	1970	British Sidac/Transparent Paper	13.11.70	Did not take place
12	1972	Beecham/Glaxo Boots/Glaxo	14.7.72	Neither took place
13	1973	British Match/Wilkinson Sword	8.10.73	Took place
14	1973	British Rollmakers/Davy United	4.4.74	Did not take place
15	1973	Boots/House of Fraser	17.5.74	Did not take place
16	1974	Eagle Star Ins/Grovewood Securities	14.5.74	Took place
17	1974	Charter Consolidated/Sadia	8.9.74	Took place
18	1974	NFU Development Trust/FMC	15.7.75	Took place
19	1975	Amalgamated Industries/Herbert Morris	—	—

The main points which emerge from this examination of action under merger legislation are: *Dept Trade & Industry*

(a) a large number of mergers have been considered by the D.T.I. but relatively few (3 per cent) have been referred to the Commission.

(b) the D.T.I. have in a number of important cases decided not to make a reference in the light of assurances given by firms about their intentions and behaviour.

(c) the Commission has reported against only a small number of mergers (one-quarter of those considered by it).

(d) in cases where the Commission found against a merger, the D.T.I. have not so far needed to make use of their statutory powers to forbid it.

It is only fair to add that each merger proposal is examined by the Commission on its merits. That is to say the Commission adopts no preconceived view of a merger by reason of its size or type or apparent motive.

As Mr M. A. Weinberg observes:

'The most serious inhibiting factor for some time to come must be the absence of precedents to guide parties to a prospective take-over or amalgamation on the view likely to be taken on the public interest. While companies in the United States can look to many years of practice under the anti-trust laws and a fair amount of informative case-law companies in this country have only a couple of monopolies commission reports to look to and the likelihood is that few, if any, cases will find their way to the Courts.'[1]

Newspaper mergers are also subject to investigation and report under section 8 of the Monopolies and Mergers Act 1965. The first reference was made on September 30th, 1966, in connection with the transfer of *The Times* and *The Sunday Times* to a new company to be set up in which the Thomson Organisation and The Times Publishing Corporation would own 85 per cent and 15 per cent respectively. The report[2] was issued on December 21st, 1966, and on the same day the President of the Board of Trade stated that he had given consent to the transfer of *The Times* and *The Sunday Times* to the proposed new company in the terms set out in the report.

The second reference concerned Thomson Newspapers Ltd and the proposed transfer of three weekly newspapers owned by Crusha & Son Ltd.

Again, some mergers may well have been stimulated by firms' belief that, with trade liberalization proceeding apace and the emergence of the European Economic Community (the 'Six') and

[1] *Take-over and Amalgamations.* Second edition. Sweet & Maxwell.
[2] HC 273.

the European Free Trade Association (the 'Outer Seven') threatening to make competition in their own fields much fiercer, it would be wise to link up with other similarly placed concerns in an effort to reduce unit costs.

The ranks of the British motor manufacturers have been severely pruned as a result of mergers. In fact, there is only one all-British group left to do battle with American-owned giants like Fords, General Motors (Vauxhall) and latterly Chrysler (Rootes).

Over the past few years or so, the British aircraft industry has been passing through a phase of readjustment after the years of high defence production and full employment. This readjustment, which is not yet completed, is marked principally by two developments: contraction and consolidation of the industry into fewer, more powerful units; and a declining labour force. It has been dictated by a number of factors: the increasing cost and complexity of modern military and civil aircraft, the falling off of military orders at home, and the intensification of overseas competition in the civil field and, not least, the imminent prospects of nationalization (1976).

Elsewhere, the pressure is equally strong. The shares of rubber growing companies have never been so active. Several factors have been operating. Amalgamations to reduce overheads on estates, bids by groups attracted to large cash holdings of companies, and an increasing tendency by the Chinese in the Far East to buy British-owned estates.

The Minister of Housing and Local Government made the first compulsory order for regrouping water undertakings under the Water Act 1945. One purpose of that Act was to effect the reorganization of water supply into undertakings of more sensible size and extent. So far the Government have relied on persuasion and prodding. But under that mild administration progress has been slow. At the end of the Second World War there were more than 1,000 local authority undertakings and water boards and 150 companies. About four-fifths of the industry is left in the hands of 370 local authorities and water boards. The substantial remaining portion is in the hands of some forty-eight companies. Amalgamation into water undertakings large enough to be efficient was accelerated by the Ministry of Housing in 1956. The reorganization of local government into larger units which came into effect on April 1st, 1973, has further hastened the more gradual process of amalgamation which had been in evidence until that date.

In publishing, so we gather,

'the most conspicuous and significant development during recent years has been the amalgamations and working associations between groups of firms. Amalgamation between publishers, of course, is an old story.

The genealogies of some of the nineteenth-century publishing houses are as tortuous as those of the Hapsburgs.'[1]

Local breweries, once the mainstay of the brewing industry, have gradually declined in importance. Today, as a result of a series of mergers and take-overs, the bulk of the trade is in the hands of the 'Big Seven' (Allied, Bass Charrington, Courage Barclay & Simonds, Guinness, Scottish & Newcastle, Watney Mann and Whitbreads). Even so, two of these companies have already fallen victim to the diversification ambitions of firms outside the brewing industry, for Courage was taken over by the Imperial Group (in 1972) while Watney Mann reluctantly gave in to Grand Metropolitan Hotels (in 1972).

After years of take-overs and mergers, the distribution of sugar in Britain has fallen into the hands of three companies. Tate & Lyle produces rather more than the other two put together, and sells cane sugar under its own name. Silver Spoon sugar comes from home-grown beet and is sold mainly in or near those areas of eastern England where beet is grown. Sankey sugar, in Northern England and Westburn in Scotland is refined from cane by Manbre and Garton, the only remaining cane rival of Tate & Lyle. Each cane company has a refinery in London, Liverpool and near Glasgow.

Most of their combined output goes to food processors – not only the obvious ones like bakers and sweet-makers, but also those who produce tinned soup and pastry casings for meat pies.

Nor is the building society movement exactly free from similar overtures. At the turn of the century there were more than 2,300 societies. By 1920 the number had dwindled to 1,300 and by 1940 to less than 1,000.

A suggestion that more building societies should merge came from Mr Keith Brading, the Chief Registrar of Friendly Societies. Addressing the Midland Association of Building Societies,[2] the registrar, who has overall control of the conduct of building societies, suggested that there could be many advantages in an accelerated rate of mergers. That course would promote greater efficiency in the movement and less proliferation of offices.

Of the 450 societies in Britain at that time, he said, about 50 did practically no business at all and 300 of the remaining 400 were essentially local. Many others were purely regional. He questioned whether the regional societies had a particular role of its own or was in the process of growing to national stature. If the latter was true, just how many societies did Britain need – 50 or 5?

Mr Brading gave three reasons for the trend towards mergers:

[1] *The Times*, February 1st, 1958.
[2] *Financial Times*, September 29th, 1973

(1) increased efficiency and economy of management.
(2) a broader base for business, serving to strengthen security and improve the spread and quality of the service provided.
(3) The scope which a larger organisation offered for better staff opportunities. Today, there are no more than 400 building societies still operating in the United Kingdom, with the biggest societies – Halifax, Abbey National, Nationwide (previously known as the Co-operative Permanent), Woolwich Equitable, Leeds Permanent – all assuming a more dominant position in the movement.

In the field of distribution, the pace of expansion via mergers has been, if anything, a good deal faster than in manufacturing. Noting the increase in the size of multiple shop firms, Mr J. B. Jeffreys observes:

'In the period of the inter-war years and down to 1950 the number of branches in existence increased more rapidly than the number of multiple shop organizations. The main reason for this was not a decrease in the number of new multiple shop firms coming into existence, but an increase in the number of mergers and amalgamations. Amalgamations took place between small and medium-sized firms, but the outstanding feature was the amalgamations between very large firms. Practically all the firms in the grocery and meat trades that had grown rapidly in the years before 1914 were involved in amalgamations in the inter-war years.'[1]

The author illustrates the trend by showing that: 'In the meat trade the leading firms joined together in 1923 to form the Union Cold Storage group, which had over 2,000 branches.' Again, in the grocery trade: 'most of the leading firms and some smaller ones amalgamated between 1924 and 1931 to form the Home and Colonial group, with over 3,000 branches, and some of the other large firms merged between 1927 and 1934 in the International Tea group, which had over 1,000 branches in 1938'. Other amalgamations took place in the chemists' trade in 1934 giving birth to the Timothy Whites & Taylors group, in the footwear trade in 1927 resulting in the Freeman Hardy & Willis group,[2] and in the dairy trade in 1915–21 giving rise to the United Dairies group. In 1939 there were twelve firms with over 500 branches each and of these five had over 1,000 apiece. Apparently only Boots Pure Drug Co and W. H. Smith & Son of the very large firms had grown in the orthodox way – mainly by opening new branches.[3] 'The increase

---

[1] *Retail Trading in Britain, 1850–1950*, by James B. Jeffreys, page 64.
[2] Just over twenty-five years later, this group was itself the subject of a take-over bid by Mr Charles Clore and his associates. Soon afterwards the Dolcis and Manfield chain of shops were added to form the British Shoe Corporation. In shoe retailing generally the pace of concentration has been vigorous – as well as in vertical integration between selling and manufacture. Apart from the British Shoe Corporation mentioned above another link-up brought Saxone and Lilley & Skinner together, controlling nearly 500 shoe shops.
[3] But even Boots succumbed in 1968 by absorbing Timothy Whites & Taylors.

in the size of the other firms was chiefly the outcome of amalgamations.' Continuing the story, amalgamations continued undiminished throughout the Second World War and on into the post-war years. Three further large groups gained ground and finally emerged with over 500 branches each – the Allied Bakeries group in the bread trade, the Moores group in the grocery trade and the Great Universal Stores group in the furniture and women's clothing trades.[1] Discussing the exact reasons for the spate of retail amalgamations and mergers in the inter-war years, Mr Jeffreys remarks that:

> 'There were in most instances advantages to be gained from amalgamation by way of increased specialization of management, economies in buying and in transport, and the elimination of redundant units. To firms wishing to expand rapidly the acquisition of another concern which had good shopping sites was a more attractive proposition than the much slower process of acquiring sites one by one.'[2]

Opinion was sometimes divided, however, on the precise advantages to be gained in terms of organization.

> 'The Home and Colonial group, for example, after experimenting with close central control and direction of the trading organization and policies of the merging companies, reverted back to a fair measure of autonomy for each company.'

In addition to the purely economic and organizational matters, financial considerations often dominated the scene in many mergers. Mr Jeffreys comments:

> 'In some instances the financial gains obtained from buying up a rival company which had met with difficulties were as important as the trading advantages that might accrue from such a merger.'[3]

The same sort of development was afoot among the department stores. A feature of the inter-war years was the number of amalgamations that took place between the firms, leading to the emergence of a few companies each controlling a great number of stores. It is clear that the trend towards mergers or acquisitions of other stores had started before 1914. Thus:

> 'John Barker acquired Ponting Brothers in 1907 and Harrods bought Dickens & Jones in 1914, and immediately after the war Debenhams acquired Marshall & Snelgrove and Harvey Nicholls. Harrods acquired Kendal Milne of Manchester in 1919 and Swan & Edgar in 1920 (the shares in this firm were resold in 1926), and John Barker bought Derry & Toms in the same year.'[4]

---

[1] Great Universal Stores has spread its tentacles even farther afield in the past few years. Burberry's, Weaver to Wearer, Rego Clothiers, Morrisons (Holdings), Penberthy's, Ryland's & Sons, Waring & Gillow, Whiteway Laidlaw and Hope Brothers (which had itself absorbed Hector Powe a short while before) have been drawn into the fold.
[2] *Retail Trading in Britain*, op. cit., page 66.
[3] Op. cit., page 66.
[4] Op. cit., page 345.

Major developments in the direction of grouping stores occurred in the late twenties and early thirties. It took two main forms. In some cases a company would acquire control of a number of separate department stores, primarily for financial reasons, and little or no change would be made in the trading or buying of policies of the individual department stores so acquired. In other instances a department store, having acquired control of other stores with the idea of developing a 'multiple' department store organization, would impose an important measure of central control over the buying and trading policies of the individual stores. The main developments in the twenties fell into the first category, and three main groups of department stores were formed. There was the Debenhams group which had taken over a number of stores from the Drapery Trust in 1927, then the United Drapery Stores group founded in 1927; and lastly the Selfridge Provincial Stores group that started life in 1926. In bringing the story up to date, it must be recorded that in April 1967 the United Drapery Stores made a bid for Montague Burton. If approved, the combined £136 million group would have formed Britain's largest retailers. Doubtless, there is still scope for rationalizing and making more profitable the 520 Burton shops, eighty Jackson the Tailor branches and United Drapery's own 1,000 outlets, which include 600 John Collier, Claude Alexander and Alexandre shops.

As long ago as 1940 the Selfridge Provincial Stores group, which numbered some sixteen stores passed to John Lewis Ltd, and a fourth group of stores now to be reckoned with – that built up originally by the Great Northern & Southern Stores Ltd, founded in 1936, which was itself absorbed by The Calico Printers' Association Ltd, along with Hide & Co.

The other type of amalgamation or growth is best exemplified by Lewis's Ltd, which partly through building and partly through buying developed a small chain of eight department stores in different parts of the country under a unified control. Mr Jeffreys sums up by saying that:

> 'The direct effect of the financial amalgamations on the economic and trading policies of the stores concerned was negligible.'[1]

The example of Lewis's Ltd did not, however, attract many imitators. Perhaps a few would deny the economic advantages of employing such a technique, but many would oppose centralized buying and unified control. The individual characteristics and reputation of department stores resulting from their long emphasis on service to the particular groups of consumers who patronized

[1] Op. cit., page 346.

them, obviously demand a high degree of local and individual control over buying and trading practice.

It is interesting to note in passing that in 1965 Mr Clore returned to the bid arena from which he had been absent since the hectic days of the 1950s when his British Shoe Corporation (itself a subsidiary of Sears Holdings) bid for Lewis's Investment Trust. Initially, the £58 million bid was opposed by the Cohen family which was said to control 20–30 per cent of the shares. In face of this and opposition from other shareholders an extra 1s a share was offered making the final bid worth £62 million. In the end, this was enough to win over the waiverers, but as the directors pointed out in a circular letter to the shareholders:

> 'Your board still regards the securities of British Shoe Corporation as fundamentally unattractive, but finds it difficult to advise ordinary shareholders that a price of 85p a share in cash is inadequate.'

Evidently, all these kinds of groupings and regroupings which took place up to 1950, were but the forerunner of other and more widely-based mergers which have since affected the distributive trades. The Co-operative movement has been similarly afflicted, for the number of societies has slowly diminished by amalgamation; in 1900 there were 1,439 with an average membership of 1,186; in 1920, 1,139 averaging 3,267; in 1956, 947 averaging 12,746. In 1968, after quite a battle, 567 retail Co-ops round Britain agreed to a blueprint for merging into 55 regional societies on the theory that bigger was better.

While take-overs and friendly amalgamations quickly followed the 1968 plan, the pace of mergers has almost come to a halt in the past few years. By 1975, there were still over 200 societies left in business.

ADVANTAGES

1. Economy in capital expenditure

It may well happen that a merger will lead to more intensive use being made of existing manufacturing assets than was the case beforehand. That factor should, in its turn, promote better and more economical planning of future capital expenditure. For one must not overlook the fact that on a merger of two or more firms, the new board of directors is probably looking far ahead rather than to the immediate future. While, therefore, two competing firms might both be tempted to over-expand at the same time and so have to carry the burden of surplus capacity, that situation would be less likely to happen if both firms had joined forces. At the same time, it must be conceded that following a merger the group as a whole may

equally overplay its hand by over-estimating the future market
possibilities for its products.

2. Economy in the use of current assets

Quite often, where two or more businesses are merged, a real saving
in stock-in-trade can be achieved, i.e., the level of the stock of spare
parts can be progressively reduced or over-stocking of raw materials
can be eliminated simply because there is a higher overall level of
stock available to draw upon. Again, the large buyer is almost
always in a better position than the small, both in regard to price
and the terms of settlement. In the case of a group consisting, say,
of a holding company and a number of operating subsidiaries, the
actual purchasing may be either centralized in the holding company
or decentralized in the operating subsidiaries. Either way, special
terms can often be negotiated with suppliers, not only in relation to
raw materials supplies but also in respect of purchases of plant and
equipment. Furthermore, another important advantage likely to
result from a merger, is that the group is put in a much stronger
position to borrow from its bankers. In the first place, the group's
size is such that it now has larger assets to offer as security for
temporary advances. Secondly, in the event of a diversity of interests,
the group would be better placed to weather trade recessions,
quotas or other import restrictions imposed by overseas countries,
purchase tax changes, and unexpected hire-purchase restrictions, etc.

Apart from this, a group may find that it is able to operate safely
with a lower average bank balance and still finance seasonal trade.
But, on this and other matters, a good deal depends upon the degree
of day-to-day control imposed as a consequence of the merger.
Sometimes the main company acts as a kind of banker to the group
by receiving surplus cash from subsidiaries and, conversely, lending
money back when this is needed. Whereas, on other occasions, a
wide measure of autonomy may exist within the merger, i.e., though
companies may be technically united under one umbrella, they are
each given considerable latitude in running their own affairs.

3. Ease of access to the capital market

A merger of interests should, if only by reason of size, possess added
financial strength. Size generally brings in its wake a certain resilience
to set-backs. Besides improving credit-worthiness, the merger
should improve facilities for raising fresh capital from the market.
As a group comes into being, the number of shareholders has a
tendency to increase along with the expansion of physical assets.
If, at some later date, the company can no longer finance its continued expansion from retained profits, it may decide to give its
own shareholders the chance of investing further money in the

by force of circumstances. Thus, the Distillers Co – famous for its
brands of whisky – launched out into the industrial field in the post-
war years and has built up a separate division devoted to chemical
and allied products, occasionally in partnership with other public
companies. Then, Arthur Guinness, Sons & Co, the well-known
brewery firm, has acquired over the last few years extensive interests
in the confectionery trade through its purchase of Callard & Bowser,
William Nuttall and the Lavell's chain of shops. The British Match
Corporation aims to extend its interests in timber utilization,
packaging and printing. Recent investments in these fields are said
to total £687,000 and include a 41 per cent interest in the Airscrew
Co & Jicwood Ltd. In the fertilizer field, Fisons Ltd have expanded
further afield by taking in Pest Control and an interest in Airwork
Ltd, besides developing a chemical and pharmaceutical group based
on Benger Laboratories and Genatosan. In the tobacco industry,
British-American Tobacco has taken over Yardley's (1967) to add to
its Lentheric range of perfumes, and also owns the Tonibell ice cream
firm. Imperial Tobacco, too, have broken away from their traditional
trade into potato crisps, teaching machines, electronic equipment,
and packaging equipment. In a declining industry like textiles,
some companies find that diversification is the answer to their
problem. Courtaulds followed this course by forming Group
Developments Ltd early in 1958 for the express purpose of pursuing
a policy of diversification. This list of its acquisitions is impressive.
Cellon Ltd (aircraft finishes, lacquers, etc.), Reads Ltd (can makers),
Pearlite Box (manufacturers of wax cartons), Betts & Co (makers of
foil bottle tops), Gossard (Holdings) Ltd (manufacturers and dis-
tributors of foundation garments) and Harbens (rayon manufac-
turers) have all been brought into the group. Later still, Pinchin,
Johnson & Associates (paint) was acquired together with many
textile firms (Lancashire Cotton Corporation, Fine Spinners &
Doublers, Bairns-wear, Susan Small, Foister, Clay & Ward, Kayser-
Bondor, Aristoc, Ballito Hosiery Mills, Cook & Watts, Wilkinson &
Riddell, Wolsey, Bell, Nicholson & Richard Lunt, Macanie, I. &
R. Morley) and six other bids – following on in close order – Prew-Smith
Knitwear, Clutson and Kemp, H. Lister, M. Duke, the Northgate
Group and Sir Thomas & Arthur Wardle.

Courtaulds has certainly been setting the pace in textile take-overs
and has already established itself as the biggest single force in British
textiles.

It is intent upon becoming a vertical textiles company – securing
for itself tied outlets comprising some 20–25 per cent of the industry –
rather than remaining primarily a fibre producer. The Monopolies
Commission report on the Supply of Man-made Cellulosic Fibres
may, however, have put a damper on these ideas since one of the

recommendations dealt with the very question of further acquisitions in the textile industry by Courtaulds.

Nationalization has also caused the rebirth of many firms in a new guise. Cable & Wireless is now a successful investment trust, and both Thomas Tilling and the British Electric Traction group have had a new lease of life since some of their transport undertakings were detached and are now firmly ensconced as industrial holding companies, while Powell Duffryn – deprived of its coal interests here – has looked overseas, to mining operations there, for ways and means of using its expertise.

The most remarkable example of a reinvigorated company, however, is demonstrated by the Hawker Siddeley group, which has been virtually transformed from a group centred upon aircraft construction to a large and diversified group which is now in the front rank of world leaders in heavy industry and engineering, in addition to its original, though diminished, interest in aircraft construction. These changes have been imposed not only through alterations in defence policy but from the group's own policy of expansion and diversification.

Some years later, Hawker Siddeley sold their half-share in Bristol Siddeley Engines for £26 million. Armed with this cache of cash, they made a bid for Crompton Parkinson worth £25 million. The initial bid of 54p a share consisting of a mixture of cash and shares was rebuffed but the Crompton board subsequently accepted a revised bid of 65p a share – all in cash this time – totalling £30 million. As *The Times* put it: 'The power of hard cash has won through'.[1]

The formal completion of Hawker Siddeley's bid for Crompton Parkinson meant a major shift in the pattern of Hawker's business. Hawker is now primarily a specialist engineering group: taking in both R. A. Lister (acquired earlier) and Crompton Parkinson, only about 30 per cent of its capital is employed in aircraft and around 40 per cent of the labour force.

Nowadays, there is far more pressure on companies to concentrate on running the mainstream of their business profitably. The fashionable diversification take-overs of the fifties have gone right out of the picture.

But there are still many different roads to nationalization. Steel, aircraft and shipbuilding (under the influence of the Geddes Report) have been reshaped by the Government. The electrical manufacturing industry is slowly regrouping itself – a process that has been set in train by the nationalized industry's determination to rationalize its buying.

[1] February 7th, 1967.

DISADVANTAGES

All the arguments, however, are by no means favourable to mergers. There are many real objections to be considered.

1. Elimination of the personal touch

Certain businesses owe their success to the strength of character and drive of the proprietor or proprietors. In fact, one of the outstanding advantages of the small one-man or two-men type of business is that the proprietor really does know the whole of his staff and they in turn know him. With the growth in size of a business, however, it is quite impossible for any one man to know more than a small proportion of the total individuals employed. Therein lies the danger that the beneficial effects of the personal touch will be lost. The control of the business, both in minor matters of policy and in day-to-day administration, must inevitably be delegated in some way. Delay in reaching a decision on a problem is often commonplace. Again, there is the ever-present danger that the general scheme of control may break down. Thus, where a business has a large output but works on a small margin of profit, any wastage due to unwieldy direction, or leakage attributable to lack of control, may prove serious in the extreme.

On the other hand, the personal ties may exist between the proprietor and his customers, just as with his workpeople. Here, the knowledge that the business is no longer under the old ownership and supervision may have an adverse effect. Goodwill on either side is a particularly tender plant.

Apart from this, there is always the disadvantages associated with large-scale business and its diversity of interests. Factories may be dispersed at home; while some may be established abroad. Control is rendered difficult even where management is decentralized, notwithstanding the comparative ease of communication these days. In such a setting, a feeling of impersonality is bound to pervade the big business: it is virtually a chronic disease, industrially speaking, and many able minds have been devoted to its cure; workers' councils, joint production committees, training courses, welfare schemes, sports and recreational centres are all symptomatic of the efforts made to create or recreate a corporate spirit.

2. Loss of trade name

The parties to a proposed merger may object to the potential loss of valuable trade names. This objection does not seem to be borne out in practice, however, for it seems to be the rule rather than the exception to preserve the trade name in some form, depending upon the exact style of merger contemplated. Thus, a merger concluded by means of the formation of a separate holding company leaves the identity of the constituent companies unaltered. To all outward appearances, each business would continue trading under its own name exactly as before.

For example, it is now ten years since McVitie & Price and Macfarlane, Lang & Co amalgamated under the name of United Biscuits Ltd, but both constituent firms continue to sell their biscuits throughout the length and breadth of this country under their own name. And the same may be said of a leading competitor in the biscuit trade, the Associated Biscuit Manufacturers, which markets biscuits through its two well-known operating subsidiaries, Huntley & Palmers and Peek, Frean. While in another type of manufacture, Raleigh Industries, which claims to have the largest bicycle plant in the world, embraces the B.S.A., Sunbeam and New Hudson trade-marks as well as Raleigh, Rudge-Whitworth, Humber and Triumph.

A merger enacted through a new company taking over the actual undertaking (i.e., purchase of assets including goodwill) of two or more other firms, poses a difficult problem. The constituent businesses may hitherto have carried on their operations under a name which has become a household word and thus possesses a sale price of its own under the heading of goodwill (which will have been paid for by the new company). Unwilling to jettison a valuable asset, the new company usually solves the difficulty by adopting a double-barrelled name which, literally, merges the names of the old businesses, viz., Birmid Qualcast, British Insulated Callender's Cables, Cadbury Schweppes, Johnson Firth Brown, Ranks Hovis-MacDougall. Failing that, the new company may assume an entirely new name quite unconnected with the old businesses but taking care to exhibit the old links in a prominent manner adding the phrase '. . . branch' or '. . . works' in all letter headings, advertisements, circulars, window displays, etc. On the other hand, a perusal of the *Stock Exchange Daily Official List* shows that many large groups do change their title at some time during their history, as the result of mergers. The use of a prefix like 'Allied', 'Amalgamated', 'Associ-ated', 'Combined', 'Consolidated', 'Imperial', 'United', or the use of the word 'International' either as a prefix or suffix and finally the introduction of a suffix like '. . . (Holdings)', is indicative of the group's objectives or origins. Masquerading under these generic titles, for instance, we find such well-known groups as:

Allied:
   Allied Brick & Tile Works, Allied Industrial Services, Allied Iron-founders, Allied Suppliers.

Amalgamated:
   Amalgamated Cotton Mills Trust, Amalgamated Limestone, Amal-gamated Metal Corporation, Amalgamated Packaging Industries, Amalgamated Roadstone.

Associated:
Associated Biscuit Manufacturers, Associated British Foods, Associated Clay Industries, Associated Commercial Vehicles, Associated Dairies, Associated Engineering, Associated Fisheries, Associated Motor Cycles, Associated Newspapers, Associated Paper Mills, Associated Portland Cement Manufacturers, Associated Television.

Combined:
Combined Electrical Manufacturers, Combined English Stores Group.

Consolidated:
Consolidated Tin Smelters.

Imperial:
Imperial Chemical Industries, Imperial Cold Storage & Supply Co, Imperial Continental Gas Association, Imperial Group.

International:
International Computers (Holdings), International Combustion, International Compressed Air, International Paint, International Timber Corporation.

United:
United Biscuits, United Canners, United Drapery Stores, United Gas Industries, United Glass Bottle Manufacturers, United Molasses, United Newspapers, United Premier Oil & Cake, United Sua Betong, United Transport, United Wine Traders.

. . .(Holdings):
APV (Holdings), British Paints (Holdings), Cannon (Holdings), William Collins & Sons (Holdings), Gratrix (Holdings), International Combustion (Holdings), Reckitt & Colman (Holdings), W. H. Smith & Son (Holdings), Wilmot-Breeden (Holdings).

International:
AD International, Bodycote International, BSG International (formerly the Bristol Street Group), Caravans International, Carpets International, Davy International, Dawson International, Letreset International, Lion International, Long John International, LRC International, Martonair International, Photopia International, Readicut International, Redman Heenan International, Staflex International, Viyella International.

If the financial history of these firms was fully documented, almost all of them would be found to have expanded by one or more mergers on the way along. For example, from *The Board of Trade Journal*,[1] we learn that:

'At an early period in the history of textiles in Scotland an important branch of the dyeing and finishing industry was set up in the Vale of Leven, which runs from the foot of Loch Lomond to the River Clyde. There a plentiful supply of the right type of water was to be found and a number of firms were successfully established. From an amalgamation of some of these firms, the United Turkey Red Co Ltd, one of the largest dyeing and finishing firms in Scotland, was formed in 1898.'

[1] March 21st, 1958.

3. Inconvenience and expense

Obviously all businesses do not readily lend themselves to a profitable merger. It is assumed, however, that negotiations would have been broken off where a real stumbling-block loomed up in the preliminary discussions. If proceeded with, such a merger would most likely fail in its object.

As to expense, much depends upon the form taken by the merger (this point is fully discussed in Chapter IV). In general, however, the expenses fall into two categories, (a) stamp duties; and (b) professional fees. The former category includes stamp duties on the transfer of assets or shares from one ownership to another,[1] and on the authorized share capital of a newly formed limited company.[2] However, relief from stamp duty can be obtained in certain well-defined circumstances.

The latter would normally take in valuation fees for property or other assets, accountancy and legal fees for expert advice.

4. Monopoly powers

In the past, mergers have often been denounced as leading to exploitation of the public or giving rise to 'unfair competition' with other traders. While it would be presumptuous to deny all these accusations, in most cases they are based on extremely scanty and inconclusive evidence. Nor have the many reports of the Monopolies Commission over the last few years caused this view to be challenged in any material respect. Moreover, the activities of the Restrictive Trade Practices Tribunal should keep a restraining hand on firms' exuberance in this direction. In the main, the evidence points to the use of resale price maintenance methods, suggesting competition in service rather than in price. The tests applied in determining whether or not a monopoly exists under the Monopolies and Restrictive Practices (Inquiry and Control) Act 1948, cannot be regarded as exacting. In substance, the terms of issue confronting the Commission are twofold:

(a) Does one person or group supply at least one-third of the British market for the goods under investigation, or is one-third at least supplied by two or more persons who conduct their business in any way to prevent or restrict competition in production or supply?

(b) Do such conditions of monopoly or restriction, if established, operate against the public interest?

---

[1] Stamp duty on conveyance or transfer on sale is at the rate of £2 per cent of any property.
[2] Capital duty is at the rate of £2 for every £100.

5. Personality problems

Another disadvantage inherent in mergers arises from loss of status or affront (imagined or intended) to personal feelings. Directors who have in the past been the dominant character in their own business, assuming the forcefulness of a petty dictator in some respects, naturally take unkindly to a change of organization in which they find themselves merely one of a group of people composing the board of directors. With executive responsibility curtailed, the prospect of finding themselves in a minority in important matters of policy – and thereby outvoted – may well rankle. Furthermore, two companies which have been operated as separate units, and are now to be merged, will both have had their own boards of directors, and reporting to them in turn their own departmental managers. Each company can be regarded as a harmonious team. If the two companies are merged, it means that duplicate boards of directors exist (apart from the resignation or death of one or more of the directors). In such circumstances, one director, say the production director, will have to be made senior to his colleague in the other company. A similar problem arises on the sales and financial sides. The problem very often resolves itself, of course, where one man, by his ability, age and reputation, stands head and shoulders above his co-director, and is appointed 'chief' by general consensus of opinion. Nevertheless, it is a very real factor which must be taken into account in any merger.

CHAPTER III

TYPES OF MERGER

In general a merger between two or more firms may be accomplished in three ways:

(*a*) the holding company method;
(*b*) complete amalgamation; or
(*c*) pooling arrangements.

These three types of merger will now be considered in detail, due regard being paid to the reasons appertaining to the choice of method, and to the procedure which should be followed.

(*a*) Holding Company Method

This is apt to be the most widely-used method in practice, judging by the number of mergers which have taken place under the auspices of a holding company scheme. It is so called, because either a new limited company is formed (a non-trading company more often than not) or one of the constituent companies is designated the holding company (thus acting in the dual capacity of trading-cum-holding company). The several companies which are parties to the merger are, as it were, annexed via the holding company through the acquisition by the latter of the whole of, or perhaps only a controlling interest in, the share capital of one or more of the limited companies owning the businesses in question. Thus it is possible to secure an identity of interests between two or more companies without really disturbing the legal entities composing the merger. On the surface, the business may appear to carry on as before, but due to the change of ownership, internal reorganization and pooling of efforts can be effected without undue publicity.

At the outset, the parties to the merger must determine whether a brand-new company shall be incorporated as a non-trading holding company or whether one of the existing companies shall be appointed to take on the function of holding company along with its normal trading activities.[1] Much depends, of course, on the circumstances of each case, but the capital structure and other technical features of the constituent companies to the merger may

[1] A sidelight on this vexed question comes from G. & J. Weir Ltd. Hitherto the parent company has functioned in a dual capacity, as it has been both a trading and a holding company. The board now considers that it would be better to separate these two functions, which would enable the board of the holding company to concentrate exclusively on policy matters affecting the group and leave the purely trading functions in the hands of the local board. (1957 Annual Report.)

have a distinct bearing on the matter. It is not unusual when a holding company is formed, for the operating companies of the new group to change their status from public companies, where they are such, to private companies. A merger must not just be seen as a neat accounting exercise. It is as much a binding together of people: diverse in their ways and outlook.

As industrial groups tend to grow larger and often widely dispersed, their organization becomes more and more important and the autonomy of the corporate unit sometimes has to give way to administrative convenience. In meeting this challenge, therefore, many large groups have resorted to a divisional basis of organization based on products. Dealing recently with the composition of the Associated Electrical Industries group and the proposed formation of product divisions, Lord Chandos said: 'It is, however, constantly necessary to adapt our organization to changing conditions. The ideal at which we aim is to devolve executive functions to subsidiary boards, whilst maintaining a strong central control of industrial and financial policy.'

New holding company
The formation of an entirely new holding company gives the company a comparatively free hand in arranging its capitalization, i.e., future expansion is made that much easier. Any additional capital which the operating companies may need for their businesses can be obtained on loan from the holding company. In this way, the latter acts as 'banker' to the group, surplus funds being accepted on loan from, say, one operating company whose funds may temporarily be in excess of current needs, while the borrowing needs of another operating company can be met from the surplus. Failing this switching of cash surpluses to meet deficits, however, a holding company might well be in a more favourable position to raise fresh capital since it is a new company unencumbered with debt in contrast with an old company saddled with an existing issue of debentures. Furthermore, sheltering behind the holding company are operating companies each owning substantial assets, which in total may provide ample assets cover for a new issue of shares or debentures.

The sentiment may play its part in choosing a holding company. Shareholders in a company might be loath to see their company engulfed by another existing company engaged in the same line of business. On the surface, it bears all the signs of absorption by a dominating concern of a rather small competitor. Where a holding company comes into being, however, exchanging shares with the shareholders of the operating companies, those shareholders now have a voice in the direction of the holding company's affairs proportionate to their old shareholdings in the operating companies.

If, on the other hand, the holding company pays out cash to the shareholders of one or more of the operating companies, the presumption is that the price is well up to or even above market expectations. That being so, the old shareholders withdraw, having no further interest in the shares or the affairs of the operating company.

As to valuation, where any new holding company is formed to acquire the share capital of two operating companies, whether for cash or by way of an exchange of shares, then both interests will need to be valued.

This method leaves undisturbed companies fortunate enough to have debentures or preference shares in issue which carry a low rate of interest or dividend.

Exisiting company

The advantage of using an existing company as an operating-cum-holding company does save preliminary and formation expenses, though this again is often more apparent than real if the merger takes the form which permits relief from stamp and other duties.

On the other hand, there are some very real objections, especially from the financial angle. If an otherwise acceptable existing company having considerable debenture capital in issue is appointed to act as holding company by purchasing the shares of another company in exchange for a further issue of its own shares, then certain disadvantages may follow. First, it must be borne in mind that the object of the holding company method is to enhance the position of those controlling the operating companies, i.e., the holders of the equity or ordinary shares in the holding company. All that would happen in the above case, however, is that the security of the debenture-holders would be improved by merger, to the detriment of the real owners: the same may be said of preference capital too. Secondly, if the operating side of the holding company should experience a spell of poor trade with reduced profit margins, the time might come when the debenture-holders could appoint a receiver. On an enforced realization of assets, albeit including the shareholding in the other operating company, both businesses could pass into new ownership, leaving the original owners practically penniless. Whereas the same grouping of interests in the hands of a separate holding company would only involve the downfall of the one operating company having debenture capital in issue, the business and assets of the other operating company would continue unimpaired.

In general, then, if an existing company is preferred as the holding company, it is advisable to select the one which has little or no prior capital, leaving the other company to continue unhindered as an operating company only. If both operating companies happen to have prior capital to any degree, then on balance the advantage lies with the formation of a new holding company altogether, so as to overcome the possible enrichment of the security behind one or other of the operating companies.

On the question of valuation, if an existing company fulfils the double function of operating-cum-holding company and seeks to acquire for cash the shares in another operating company, then the merger only requires valuation of the one block of shares to be taken over. Conversely, if the interest in the second operating company is acquired through the medium of an exchange of shares then both classes of shares would have to be valued. One practical advantage of using an existing company as a holding company instead of forming a new holding company, is that its accumulated reserves are free for use. Whereas a scheme involving the formation of a new holding company to take over two operating concerns does freeze the major part, if not the whole, of the free reserves of the operating companies. In this case, the reserves are, as it were, immobilized as capital. The original intentions of the two carpet-making interests, John Crossley & Sons Ltd and Carpet Trades Ltd, to form a holding company foundered on this very point. The decision was taken instead to form a new operating company to take over the Carpet Trades' business, Carpet Trades itself becoming a holding company. By a share exchange the holding company then acquired the John Crossley capital. In this way the merger freed the reserves of the Carpet Trades company and only immobilized those of the Crossley concern. Either concern, of course, could have been designated the holding company.[1]

Treatment of share premium accounts

While on the subject of holding companies, mention must be made of a new section of the Companies Act 1948, of special interest to accountants, which was judicially considered for the first time in 1951.[2] It was section 56, which deals with the issue of shares 'at a premium, whether for cash or otherwise' and requires the transfer to share premium account of 'the amount or value of the premiums'. The balance of this account has then to be treated as though it were paid-up share capital, with certain minor modifications. In this particular case, the plaintiff sought an injunction restraining the defendent from retaining just over £5 million as a sum credited to share premium account, or treating it other than as a general reserve.

The facts were that Ropner Holdings Ltd, which was incorporated as a holding company, had for its main object the acquisition for

---

[1] *The Accountant*, July 10th, 1954, page 46.
[2] *Henry Head & Co Ltd v. Ropner Holdings Ltd* ([1951] 2 All E.R. 994).

the purpose of amalgamation of the whole of the issued capital of two shipping companies which, although carrying on business separately, were under the same management. A valuation of the assets of the two shipping companies was procured, and, in order to equalize the assets of each, the company which had the greater assets made a capital distribution equal to the excess. Ropner Holdings Ltd then issued the whole of its authorized capital of £1,759,606 (being the sum of the issued nominal capitals of the two shipping companies) to the shareholders of the shipping companies on the basis of one £1 share for each £1 of the nominal value of the shares of the shipping companies. The aggregate value of the assets of the shipping companies at the date of the acquisition of their shares by Ropner Holdings Ltd was £6,830,972. The excess over £1,759,606 was shown, less £4,860 attributable to formation expenses in the annual balance sheet of Ropner Holdings Ltd as 'capital reserve, share premium account' in conformity with section 56 (1), Companies Act 1948.

The directors had been advised that they were bound to show their accounts in this way but they and the plaintiff in the action, who was a large shareholder, regarded that as very undesirable, because it imposed rigidity on the structure of the company having regard to the fact that a payment out of an account kept under that name, that is, a share premium account, can only be effected by means of a transaction analogous to a reduction of capital. It was, in effect, as if the company had originally been capitalized at nearly £7 million instead of £1,759,606. Counsel for the plaintiff asked who in the world would suppose that a transaction of this kind, a common enough type of transaction, was the issue of shares at a premium? He argued that nobody in the commercial world would dream of so describing it and Mr Justice Harman felt constrained to agree that at first sight it was with a sense of shock that one heard it said that the transaction was the issue of shares at a premium. Everybody, he supposed, who hears these words thinks of a company which, being in a strong trading position, wants further capital and puts forward its shares for subscription by the public at such a price as the market in those shares justifies. The amount of the price above the nominal value of a share is, no doubt, a premium.

That is what is ordinarily meant by the issue of shares at a premium, but section 56 (1) goes further, for it relates to a situation in which a company issues shares at a premium 'whether for cash *or otherwise*'. What 'otherwise' can there be, if the transaction in this case is caught by the word? It must be a consideration other than cash. The section continues with the words, 'a sum equal to the aggregate amount *or value* of the premiums'. Apparently, if the shares are issued for a consideration other than cash and the value of the assets so acquired is more than the nominal value of the shares issued, shares have been issued at a premium. It was argued for the plaintiff that the section cannot apply where the issuing company has no assets at all other than those it will acquire as the price of the issue of the shares because 'premium', it was contended, meant some premiums resulting from the excess value of its already existing assets over the nominal value of its shares. Mr Justice Harman, however, declared that although he had every desire to reduce the effect of the section to what he could not help thinking would be more reasonable limits, he could not see his way to limiting the section in that way. It is clearly not a section which only applies after the company has been in existence a year, or after the company has acquired assets, or that it does not apply on the occasion of a holding company acquiring shares on an amalgamation. Whether that was an oversight on the part of the Legislature or whether it was intended to produce the effect it seemed to have produced, it was not for his lordship to speculate. The transaction was within the scope of the section. He accordingly dismissed the action.

It is to be observed that the assets were valued at nearly £7 million expressly for the purpose of the transaction and the physical assets were valued without including anything for goodwill.

(b) Complete Amalgamation (or Absorption)

This particular form of merger connotes the full integration of one or more undertakings within the legal framework of a limited company, in the sense that the assets of these undertakings are taken over and at the same time the company assumes responsibility for payment of all liabilities. The business or undertakings which are the subject of a complete amalgamation may be owned by individuals, or unincorporated firms, or limited companies as the case may be. Whatever the status of the businesses to be taken over, it is usual for a limited company to be formed as the owner of the combined undertakings.

Once the merger becomes operative, the constituent firms, undertakings or limited companies fade out – the firms and undertakings throwing in their lot, as it were, into the common pool of assets while limited companies would simply go into liquidation.

Once again one is faced with the problem of either forming a new limited company to acquire the businesses or using any existing limited company (if there is one). In the ordinary course of events the advantage seems to lie with using the existing company. The formation of a new company inevitably entails expense even when relief can be claimed from duty on share capital and stamp duty on the conveyance of assets. Furthermore, the sale of the assets of the existing company with all its attendant legal formalities, and the costs arising from the subsequent liquidation of the company, would all be avoided if the company in possession was allowed to continue in existence. Nevertheless, before pronouncing finally upon this matter, inquiry should be made as to the precise rights attaching to the share capital of the existing company; the provisions of its memorandum and articles of association, etc.

An existing company taking over other businesses can pay for them as follows:

(i) In cash. The necessary finance being found either out of existing surplus liquid resources or out of the proceeds of a new issue of shares or debentures.

(ii) In its own shares (or debentures).

If payment is made in cash, only the business or businesses to be taken over need be valued. On the other hand, if payment is made in the shares or debentures of an existing company then a fair value will have to be arrived at, involving a valuation of the business of the purchasing company. One of the main objections to a scheme for complete amalgamation is that the benefit of low interest and/or dividend rates on debentures and/or preference shares in an existing company may be lost for good. Thus, in the case of such a company merging completely with another business and subsequently going into liquidation, its assets would presumably be distributed among its debenture-holders and preference shareholders in that order. The company's assets would now comprise whatever consideration had been received on the sale of its business, namely, cash or shares. Owing to liquidation, the company would be obliged to pay out its debenture-holders and preference shareholders in accordance with the terms of issue, i.e., at par, or, perhaps, at a premium. Bearing in mind, however, that these debentures and preference shares carry a low rate of income, then their true market value (on a going-concern basis) would be well under par. The result is that liquidation may impose a penalty on the ordinary shareholders since they would lose the benefit of the use of capital raised, say, in a period of comparatively cheap money. Thus, instead of buying the undertaking, the merger could be secured by giving the purchasing company the chance of acquiring the ordinary share capital. In this way, the debentures and preference shares remain undisturbed as part of the capital stucture of a going concern, while the consideration for the ordinary shares would be duly enhanced.

A complete amalgamation also suffers from another serious disadvantage, that is the difficulty (not to mention the trouble and expense) of transferring assets and valuable contracts from the name of one company to the name of another. All this can be avoided under the holding company method.

(c) Pooling Arrangements

Pooling arrangements are not very common in industry these days, and one is more likely to meet the holding company or complete amalgamation version of a merger. However, pooling arrangements still exist even if the form they take is sometimes radically different from that followed in the past. In pre-war days, such an arrangement applied where two or three companies continued to operate as separate units, with their separate boards of directors, but undertook to pool their activities – whether manufacturing or sales – and share the profit in some agreed ratio. An alternative basis for pooling is where the two or three companies coming together set up a common research establishment, serving all the constituent members. In practice, this form of pooling is often conducted through the appropriate trade association, especially when none of the constituent members is strong enough to commence its own research activities. But pooling arrangements are on the decline even where only two or three companies are involved. A contributory factor to this decline has clearly been the mounting legislation against monopolies, first in the form of the Monopolies and Restrictive Practices Act 1948, and later reinforced by the Restrictive Trade Practices Act 1956 and the Monopolies and Mergers Act 1965. With very few exceptions, pooling arrangements today would have to run the gauntlet of one or other of these Acts. Without attempting to prejudge the issue, it might prove extremely difficult to show that such arrangements were introduced in the public interest.

Nevertheless, there is still some grouping of resources among firms which have all the features of a pooling arrangement but which operate under more formal auspices.[1] For instance, the construction of nuclear power plants is beyond the capacity of any one engineering firm. The result is that two major groups of nuclear power constructional companies emerged in the United Kingdom, representing the banding together in each case of civil, electrical and mechanical engineers for this specific purpose. The names and composition of the two groups are given below:

NUCLEAR POWER COMPANIES

NUCLEAR POWER GROUP

C. A. Parsons & Co	Electrical Engineers
A. Reyrolle & Co	Electrical Engineers
Head Wrightson & Co	Chemical Engineers
Sir Robert McAlpine & Sons	Civil Engineers
Clarke Chapman & Co	Boilermakers
Whessoe	Boilermakers
Strachan & Henshaw	Steel Hoists
John Thompson	Boilermakers
Associated Electrical Industries	Electrical Engineers

[1] For a full description, see 'Concerning Consortia'. *Board of Trade Journal*, September 26th, 1958.

NUCLEAR DESIGN AND CONSTRUCTION

British General Electric	Electrical Engineers
Babcock & Wilcox	Boilermakers
Taylor Woodrow	Civil Engineers

A further change was announced in March, 1973, when one company replaced Britain's two existing nuclear construction consortia. GEC would hold 50 per cent of the new £10m company, while the Nuclear Power Group and British Nuclear Design and Construction were given the opportunity of taking up a 35 per cent share. The remaining 15 per cent share to be taken up by the Government through the United Kingdom Atomic Energy Authority.

Another slant on pooling arrangements manifests itself in the linking-up of businesses in this country and elsewhere through royalty agreements and licensing arrangements. An example of the former is to be found in the production of the man-made fibre, terylene, which is manufactured by Imperial Chemical Industries Ltd, under a royalty agreement with Calico Printers Association Ltd (who own the patent). As for licensing arrangements, aircraft firms in several countries are making jet engines under licence to Rolls-Royce Ltd.

In recent years, pooling arrangements and joint venutres have been largely carried on through the corporate structure, i.e., associated companies jointly owned by two or more trading companies and this method will probably supersede the less formalized joint ventures and pooling arrangments of old.

CHAPTER IV

FISCAL CONSIDERATIONS

RELIEF FROM STAMP DUTY

A merger of companies almost invariably involves the conveyance of the property of at least one of the companies concerned, and that conveyance is usually a conveyance on sale, whether effected by agreement[1] or pursuant to an Act of Parliament. A wide measure of relief from duty (conveyance on sale duty and companies capital duty) on amalgamations and reconstructions is afforded by section 55 of the Finance Act 1927, provided certain complicated conditions are satisfied. The amalgamations and transfers of assets effected by nationalization and denationalization schemes are separately relieved from duty (e.g., Finance Act 1946, section 52; Finance Act 1948, section 74).

The conditions are laid down in section 55 of the Finance Act 1927, which is a long and somewhat tortuous section. An attempt will be made here to summarize its provisions and to clarify the subject-matter.

Broadly, for stamp duty purposes, a reconstruction is the taking over of an old company by a new company, and an amalgamation is the blending of the undertakings of two existing companies. There is a grave lack of precision, however, about the terms used in this section and it is possible that both 'reconstruction' and 'amalgamation' have a wider and more popular connotation here than in other cases. Two common methods of amalgamation are covered: one, where a company acquires the undertaking of another company; the other, where a company acquires not less than 90 per cent of the share capital of another company, in each case in consideration of an issue of the acquiring company's shares. The Finance Act 1927, section 55, as amended by the Finance Act 1928, section 31, and the Finance Act 1930, section 42, deals with the matter of relief from stamp duty,[2] stipulating that where companies carry out a scheme of reconstruction or amalgamation relief may be obtained from all, or at least part, of the stamp duty normally payable on the capital of a company and on the transfer of shares. Put briefly, the object of subsection (1) of section 55 is to eliminate the hardship of paying duty in a case where there is a transfer of property from one legal entity to another, but that transfer is technical in character and the ownership of the property in substance remains the same.

[1] *Brotex Cellulose Fibres v. Commissioners of Inland Revenue* ([1933] 1 K.B. 158).
[2] See Appendix I.

The full section provides that where in connection with a scheme of reconstruction or amalgamation a limited liability company (called 'the transferee company') is incorporated or increases its capital with the object of acquiring the whole or part of the undertaking, or not less than 90 per cent of the issued share capital, of a particular existing company (called 'the existing company') –

(*a*) no capital duty is to be payable on so much of the initial capital or of the increase of capital of the transferee company as equals whichever is the less of:

(i) the capital of the existing company, or where part only of the undertaking is taken over, the proportion of its capital corresponding to the fraction of the undertaking acquired; or

(ii) the amount to be credited as paid up on the shares issued by the transferee company as consideration for the acquisition and on the shares issued to the creditors of the existing company in consideration of their releasing their debts or assigning them to the transferee company;[1]

(*b*) *ad valorem* duty under the heading 'conveyance on sale' is not to be charged on any instrument made for the purpose of, or in connection with, the transfer of the undertaking or shares or on any instrument made for the purposes of, or in connection with, the assignment to the transferee company of any debts of the existing company.

For the exemption to be available, therefore, the following conditions must be fulfilled:

(1) the particular existing company which is being acquired must be incorporated in England or Scotland;[2]

---

[1] As amended by Finance Act 1928, section 31.

[2] *Nestle Co Ltd v. Commissioners of Inland Revenue* ([1952] 1 All E.R. 1388).

(*a*) This case was decided on exemption from capital duty only. Even so, it would appear to extend to relief from conveyance on sale duty.

(*b*) Prima facie, the expression 'existing company' used in section 55 appears to mean a company wherever incorporated, but in the above case, Danckwerts, J., in the Chancery Division, held that the expression related only to a company regulated by the laws of Great Britain. The appellant company, which was itself incorporated under the laws of Great Britain, increased its capital with a view to the acquisition of not less than 90 per cent of the issued share capital of each of four other companies, two of which were incorporated under the law of Northern Ireland. The Commissioners of Inland Revenue were willing to admit that the transferee company was entitled to exemption from stamp duty in respect of its acquisition of capital of the two companies incorporated in Great Britain, but were unwilling to extend exemption to the capital of the two Northern Ireland companies. Danckwerts, J., said that the point at issue was the meaning of the expression 'existing company'. That expression was nowhere defined, but the learned judge expressed the view that, as the Statute concerned was one which gave relief from fiscal dues, it was not likely that Parliament in passing it was concerned with a company formed abroad. He drew

(2) the consideration for the acquisition (except such part thereof as consists in the transfer to or discharge by the transferee company of the liabilities of the existing company) must consist as to not less than 90 per cent thereof in the issue of shares in the transferee company:

   (a) where an undertaking is to be acquired, to the existing company or its shareholders, or

   (b) where shares are to be acquired, to the shareholders in the existing company in exchange for the shares held by them in the existing company;[1]

(3) the existing company, or its shareholders, must be registered as the holders of shares allotted to them;[2]

(4) the memorandum of association of, or the letters patent or Act of Parliament incorporating, the transferee company must provide that one of the objects for which the company is established is the acquisition of the undertaking of, or shares in existing company, or it must appear from the resolution, Act of Parliament or other authority for the increase of the capital of the transferee company that the increase is authorized for the purpose of acquiring the undertaking of, or shares in, the existing company. Section 55 (2) of the Finance Act 1927, however, provides that for the purposes of the exemption from conveyance on sale duty, a company which has, in connection with a scheme of reconstruction or amalgamation, issued any

---

support for this conclusion from the provision in subsection (1) (a) before its amendment by the Finance Act 1930, section 41, which seemed to make it plain that the prime object of the exemption was to prevent stamp duty being levied afresh where there was merely an increase of capital for the purpose of acquiring existing shares. Although the words 'in respect of which stamp duty has been paid' were repealed by the Act of 1930, the explanation of counsel for the Commissioners made it plain that the reason behind that repeal was *not* to extend the relief to the taking over of shares of a company *in any part of the world*, but simply to make it available to those companies which had been formed or had increased their capital before the Customs and Inland Revenue Act 1888 introduced the stamp duty in question, and in respect of whose capital it could not be said that stamp duty had already been paid.

[1] As to issues to nominees in relation to section 55 (1) (c) (ii), see *Murex Ltd v. Commissioners of Inland Revenue* ([1933] 1 K.B. 173).
[2] *Oswald Tillotson Ltd v. Commissioners of Inland Revenue* ([1933] 1 K.B. 134). The decision in this case turned on the meaning of the word 'issue', a word of which Lord Hanworth, M.R., remarked in the above case that it was impossible to say that it was used in all Acts of Parliament and in all circumstances with the same meaning. He came to the conclusion that 'issue' meant something more than the mere giving of an allotment letter to a member of the existing company enabling him to deal with the shares offered to him as he wished. It must, he held, mean a later stage (viz. placing him on the register of members), and the test to be applied was whether the shares ultimately belonged to some person who was the holder of the shares in the old company so that the identity of the old corporators and the new was maintained.

unissued share capital shall be treated as if it had increased its nominal capital. Where a company has, therefore, simply issued previously unissued share capital, condition (4) obviously does not apply to a claim for exemption from conveyance on sale duty.

Where exemption is claimed from conveyance on sale duty, three further conditions must be satisfied:

(a) the instrument must be adjudicated;

(b) where the transferee company is incorporated under the Companies Acts, the instrument must be:

    (i) executed within twelve months from the registration of the transferee company or the date of the resolution for the increase of its capital; or

    (ii) made in pursuance of an agreement which has been filed, or particulars of which have been filed, with the Registrar of Companies within such period of twelve months;

(c) any debts taken over as part of the consideration must, except in the case of debts due to banks or trade creditors, have been incurred at least two years before the proper time for making a claim for exemption.

The Commissioners are entitled to call for a statutory declaration by a solicitor that the provisions of the section have been complied with, and in practice they usually insist on being supplied with such a declaration. Since, however, the declaration cannot be made until the reconstruction or amalgamation has become effective, it is usual to pay the capital duty in the first instance and to recover it when the transfers are adjudicated. Section 55 (5) further provides that, if at the appropriate time for making a claim for exemption from duty there were in existence all the necessary conditions for such exemption other than the condition that not less than 90 per cent of the issued share capital of the existing company should be acquired, the Commissioners may repay the duty, if it is proved to their satisfaction that not less than 90 per cent of the issued share capital of the existing company has under the scheme been acquired within six months from the earlier of the two following dates:

(a) one month after the first allotment of shares made for the purpose of the acquisition;

(b) the date on which an invitation was issued to the shareholders of the existing company to accept shares in the transferee company. (It will be seen that this provision allows time for the shares of dissentient shareholders to be compulsorily acquired under the provisions of section 209 of the Companies Act 1948.)

The benefit of the exemptions conferred by section 55 will be lost, however, and the duty will become payable as a debt due to the Crown, together with interest at 5 per cent per annum if:

(a) any declaration or other evidence furnished in support of the claim is subsequently found to be untrue in any material particular; or

(b) where shares in the transferee company have been issued to the existing company in consideration of the acquisition of its undertaking, the existing company within a period of two years from the date of the registration or incorporation, or of the authority for the increase of the capital, of the transferee company, as the case may be, ceases, otherwise than in consequence of reconstruction, amalgamation or liquidation to be the beneficial owner of the shares so issued to it; or

(c) where the exemption has been granted in connection with the acquisition by the transferee company of shares in another company, the transferee company within the same period ceases to be the beneficial owner of the shares so acquired, otherwise than in consequence of reconstruction, amalgamation or liquidation.

For the purposes of the last two foregoing cases a company ceases to be the beneficial owner of the shares if it ceases to be the beneficial owner of *any* of them.[1] Where, however, the shares are issued to individual members of the company instead of the company itself, the section does not impose any obligation on the members to retain the shares after they have been issued to them. Consequently, once he has become the registered holder, the member may freely dispose of the shares at any time, without the benefit of the exemptions being lost.

It will be apparent that the conditions of the section are construed very rigidly and exemption will only be granted if the merger or reconstruction is carried out in exact accord with the statutory provisions. For example, it will not apply on an acquisition wholly or largely for cash. It has also been established that even where an exchange of shares takes place, the whole 90 per cent must be obtained under *one* reconstruction. The circumstances in which

---

[1] *Attorney-General v. London Stadiums* ([1950] 1 K.B. 387). The defendant company was incorporated with the object of acquiring and amalgamating the undertakings of three other companies and obtained relief from stamp duty under section 55. Some four months later the three companies sold to a firm of stockbrokers a large proportion of the shares allotted to them in payment for the acquisition of their undertakings and the stockbrokers shortly afterwards sold the shares to the public. The Commissioners of Inland Revenue thereupon brought an action, through the Attorney-General, claiming, under section 55 (6) payment by the transferee company of a sum equal to the duty which had been remitted.

this latter ruling was given are instructive if only to show how important it is to comply with section 55 to the letter. A transferee company which already owned 42 per cent of the share capital of the transferor company (which it had acquired for cash some years before) acquired the bulk of the remaining 58 per cent in consideration of an allotment of its own shares, so as to become the holder of over 90 per cent of the transferor company's share capital. The exemption conferred by section 55 did not apply because the transferee company did not by virtue *of the scheme* acquire 90 per cent of the share capital, and in any event the 90 per cent was not acquired, as to not less than 90 per cent for a share consideration, as required by section 55 (1) (c) (ii).[1]

In cases not falling within the purview of section 55, however, exemption from transfer duty – though not from capital duty – may sometimes be obtained.

This important exemption from the *ad valorem* stamp duty normally payable on any transfer of property is one which relieves from all duty such transfers when made between associated companies. Broadly speaking, for this purpose the companies are associated if one is a 90 per cent or more subsidiary of the other, or if both are 90 per cent or more subsidiaries of a third company. The exemption is conferred by section 42 of the Finance Act 1930,[2] as amended by section 50 of the Finance Act 1938.

In *Escoigne Properties Ltd v. Commissioners of Inland Revenue* an attempt was made to push this exemption to extreme lengths. To simplify the facts, in 1950 the owner of some freehold and leasehold property contracted to sell this property to a limited liability company for a sum to be satisfied by the issue of shares. The shares were duly issued, but no formal conveyance of the properties was ever made.

Four years later the original company arranged to sell these properties to a wholly owned subsidiary company. The original vendor had in the meantime died (a fact of no legal significance) and his personal representatives duly transferred the properties to the subsidiary company. The question then arose as to the proper amount of stamp duty payable on such transfers. Mr Justice Vaisey thought that the transfer was a transfer effected between associated companies and therefore fell within the ambit of the relieving provisions, and that consequently no duty was payable.

The Court of Appeal, however, took a different view. They thought that while the effect of the transfer was such as fell within the relieving provisions, this was not its *only* effect; and that as part of the effect was the completion of the original contract for sale

---

[1] *Lever Brothers Ltd v. Commissioners of Inland Revenue* ([1938] 2 K.B. 518).
[2] See Appendix II.

between the individual and the parent company, this transfer was not relieved from liability for duty.

The majority also expressed the view that, even if the original relieving section in the 1930 Act would have applied if it had stood alone, the exemption would have been lost under the amending section in the 1938 Act which denied the benefit thereof to a case where the final conveyance was executed in pursuance of or in connection with an arrangement whereunder the beneficial interest in the property had previously been transferred by a third party. The original sale, they held, was clearly 'an arrangement', and the original vendor was the 'third party'. Furthermore, in the Court of Appeal, the Master of the Rolls went on to say that if he was wrong, it was plain that whenever an individual desired to transfer property to a company he could avoid all stamp duty by the device of incorporating two companies. The company appealed to the House of Lords, which unanimously dismissed the appeal.[1]

A similar case was heard in the Chancery Division on December 18th, 1958, relating to the conveyances of freeholds and leaseholds from one associated company to another, which turned on the question whether a 90 per cent beneficial interest was held on the relevant date (*Holmleigh (Holdings) Ltd v. Commissioners of Inland Revenue; Metropolitan Boot Co Ltd v. Commissioners of Inland Revenue; The Hale (Holdings) Ltd v. Commissioners of Inland Revenue*).

Another stamp duty case was *Rodwell Securities Ltd v. Inland Revenue Commissioners* ([1968] 1 All E.R. 257). The duty in question was that chargeable on conveyances of land. Section 42 of the Finance Act 1930 exempts from duty any such transfer between companies when one of the companies is beneficial owner of not less than 90 per cent of the issued share capital of the other, or when not less than 90 per cent of the issued share capital of each of the companies is in the beneficial ownership of a third company.

In the admirably succinct headnote to the report of the case, 'a wholly-owned subsidiary of a parent company conveyed land to the wholly-owned subsidiary of another wholly-owned subsidiary of the parent company'. Put otherwise, company A owned company B and company C. Company C owned company D. The transfer was between B and D. Pennycuick, J., held that the transfer was not exempt; where A owns C and C owns D, A does not own D. There can perhaps be little enough dispute on the strict meaning of 'beneficial ownership', but one may sympathize with counsel for the plaintiffs, who argued that the term should be interpreted liberally. The judge agreed that if the Act had used the words 'controlling interest',

---

[1] *The Financial Times*, November 22nd, 1957.

or had added the words 'directly or indirectly', the circumstances here would have been covered. He pointed out too that 'where you have a chain of companies it is always possible, by arranging the transfer in a certain way, to obtain the benefit of exemption under the section'. The duty in question here was £762·50. It is obviously worth while in such cases for B to transfer to C, and then C transfer to D.

This particular relief falls a long way short of the full benefits obtained by compliance with section 55. As stamp and capital duties can be a heavy item on a merger or reconstruction, the greatest possible care should be taken to ensure that the draft scheme complies with the statutory conditions for exemption in every respect. As another illustration of the way one needs to be absolutely meticulous in offering advice on this matter, the scheme for the merger of the Austin Motor Co Ltd and Morris Motors Ltd (under the title of the British Motor Corporation Ltd) as originally announced, merely provided for the new holding company taking over the *ordinary share capital* of the two operating firms, thereby acquiring full control. Unfortunately, both operating companies had substantial preference capital in issue, with the result that in neither case was the requisite 90 per cent of the *issued share capital* being acquired. Once this fact was brought to the notice of the companies concerned, the original scheme was withdrawn and a revised scheme put forward later which entailed an exchange of shares for both the preference and ordinary share capitals of the Austin Motor Co Ltd and Morris Motors Ltd. At the time, it was said that about £650,000 in duty was saved through this amendment of the original scheme.[1]

Example 1

A Ltd has a share capital of £200,000.

B Ltd is incorporated with a share capital of £300,000 to acquire the whole of A Ltd's undertaking, and issues to A Ltd £200,000 fully-paid shares. B Ltd is entitled to relief from capital duty on £200,000 – the amount credited as paid up on the shares and incidentally the amount of A Ltd's share capital. Duty remains to be paid, however, on the balance of £100,000, i.e., part of B Ltd's share capital.

If B Ltd had issued only £180,000 fully-paid shares together with a sum of £20,000 in cash, relief would, of course, only be granted on £180,000, the amount credited as paid up on the shares being less in this case than the share capital of the transferor company. In both cases, the transfers of the undertaking will be stamped

---

[1] *The Economist*, March 8th, 1952, page 610. For the original scheme see *The Economist*, December 1st, 1951.

under the head 'Conveyance or transfer of any kind not hereinbefore described'.

It will be realized that the £180,000 fully-paid shares mentioned in the second paragraph constituted 90 per cent of the total consideration of £200,000. Had the position been otherwise, i.e., £150,000 in fully-paid shares and £50,000 in cash, the exemptions would have been inapplicable.

Example 2

A Ltd increases its capital from £200,000 to £290,000 in order to acquire 90 per cent of the issued share capital of B Ltd, which has an issued share capital of £100,000. A Ltd issues to the holders of 90 per cent of the issued share capital of B Ltd £90,000 fully-paid shares in exchange for their shares in B Ltd. Exemption from capital duty will be granted on the £90,000 which is credited as paid up on the shares issued by A Ltd. If B Ltd had had a share capital of £80,000, however, and A Ltd issued £90,000 fully-paid shares to *all* the shareholders of B Ltd in exchange for their shares in B Ltd, relief from capital duty would be obtained on £80,000 (the amount of B Ltd's share capital) and duty would thus be payable on the balance of £10,000. If, in the last situation, the shares in A Ltd had been issued to the holders of only 90 per cent of the issued share capital of B Ltd (i.e., holders of £72,000 out of the total of £80,000 shares) then relief would still have been granted on £80,000 (the amount of B Ltd's capital).

The transfers of the shares in all the above cases will be stamped as before.

Example 3

A Ltd has an issued share capital of £500,000 divided into £60,000 5 per cent cumulative preference shares and £440,000 ordinary shares. B Ltd, which wishes to take over A Ltd, has a nominal share capital of £1 million – all of which has been issued as ordinary shares. If B Ltd wishes to obtain exemption from capital duty on any increase in its own capital it must make an offer (by way of an exchange of shares) for at least 90 per cent of the issued share capital of A Ltd. If an offer for the £440,000 ordinary share capital was made (which would be more than sufficient to acquire effective control of A Ltd) that would only constitute 88 per cent of the issued share capital and would not, therefore, comply with the requirements. In the circumstances, it would be necessary to make an offer to acquire either £10,000 preference shares *for cash* (thereby bringing up the holding to 90 per cent of the issued share capital of A Ltd), or, if need be, the whole of the preference shares in issue by way of an appropriate exchange of shares. .

Example 4

A Ltd has an issued share capital of £100,000. B Ltd, which wishes to take over A Ltd, has an authorized share capital of £1 million of which £500,000 has been issued. B Ltd issues £100,000 of its hitherto unissued share capital to A Ltd. No capital duty is payable because there has been no increase in A Ltd's share capital, while exemption will be granted from *ad valorem* conveyance on sale duty on the transfers of the undertaking.

Example 5

A Ltd has acquired the undertaking of B Ltd in consideration of the issue of shares to B Ltd and exemption from both conveyance on sale and capital duty has been duly granted under section 55, Finance Act 1927. B Ltd ceases within, say, six months, to be the beneficial owner of the shares issued to it in the first place. The amount of the duty under both heads becomes payable as a debt due to the Crown (together with interest at 5 per cent).

TAXATION

Mergers and take-overs are seldom, if ever, motivated by tax considerations but once the decision to make an offer for another company has been made, tax implications are bound to exert some influence over the terms of the offer and the procedure to be adopted for bringing the other company into the fold.

The tax angle, always complex, has been bedevilled by the introduction of the corporation tax and the capital gains tax, so much so that the involved technical aspects nowadays deserve extended treatment and expert advice beyond the scope of this book.

Suffice it to say that those interested will find a useful and reliable summary of the present position in *Take-overs and Amalgamations*, by M. A. Weinberg.[1]

In particular, Mr Weinberg examines the tax effect of take-overs and amalgamations from three points of view:

(a) The effects, primarily as regards shareholders, but also to an extent as regards the companies, of the various methods of effecting take-overs and amalgamations.

(b) The special safeguards necessary when a close company is taken over.

(c) The tax positions applicable to a group of companies, which facilitate the rearrangement of the affairs of the companies after a take-over or amalgamation.

---

[1] Sweet & Maxwell. Second edition, 1967. Chapters 16 and 17.

CHAPTER V

VALUATION – PRIVATE LIMITED COMPANIES

In the long run the prime determinant of the market price of a share is the amount the company can first earn – and thence pay out as dividend. If, therefore, one adopts this criterion of value, it resolves the apparent conflict between choosing a 'net assets' basis or a 'maintainable net profits' basis. At the same time, one cannot dismiss the 'net assets' approach altogether because the nature and circumstances of the business may require the application of this method. In general terms, however, assuming a 'going-concern' basis, earning power must have a profound effect upon asset values, in fact it is not too much to say that earning power really dictates asset values to a large extent. To take an extreme case, a company might spend £1 million on building a refrigeration plant at the North Pole. Its shares might have a high asset value but with earnings non-existent the price of the shares would probably be nil or thereabouts (near the 'break-up' value of the assets, for instance). The reason for this is not hard to find. There is literally nothing to go for so far as a potential investor is concerned. The evidence of past earning power is unlikely to inspire confidence; while future prospects are just as gloomy. Thus, even where asset values are important, they are important only in so far as they can be related to the ultimate earnings on them. This explains the apparent incongruity of an official Stock Exchange quotation for shares in a public company being lower than the estimated 'break-up' value, even when based on book values taken from the current balance sheet, of those same shares.

First, the 'break-up' value can only be of a transitory or academic interest to shareholders in a 'going concern', and one which firmly intends to stay in business in the future, i.e., the possibility of actual breaking up is so remote that the shareholders have little chance of encashing the paper values so disclosed.

Secondly, the earning power of those assets *under existing management* is insufficient to support a rate of dividend which would represent a fair return on the assets taking into account the nature of the trade and the element of risk involved. Accordingly, the market price of the shares (and through that the market value attaching to the net assets) simply reflects the known earning power or actual income derived from an investment in such a company. It must be remembered that share market quotations, which are 'prices' not 'valuations', appear to follow the generally accepted principle that the worth of the assets of a company is determined by what these assets are earning or are likely to earn for the shareholders. In the latter case, of course, the current price does to some extent discount future prospects.

All public company share transactions take place framed against the economic and political climate prevailing at the time in the stock markets. This background exists no less in the valuation of private companies' shares. It is apparent that, after making due allowance for the many extraneous factors which may affect the market for quoted shares, the investor in an established company looks first for earnings sufficient to satisfy his expectations of a yield on capital invested commensurate with the risk involved; secondly, at the trend of profits over the years. In short, he gives much less consideration to the asset values (whether based on book values or current values) when he is once convinced that earnings amply cover his income (represented by actual and prospective dividend requirements). In other words, neither earnings alone, nor net assets alone will reveal the market price of shares; but earnings related to the net assets employed will determine the approximate market value. That is why both avenues have to be explored before a firm valuation can be given, although the accent is on maintainable earnings rather than asset-worth.

The merits of this argument are not always apparent to shareholders in a private company, who are not usually so completely divorced from all contact with the management as in a public company. They may have formulated their own optimistic views as to the intrinsic value of the assets – a view, perhaps, sanctified by time and repetition – irrespective of whether these assets are employed to the best advantage or not. When it comes to an independent valuation, those lofty ideas of value are only too often shattered in the cold light of reality.

GENERAL PRINCIPLES

The basic principle in share valuations of all kinds may be stated as the determination of a fair price for the shares as between a willing buyer and a willing seller, the business being regarded as a going concern. The expression 'going concern' suggests not merely continued existence, but betokens the continuance of a vigorous and healthy existence. It implies that the company is in possession of such resources, and is being managed in such a way, that it earns a commercial reward for the capital invested, that reward including compensation for the general risks of the trade and the specific risks of the company, as well as adequate remuneration for all persons who are employed in the business; if the company's earnings are insufficient to uphold such a commercial reward, it cannot be considered on a 'going concern' basis. In such an event, resort must be had to a potential 'break-up' value.

VALUATION OF ORDINARY SHARES

The approach to a valuation of shares in a private company is much the same as that which would be adopted in the preparation of a prospectus, that is to say, most careful attention must be given to the past history and present background of the company and statistical details must be prepared in respect of the asset position at the relevant date together with a review of the trading results over a period of years. The length of the period will be chosen so as to give a representative survey over the years immediately preceding the date of valuation. Too long a period may easily be misleading by going back to years in which conditions existed which were radically different from those ruling today. While a good profit record over many years is a satisfactory proof of the stability of a business, the valuer should concentrate on the more recent period, being basically concerned with the present.

In the first instance, the valuer must carry out a close examination of the memorandum and articles, which should not be confined only to sections devoted to share capital and the rights of shareholders. In private companies the rights of directors are quite likely to be equally if not more important.

He will then proceed to an examination of the assets position as disclosed by the last accounts of the company, and a summary of trading results for the determined period. The asset position may be dealt with first, not because it is more important, but because it may provide some of the evidence required to indicate the adjustments necessary to the summary of trading results, besides affording an immediate indication of certain necessary aspects of the company's affairs.

ASSETS STATEMENT

The assets statement will be based on the most recent audited balance sheet (with any notes or qualifications) and may now be considered in some detail.

Investments in subsidiaries

While it is not usual to find subsidiary holdings in private companies, such cases do occur. A preliminary step to valuation is a consolidation, in the usual manner, of the group concerned, omitting members of the group which are not operating it. The consolidated balance sheet, with consolidated profit and loss accounts for the requisite period, will then form the basis of the valuation. Shares in subsidiaries excluded from consolidation will be considered as investments not employed in the business.

Fixed assets (*tangible*)

It is preferable to have land and buildings, whether freehold or leasehold, separately valued where this asset is relatively important, or where the number of shares involved is large; usually, unless control is passing with the shares, the cost of valuation of the asset renders such a step unjustifiable. The balance sheet amount should be taken in the absence of a separate valuation unless there is evidence of abnormality in the methods of depreciation adopted by the company.

If the circumstances are such as to require it, in the interests of fairness, an adjustment (which must be arbitrary in its nature) based on the date of acquisition, original cost and adequacy of maintenance compared with present-day values, if these can be ascertained, should be made at the time of the share valuation.

Much the same procedure will apply to items such as plant and machinery, furniture, and similar fixed assets; in the absence of a separate valuation, the depreciation rates employed during the period of review must be looked upon as the evidence most indicative of the closeness of the approximation of the net book amount to a reasonable value. It is usual for private companies to depreciate fixed assets very heavily and close scrutiny of this charge, over as long a term of years as is practical, is invariably necessary.

Investments

Shares and securities which are quoted will be valued at the middle price if held for permanent investment, or at lower price if included with the current assets. Unquoted stocks or shares, when the amount involved is material, must be the subject of a secondary valuation by methods similar to those used for the main valuation. In cases where the number of shares concerned is not important, such evidence as is available in the last balance sheet and accounts of the company or business concerned may be accepted.

If the theory that value is determined by earning capacity is adopted, a distinction must be made between assets which earn by trading or manufacturing activity and those which are expected to produce income independently of such activity. If material, therefore, any assets of a private company which belong to the latter class would be segregated from the other tangible assets. Such assets will include investments or loans (other than those of a temporary nature) and amounts expended with the intention of creating a future advantage or asset. Segregation is not called for unless the assets are material and are separable from the working capital of the business.

Current assets

As a general rule the balance sheet values may be accepted without extensive investigation; stock-in-trade and work in progress will be examined in connection with the trading records. As a result of this examination the person valuing the shares will be aware of the method of stock-taking and the consistency or otherwise in application which will determine his opinion about this asset. An accountant other than the auditor must, of necessity, devote close attention to this matter; an auditor who is valuing the shares will have already done so.

Difficulties, which may be awkward to deal with when material, may occur in a private company's balance sheet in relation to loans to associated companies or loans to directors or persons employed, sometimes free of interest. If the loans are not temporary they should be considered as investments. In any case diplomacy must be necessary in order to form an estimate of the provision, if any, required against possible loss; if the loan is to an associated company, an estimate of the extent of security must be made from its last balance sheet. The position as regards trade debtors can usually be ascertained without trouble.

Intangible assets

The question of goodwill is taken up later, but, whatever the method of goodwill valuation adopted by the valuer, any existing item of goodwill shown on the balance sheet will be eliminated in marshalling the assets, together with items of patents, trade-marks, and so on which are normally so analogous to goodwill that their values are almost inseparable from goodwill.

There should also be eliminated any expenditure, appearing as an asset on the balance sheet, which has not brought into existence, at the date of the valuation, an advantage for the enduring benefit of the business. Such assets may have a value apart from the goodwill, but it is more prudent to include them in a 'goodwill' composite item. If there is expenditure on a potential asset or advantage, the results of which are not yet available, the item may at this stage be considered as an investment, at cost or suitable valuation.

When patents and similar rights have a value independent of the trading of the company, that is to say when they can be realized separately and, therefore, are not entirely intangible, they ought not to be classed with those which are inseparable from the business as a going concern. In such cases, if material, an independent expert valuation may be necessary, and the amount will be included with the tangible assets.

Marshalling the assets

After consideration of the balance sheet items on the lines suggested it will be possible to marshal the assets into three groups.

The first group will consist of the tangible assets directly employed in the business, which fall naturally into two classes:

(a) net fixed assets, after eliminating the values of investments not employed in the business permanently held under this heading whether quoted or unquoted, and after deducting long-term liabilities;

(b) net current assets, after eliminating any permanent investments included in current assets, and long-term loans, and after deducting actual liabilities.

The second group consists of investments not directly employed in the business whether regarded as fixed or current assets, the value of which must be included in the final value of the shares concerned but possession of which produces income which is independent of earnings of the company from the trading business on which it is engaged.

An important factor in estimating the risk attaching to an investment in shares in a limited company is the existence or otherwise of surplus funds, usually taken to mean assets which could be distributed to shareholders without detriment to the earnings of the company as a going concern. The extent of the value of the net current assets, which will be further augmented by assets of the second group, is of significance in this estimate.

The third group consists of the intangible assets, the balance sheet values of which will be replaced by an amount computed by one or other of the methods of determining goodwill.

Current liabilities and provisions

The balance sheet figures may be accepted without alteration in the absence of unusual circumstances, but provisions should be scrutinized. It is still very evident that the word 'provision' is used in a much wider context than that envisaged under the Companies Act 1948, even in the accounts of some public companies. Only provisions that fit the statutory definition can be included; all else must be treated as reserves.

Arising out of this last comment it may be noted that the reserve for future taxation or provision for current taxation, or both, may call for revision and adjustment in the light of more up-to-date information so that only the actual liability at the balance sheet date is included.

The concept of goodwill

In many ways, it is a good deal easier to know what goodwill is than to define it. Back in 1901, three learned judges each gave a definition of goodwill in connection with a case before them.[1] Lord Macnaghten said: 'What is goodwill? It is a thing very easy to describe, very difficult to define. It is the attractive force that

[1] *Commissioners of Inland Revenue v. Muller & Co's Margarine.*

brings in custom. It is the one thing which distinguishes an old-established business from a new business at its first start.' In the same case Lord Davy said: 'The term goodwill is nothing more than a summary of the rights accruing to the purchasers from their purchase of the business and the property employed in it.' While Lord Lindley followed up by stating: 'I understand the word to include whatever adds value to the business by reason of situation, name and reputation, connection, introduction to old customers, and agreed absence from competition, or any of these things.'

Mr Ralph A. Hadrill, F.INST.D., discussing the question of goodwill in an article in *The Times Review of Industry*, pointed out that:

'Numerous textbooks have been written on the subject of commercial goodwill and the valuation thereof. Most of them contain mathematical formulas, more or less complicated, designed to bring out the required answer. But these are all more academic than practical; with a few exceptions it is impossible to lay down any hard and fast rules for the valuation of the goodwill of a business. Every case has to be judged on its merits, and while the opinion of a professional valuer specializing in the trade concerned may be of assistance as a guide, it is not necessarily final. In the ultimate analysis, the value of goodwill is what you can get for it, and amongst honest men that is as fair an assessment as any.'[1]

The real purpose underlining the various methods used to evaluate goodwill is simply the necessity for arriving at a figure – a starting point based on some tenable evidence that will serve as a basis for negotiation. More often than not, the price at which the bargain is eventually struck represents a compromise between the value sought by the vendor and the value upheld by the purchaser (or their respective professional advisers).

During the past thirty years or so, the problems associated with the valuation of goodwill have been given great attention by accountants in this country, the main protagonists in the discussion being the late Sir Arthur Cutforth,[2] the late Mr P. D. Leake,[3] and the late Mr H. E. Seed,[4] all of whom concentrated upon the commercial worth aspect. It is this special angle of goodwill which will now be examined, however interesting and thought-provoking the judicial dicta on the intrinsic meaning and elusive nature of the concept of goodwill may be.

The valuation of commercial goodwill
The late Mr P. D. Leake would, no doubt, receive a wide measure of agreement from accountants on his concise statement that:

[1] 'No Formula for Goodwill Valuation', March 1958.
[2] *Methods of Amalgamation and the Valuation of Businesses.*
[3] *Commercial Goodwill.*
[4] *Goodwill as a Business Asset.*

'without the reasonable probability of the earning of future super-profit no present value in the form of goodwill can exist'.

The idea of super-profit is of comparatively recent origin but most accountants are agreed that super-profit is a definite factor in goodwill. Super-profits were defined by the late Mr H. E. Seed as 'profits in excess of those required to provide an economic rate of remuneration for all labour and capital used in a business'.

The more advanced idea of 'super-profits' basis for goodwill has found ready acceptance among accountants, although in its simplest form it depends upon an estimate, not always easy to make, of the probable duration of the super-profits and, consequently, the number of years' purchase appropriate to a specific case. This key duration factor is a result of economic forces which tends to attract competition in a field which shows an above-average return. Therefore it is unwise to expect super-profits to continue as a permanent feature of future trading. In fact, the permanence may diminish as the super-profits increase. The relative probability of duration, as between different types of business, is largely a matter of opinion, and the number of years' purchase may be so arbitrary that the valuer's decision, if challenged, is very difficult to uphold.

To meet this very real objection to the basic theory certain refinements have been put forward. The late Sir Arthur Cutforth suggested a sliding-scale method which recognizes the economic case that the probable duration of super-profits is likely to diminish as super-profits increase. The sliding-scale method divides super-profits into stages with a diminishing number of years' purchase applied to each successive upward stage. Although it allows for the economic forces at work, the basic weakness persists in that it still depends on a quite arbitrary choice of periods.

The late Mr P. D. Leake was the chief advocate of a method which is in the nature of an annuity valuation. He took his stand on the fact that:

'The value of goodwill being nothing but the present value of super-profit expected to arise out of the business in future years, it is clear that as those profits arise in future years the value of the original goodwill which was purchased will be gradually worked off and will ultimately disappear. It is true that valuable goodwill may then exist but this will have arisen out of the good work done in the meantime. . . .'

In effect, he is saying that the drawing power of purchased goodwill slows down and ultimately fades away altogether, while newly created goodwill may simultaneously arise out of the ashes of the old and eventually prove a thriving new asset once more in the hands of the new owner. An example may suffice to illustrate the various methods; assuming estimated super-profits of £9,000 and an anticipated return of 10 per cent on the capital invested:

			£	Goodwill £
(a) Direct super-profits method:				
£9,000 at, say, five years' purchase ..	..	..		45,000
(b) Sliding-scale method:				
£2,000 at, say, five years' purchase ..	..	..	10,000	
£3,000 at, say, four years' purchase..	..	..	12,000	
£4,000 at, say, three years' purchase..	..	..	12,000	
				34,000
(c) Annuity method:				
Present value of an annuity of £9,000 for five years:				
interest at 10 per cent ..	..	..	..	34,117

It will be observed that all these methods are based on an arbitrary determination of the probable duration of super-profits. That is where all these methods founder because the probable duration of super-profits must be a matter of conjecture. Thus the refinements of technique embodied in some of these methods ultimately give way once again to sheer guesswork.

Recent years have witnessed yet another approach to the problem. Mr T. Greenwood first enunciated the new concept in an article in *The Accountant*,[1] and this was subsequently amplified by the late Mr H. E. Seed in 1937. The latter wrote:

'Since then the purchaser of goodwill must preforce be the purchaser of a business, it is the price he is to pay for the business which primarily concerns him, rather than the price he is to pay for goodwill as such. The matter in which the purchaser is primarily interested is the rate of return, which the profits which he expects the business to earn (after providing for his own remuneration if he is to work in the business) will yield on the price he is paying.'

This concept closely follows Lord Macnaghten's description of goodwill as 'the very sap and life of the business without which the business would yield little or no fruit', and categorically refutes the idea that goodwill can have a value apart from the value of the whole tree. As a method, it is realistic enough to eliminate any guesswork over the probable duration of super-profits.

Consideration will be given at a later stage to the means of determining appropriate rates of earnings suitable for this treatment of goodwill as a general rather than a particular item of the assets, the total value of which is ascertained by capitalization of earnings.

Adopting this general method, assuming that a company earns trading profits of £10,000, and the expected rate of earnings is 10 per cent on the price paid, the total value of that company's business assets would be £100,000. If the value of the net tangible assets is in excess of that amount, no goodwill exists, and a negative goodwill ('badwill') may be said to reduce their value to the extent of the excess; if, however, the net tangible assets are less than £100,000, goodwill exists to the amount of the difference.

[1] June 17th, 1933.

A variation of this general method aims at differentiating between earnings from tangible assets and earnings attributable to the goodwill, or intangible assets. It is based on the consideration that the higher the proportionate value of the tangible assets to the total value of the business, the higher should be that total value. For example, a company may have net tangible assets of £100,000 with profits of £22,000. If a return of 10 per cent is regarded as a reasonable one for the purchase price represented by the value of the tangible assets, the profits attributable to these assets will be £10,000. The remaining profits of £12,000 may be considered as derived from the intangible assets, in respect of which a return of 12 per cent on the purchase price might be regarded as reasonable. The intangible assets, that is the goodwill, would thus be valued at £100,000 which, added to the tangible assets, results in a total price of £200,000 for the business as a whole.

This method is said to recognize the fact that tangible assets can be sold separately and are reasonably permanent, neither of which advantages normally adheres to intangible assets. Yet piecemeal realization of assets seems more appropriate to a liquidation than to a sale of a business as an entity, and seems to cut right across the original concept of the valuation of a business as a whole rather than of its component parts. Another drawback to this method is that two appropriate rates of return have to be estimated. One rate is arbitrary enough; two rates simply defeat the object of the exercise and also widen the possible margin of error.

Another variation put forward by Mr W. G. Campbell, B.A., F.C.A.,[1] is applicable to cases where there exists a material difference between the amount arrived at on a capitalization of earnings and the value placed on the tangible assets. In such cases the difference can be, at least partly, reduced by taking the mean between the tangible assets value and the yield value. Nevertheless, this is at best a compromise solution and cannot be upheld on logical grounds.

'For a company with £100,000 capital in £1 shares, making £7,000 profits, if earnings of 14 per cent on capital invested are regarded as appropriate, a value of 50p a share results on application of the earnings basis; this value is unrealistic if the balance sheet value of the net tangible assets is considered reasonable and approximates to the amount of nominal capital. In such cases a share value of the mean between 50p and 100p is perhaps, if still only an estimate, a closer approach to the "fair" value, however that word is interpreted.'

Against that, it may be argued that the purchaser is buying a collection of assets which happen to show a below-average return. There may be various reasons for this, such as lack of orders suggesting that the capacity of the firm is under-employed, unusually

[1] 'The Valuation of Holdings in Private Limited Companies'. *The Accountant*, October 20th and 27th, 1951.

high overheads due to poor or inept management, selling prices too low, or inflation has pushed up the value of one or more assets thereby bringing to light the inadequacy of profit margins (which had hitherto seemed ample when calculated on balance sheet book values).

In any event the purchaser should be required to pay even nearer today's price for the assets irrespective of their revenue-earning capacity, since the intrinsic worth is there, and that is what they are worth in the open market as assets alone. The new owner may or may not have a chance of reaping the fruits of his collection of assets in the future. That is his risk. But to sell on the basis of a poor earnings record is to perpetuate the very under-valuation that gives rise to so many take-over bids (which are discussed in Chapter VIII) in the public company sector.

In 1952, the Incorporated Accountants' Research Committee gathered together the views of their members in a booklet under the title of *The Valuation of Goodwill*. This booklet shows examples of the six suggested methods of valuing goodwill, which were examined earlier on.

Summary of trading results
The survey of past results will be directed to obtaining evidence and data for a reasonable judgement to be made of the current maintainable profits earned by the company, adjustments being made, if necessary, suitable to the actual circumstances prevailing at the date of valuation.

The general principles in preparing the profits statement will be those applicable to prospectuses, which are fairly well established. The period chosen for the survey need not, usually, be so long as for prospectuses and need not necessarily be unbroken, since it is often safer to leave out abnormal years affected by exceptional circumstances. A period of from three to five normal years is usual in modern conditions; in certain cases it may be essential to go farther back, but, whatever period is chosen, the last two or three years will certainly be the most useful in determining the trend of current profits and in showing whether the company's activities are growing or diminishing.

Specific matters, which will usually require close attention for adjustment purposes, may now be considered.

Remuneration of management
Difficulties are usually found in connection with management charges in private companies' accounts. These charges tend to bear little resemblance to what might be regarded as a notional market remuneration for the services rendered. The valuer cannot escape a difficult and invidious attempt to eliminate these charges, and

substitute a more reasonable figure, if he is to arrive at a commercial profit for the purpose of his survey.

Transactions not at arm's length

A similar necessity exists to scrutinize all dealings between the company and its associates, whether within the company or outside, which are not arm's-length transactions, that is, when the consideration given or taken is not a true commercial consideration for goods or services, in the circumstances. It is easy to eliminate an amount but always very difficult to replace with a more reasonable one, especially when related to past events. When material items of this kind occur very frequently in the survey of profits, it may be necessary to look less to the earnings aspect than to the intrinsic asset position for valuation purposes.

Depreciation of fixed assets

This is, perhaps, the most difficult of all matters to adjust, if only because of the different policies which private, to say nothing of public, companies adopt for depreciation purposes. So far as orthodox depreciation is concerned, i.e., based on original cost, the policy may have been based on custom or caution, often both, and the resultant charge against revenue may be even more unrealistic than the charge made in respect of management remuneration. Provided the charge has been made on some systematic basis, however, the exact form of the method used, whether it be straight-line, reducing balance or some other method, seems immaterial. In any event, a useful cross-check on the adequacy of the charge can be made by comparing the capital allowances granted for tax purposes – though even here investment and initial allowances can upset the year-by-year comparison.

After nearly twenty years of persistent inflation, however, the real problem is no longer centred on orthodox depreciation. Instead, one has to try and assess what extra sums *should have* been set aside in the past (and *must* be set aside in the future) to close the gap between orthodox depreciation and a notional figure based upon estimated replacement cost. Unless this vital adjustment is made it means that past profits have been overstated simply because insufficient provision has been made for the eventual replacement of existing capacity at the new price-level then ruling. Inflation may have been a gradual process, but it has also been a continuing process. Consequently, it represents a *permanent* fall in the purchasing power value of money. Even if the Government has at last come to grips with inflation and halts the rise in prices, the twenty-year backlog has still to be surmounted. In short, some part of past earnings ought to be 'hived-off' as it were, to prepare for the day of reckoning, just as some part of future earnings have been

mortgaged, as it were, in order to take care of the continuing existence of the firm at its present level of capacity, without any question
of expansion arising.

If the fixed assets have been revalued, the task is made that much
easier, but even where no revaluation has been made, these adjustments still cannot be disregarded.

Stock-in-trade and work in progress

The valuer will be guided by the principles which apply equally to
all trading accounts, whether for balance sheet or prospectus purposes. During the period under review the methods of valuing stock
and work in progress must remain consistent; if they have been
varied at any time, consequential adjustments will be made to carry
the variation back to the beginning of the period. A valuer not
previously acquainted with the company's business will be obliged
to make a close comparative survey of the trading or manufacturing
accounts for the period in order to detect results which may point
to material variations in stock-taking.

Taxation

For the purpose of preparing a profits statement it is permissible
to ignore direct taxation, both profits tax and income tax; the distribution element of the former was so dependent on the appropriation
of profits as to merit inclusion as an appropriation itself. It is more
convenient to ascertain the results before all taxation as a means
and basis for computing the current maintainable profits.

Repairs and maintenance

The scrutiny of this item demanded by present conditions will
depend on its relative importance and no definite rules can be given
except that some kind of spread-over was inevitable in material
cases during a period when a regular policy of maintenance could
not be maintained.

Not only in this instance but in general it is wiser to confine
adjustments to items which manifestly distort the trend of profits.
It is possible to regard certain abnormalities as normal for any
business, in that their occurrence, or recurrence, is bound to happen
sooner or later. The unusual should not, without consideration, be
treated as abnormal.

Income excluded

The usual methods of adjustment will have dealt with non-recurring
material items, but it is necessary to consider that portion, if any,
of the company's income which is derived from funds invested
outside the business, since earnings are, generally, interpreted as
the results of the trading activities, apart from other sources of
income, at least for the purpose of valuation based on their capitali-

zation. Some companies combine trading operations with the holding of investments and it may be impracticable to draw a distinction between the two activities, but for cases in which the investments are more or less permanent they represent employment of surplus funds outside the business and their value, and the income derived from them, cannot be related to the trading of the business. Income from this source should, therefore, be deducted in the earnings statement, the value of the assets concerned having been already segregated.

Adjustments for subsequent events

It may now be assumed that the valuer has informed himself of the relevant facts regarding the general background and that he has prepared a statement of the assets together with a summary of the trading results, before taxation, for a period sufficient for his purpose. The adjustments, if any, made to both statements will be those normally applied for a prospectus certificate in respect of any events occurring between the date of the last balance sheet and that of the share valuation, which directly affect the asset position at the former date or which directly affect the 'maintainable' element of the results based on post trading. Such events, for example as realization of fixed assets, or sale of sections of the business, must entail elimination of the past results which were directly attributable to their retention in the business, while the declaration of dividends or distributions not provided for in the last balance sheet will directly reduce the net assets presented at that time.

If, however, the events are connected with anticipated trends, affecting the future and not the past, it is suggested that no adjustments should be made. Such events, for example, a change of management or the acquisition of new resources or assets, which cannot affect the past factual results, or a maintainable earnings estimate based on them, should be regarded as affecting only the future, proper weight being given to them in computing the risk element in due course.

Current maintainable earnings

Having completed the adjusted earnings summary, one must decide on the past results to be adopted as foundation for the estimate of current maintainable earnings at the valuation date. It is usual to take a straight average of the annual results of the period and, for a steadily maintained business, this is a reasonable method. If, however, there have been violent fluctuations in any years it may be fairer to eliminate years which were materially affected by non-recurring factors and are, therefore, not a sound indication of normal earnings. In such cases (whether eliminated or not) a lengthened period for review is necessary, so as to leave a reasonable number of normal years for averaging. Where extreme fluctuations are absent but the trend of profits is, markedly, upwards or downwards, only a weighted average, giving more emphasis to recent than to remote years, can overcome the faults inherent in a straight average.

As a guide to the weighting of the average, if some time has elapsed since the last balance sheet, the trend of current results may be useful if this can be accurately estimated. Private companies do not always keep accurate interim statistical records, but it is usually possible to obtain a reasonable close approximation, which can be of use also in the risk computation.

The average adopted represents the current maintainable earnings, before taxation, of the company in its trading capacity.

Risk

There is no such thing as a riskless investment but, for the determination of the appropriate rate of capitalization for a valuation of company shares, it is generally assumed that the rate of yield to be obtained from gilt-edged stocks represents the minimum yield sought by an investor who wishes to eliminate the risk element as far as possible and who expects a continuously maintained return. The augmented yield expected from an investment in shares of a public company represents largely the risk attaching to the type of business, and the risk of fluctuation in profits and dividend. In the case of a private company, to these general risks must be added certain special risks which call for a further addition to the yield; upon reasonably accurate estimation of supplementary risks depends the valuation of the shares.

The personal element assumes primary importance, after the general risk elements common to all investments are taken for granted. In private companies the separation of ownership and control is less than in public companies but the continued maintenance of efficient control is more difficult to ensure. It follows that the probability of continuity in management assumes great importance as a risk factor.

The asset position is important in this connection not only as determining the available cover, but also when there is a material difference between capitalization (which will include the goodwill element) based on a suitable yield and that based only on the amount of net tangible assets. The greater the difference the more necessity exists for the yield to be maintained at a level high enough to enable the investor to write off, in a reasonable time, the goodwill element latent in the purchase price in addition to compensating him for the other risks of any particular case.

The factors which must be considered in measuring the risk

elements of private companies' shares may be divided into those generally applicable to all investments in limited companies, and those which specially affect private companies. The general factors may be summarized:

(a) type of business carried on, and its place in the range between necessities and luxuries;

(b) locality and security of tenure of premises;

(c) length of time established;

(d) competition, actual and potential, and spread of customers;

(e) present state of the order-load;

(f) capital structure with special attention to priority classes of shares and to long-term liabilities, and the terms under which these have been issued or borrowed;

(g) management, particularly with regard to the prospects of continuity of management, and whether one or several persons are actively managing the business;

(h) the nature and value of the tangible asset backing and whether the assets are likely to be difficult of realization, are especially subject to obsolescence or are mainly of value only in the particular business involved;

(i) extent of the cover given by earnings in relation to dividends on shares to be purchased;

(j) the steady maintenance, or otherwise, of available profits over the period and the trend of these profits at the date of valuation, the absence of material fluctuations in annual profits being a major factor;

(k) repayment obligations, if any, in respect of prior capital and loans.

In addition to these general items the most important additional elements of risk attaching to private companies' shares deal with:

(l) marketability of the shares, as affected by special restrictions on transfer, usually specified in the articles;

(m) the powers of directors under the articles, especially where there is control by one individual only;

(n) the value of the personal contacts of the management, if these are a material element in the business.

Detailed consideration of these points is not possible nor would it necessarily be useful, owing to the numerous variations in each individual case.

Having considered the risk elements, taking care not to give attention only to factors which increase the risk to the neglect of those which diminish it, it is necessary to determine the rate of return, on the amount invested, which would satisfy a willing purchaser. For private companies the rate of return must allow for three elements:

(*a*) the minimum 'risk-free' rate which may be taken as represented by the return from gilt-edged stocks at the time;

(*b*) an increased return, applicable to shares of various classes in public companies, representing the risk compensations for such shares; the market quotations give a return compounded of these two elements which may be used for comparison and as a standard for our purpose;

(*c*) a further increased return to compensate for special risks inherent in a private company's shares, as compared with quoted shares, i.e., lack of marketability and greater degree of risk.

It is unfortunately, not possible to express, in numerical form, the amount of supplementary return which should be added to the chosen standard to compensate for the appropriate risks in any company whose shares are being valued. In the case of public companies the differences between the gilt-edged minimum rate and the market return vary widely even among companies in the same class, and even with apparently similar records. This wide margin is wider still in the case of private companies, aggravated by the small number of share transactions and the still smaller number of arm's-length transfers.

The valuer must exercise his judgement and be prepared to justify it from his experience, after giving due weight to all the evidence available, but it might be suggested that an increased earnings yield of at least 3–5 per cent would be expected from the equity shares of a good private company as compared with shares of a similar class in a public company.

Methods of estimating yield required

Although, in previous considerations of the principles of valuation involving rates of return, it has not been necessary to draw a distinction between dividend yield and earnings yield, this distinction must now be discussed.

In market price lists of quoted shares the 'yield per cent' given relates to the return of the buyer's price, based on recent dividends and is, therefore, a dividend yield. To compute the corresponding earnings yield is not possible without recourse to the company's record, usually conveniently available in the form of an Exchange Telegraph card.

In the case of private company shares (other than shares relating to prior capital which will be considered later) the earnings yield is more important than the dividend yield, chiefly because the dividend policy of private companies is apt to be somewhat irregular.

Apart from the smaller private companies where it is customary to 'absorb' profits in the form of directors' fees in order to obtain the benefit of earned income relief for tax purposes, the others often pursued an erratic dividend policy from motives of self-preservation rather than choice. For instance, the proprietors of private companies have frequently allowed reserves to grow, not because they were required to finance future expansion, but specifically because there has been no point in distributing them (thus attracting surtax and the withdrawal of non-distribution relief). If they had been able to distribute without a penal tax charge, they would have done so. These companies are thus in a wholly different category from companies which have retained profits to finance their own growth.

In inducing these companies to withhold their profits, the incidence of profits tax at the distributed rate has been in the majority of cases a more compelling factor than the surtax liability of the proprietors. This is either due to the shareholders' individual surtax positions or because of the possibility of getting money out in the form of capital, which would not bear surtax, but would have attracted a distribution charge. When, however, it is found that the continued policy of a private company in regard to management remuneration and dividend distribution has been consistent and sound in relation to the profits earned, a valuation based on dividend yield may be considered as an alternative no less equitable.

In the absence of a sound and consistent policy, it is more equitable to deal with private company shares on an earnings yield basis, for which purpose the standards of comparison, in normal cases, must be discussed.

(a) Perhaps the most satisfactory method, which, however, is not always available, is to take, as the basis of comparison, shares involved in a public issue. If the type of business is reasonably similar, and the market conditions at the date of the issue are not too remote from those of the date of the valuation, the prospectus will disclose sufficient information to determine the expected earnings yield on the issue price and the background history should afford some evidence of the comparative general risk factors. Even if some time has elapsed since a prospectus was issued, this method may be suitable if material changes in share market prices are taken into account.

(b) An examination of the market lists will permit the selection of two or three public companies, as nearly as possible similar to the private company for which the share valuation is required. The Exchange Telegraph cards of each company can be scrutinized with a view to selecting the most nearly comparable. Information sufficient for general risk appraisement can be made from the records available on the card and the earnings yield on the market price can be ascertained.

(*c*) Where the valuation concerns a small number of shares an average method may be employed by taking the average equity dividend yields of several quoted shares, reasonably similar in character to those to be valued, and multiplying by a figure which, allowing for normal taxation and reserves, will give a notional earnings yield. For example, with taxation at present rates and a reasonable distribution policy, equity earnings might be as much as three times the amount distributed to equity shareholders. An average dividend yield of 10 per cent might thus represent an earnings yield of 30 per cent for the chosen sample.

It will be agreed that comparison is easier and more realistic with an actual company as standard than with the notional undertaking represented by an average, and this method is only useful as a short cut in cases where the amounts involved are small.

Whichever method is adopted, the percentage earnings yield chosen as standard must be augmented by the percentage judged appropriate to compensate for the risk factors of the private company shares concerned in the valuation, so as to obtain an appropriate earnings yield for such shares.

Capitalization of yield

Capitalization of the net maintainable earnings in accordance with the earnings yield judged appropriate will produce an amount representing the total value of the net assets, tangible and intangible, employed in the business.

Tangible assets not employed in the business, together with the income derived from this source, will have been previously segregated. Such assets will be valued by market prices if available, or by independent valuation, if unquoted, on the principles indicated above. The total of the values so obtained will be added to the above asset total and, from this aggregate, will be deducted, if necessary, the nominal amount of capital ranking prior to the equity shares. The resulting amount, divided by the number of equity shares, will give the share value required.

If a material time has elapsed since the last balance sheet, an addition will be required, since private company share valuations are usually 'cum div. and rights', of the estimated net dividend or rights accrued on each share on a day-to-day basis. For equity shares the previous distribution, other things being equal, may conveniently serve as standard.

VALUATION OF PREFERENCE SHARES

Fully-paid preference shares

The discussion up to this point has been directed to the general valuation of private company shares, without special consideration for priority classes of shares, since most difficulties occur in connection with equity shares. When we turn to the fixed interest bearing or preference shares, the problem is, in several respects, more easily solved.

The record of profits is important mainly for the indication it gives whether and to what extent the yearly earnings have exceeded the amount required to ensure the continuation of the fixed preference dividends. If this essential is present the rate of dividend is the yield to be adopted for the purpose of valuation. An examination of prices of similar shares in public companies and the dividend yield derived from them will be made and the risk element will determine the additional yield required for any particular private company.

While the general risk element and the special private company risk element such as difficulty in marketability remain even for preference shares, for practical purposes the main considerations are the extent of the asset cover, and the security afforded by the total earnings of the company.

Should the profits summary result in estimated maintainable profits less than that necessary to met the fixed preference dividends, the valuation of preference shares will be on the methods suggested for equity shares since the preference shareholders will have a direct claim to the whole of the trading profits.

Participating rights may cause difficulty unless the shares are already participating to the full extent and the continuation seems reasonably secured. When participation has been achieved only to a partial extent the most prudent course is to have regard only to the rate of dividends already paid and to ignore future possibilities, but in exceptional cases some enhancement of value due to future prospects may have to be recognized.

In determining the risks attaching to preference shares, assuming that the background of the company is satisfactory, the chief attention should be given to the net tangible asset backing. Preference shareholders demand greater asset security than equity shareholders and it may be taken as a working rule that a preference share issue should be covered at least twice before it can qualify as a normal risk in that class of investment. Additional cover over and above that point need not greatly affect this element of risk but reductions below that level will increasingly justify higher yields.

Similarly, in relation to maintainable profits the amount should be several times that required to cover the fixed preference dividend, a less adequate cover will indicate the necessity for a higher yield.

As in the case of equity shares selection of a suitable standard of comparison from quoted shares of a similar type will be made. If the dividend yield of the selected standard shares is, for example, 5 per cent, and 2 per cent is judged adequate reward for the additional risks of the shares to be valued, a dividend yield of 7 per cent will be required to justify a par value for these shares. An 8 per cent £1 preference share would be valued at £1·14 and a 6 per cent share at 86p to each of which would be added the net dividend accrued on the share.

An adequate supplementary yield is no easier to express in general terms for preference than for equity shares. In special cases an additional 1½ per cent might be judged sufficient, but, normally, 2 per cent would, perhaps, be regarded as the minimum additional yield expected.

A difficulty in valuation may be met with when the preference shares in a private company bear a high rate of interest. If the company is well established, with a low risk factor, a valuation on a yield basis may give the preference shares a value considerably above par. In most cases the preference shareholders have no right to participate in assets available for distribution beyond the amount paid up on their shares. Voluntary liquidation is not so remote in the case of private companies as it is, normally, for public companies, and this fact must be borne in mind when the yield basis value exceeds an arbitrary amount.

For example, preference shares may participate in profits to the extent of 10 or 12 per cent, which, on a dividend yield basis, might justify a valuation of £1·50 or more. If, however, on a reconstruction or liquidation, the shareholders were entitled only to the par value of the share, a valuer must feel that some reduction in the yield valuation is called for. Opinions will differ on the reasonable limit in such cases but it may be suggested that, even if the chance of liquidation is remote, only very exceptional circumstances would support a value exceeding £1·25.

In addition to the above considerations the valuer must have in mind any special rights which would pass with the preference shares, for example, equal voting rights with equity shareholders, rights to subscribe for other shares on favourable terms or to share in bonuses. Such rights are difficult to evaluate but they justify an additional value being placed on such shares as compared with otherwise similar shares without these rights.

Redeemable preference shares

The importance of a revision to and the extent of the consequent adjustment of a redeemable preference share valuation will be in direct proportion to the nearness of the date of the obligation, or of the option, to redeem such shares, either at par or at a premium.

It is a matter of opinion when the influence of a fixed redemption date should begin to affect a share valuation. In the case of a prosperous company the redemption will be reasonably certain and a valuation occurring five years or less before the due date should take into account the redemption as affecting the risk element giving due weight to the relative nearness of the due date in estimating the supplementary yield expected.

This risk element may be regarded as reduced, or increased, as the date of redemption approaches according to whether the amount payable on redemption is greater, or less, than the share value indicated for a non-redeemable share.

For example, if the shares valued above £1·14 and 86p were redeemable at par in three years' time the expected yields might be adjusted to $7\frac{1}{2}$ and $6\frac{1}{2}$ per cent, respectively, justifying values of £1.06$\frac{1}{2}$ and 92$\frac{1}{2}$p, the net accrued dividend being added as before.

Any premium payable on redemption may be regarded as accruing over the five years before the due date, the accrued amount being added to the normal valuation.

If the circumstances of the company are such that redemption at the due date is likely to be in jeopardy it is prudent to ignore the redemption element until that date is sufficiently near for a realistic estimate of the probabilities to be made.

An alternative method, if redemption is reasonably certain, is to calculate, from compound interest tables, the present value of the amounts of capital and interest which the shares will produce to the owner during the remaining period.

For example, 8 per cent preference shares of £1 each redeemable at £1·05 in five years' time, assuming an expected rate of interest of 7 per cent, and calculating, for convenience, on a holding of £100 show the following result:

	£
Present value of £8 per annum for four years (interest 7 per cent) ..	2?
Present value of £113 in five years' time (interest 7 per cent)	8?
	108
Accrued net interest, say	?
	£110

The value of each share is thus £1·10.

Where an option to redeem exists there are factors more difficult to compute. Outside influences, such as trends in interest rates, as well as internal conditions in the company itself, will influence the directors in decisions relating to the exercise of the option. The valuation of the shares is, therefore, affected by probabilities, the relative importance of which is not always easily resolved. All that the valuer can do is to consider whether the known relevant factors point to an inducement to exercise the option at an early date. If, in his judgement, they do so, he will adjust his value accordingly; it is tempting, but not justified, to consider the length of time the option has remained unexercised, and to give this consideration too much importance. The factor of probability does not greatly affect the case of shares which, on any selected basis, are valued at an amount materially below par. There is little likelihood of the option being exercised, for obvious reasons, even if the company, in such cases, were in a position to finance the transaction.

OTHER METHODS OF VALUATION

Companies recently formed

The valuation of shares in new businesses, formed within five years or less before the date of valuation, must be treated as a special case in that the available data for determining maintainable profits may be insufficient. In some cases it may be possible to make cautious estimates of future results after consideration of the scope for increased production, diminished costs, and probable markets. Such valuations must always be arbitrary and contentious, and the intrinsic value of the assets must be the most important factor until it is judged that the company is sufficiently well established to apply the method of capitalization of profits with advantage.

Partly-paid shares

Valuations, on whatever basis, of partly-paid shares are subject to revision to allow for the circumstances on which further calls may arise. The revision must depend on an estimate, or perhaps judgement is a better word, of the most likely trend of events from the company's known position at the time of valuation. A well-established company with a prosperous record may make further calls with a view to expansion and with a greater degree of certainty of increased prosperity as a result. In such a case, against the contingent liability on the shares, there may reasonably be set off the consequential benefits which will ensue, or, at most, the adjustment of the valuation need be a nominal one only. More difficult, however, is the case of a company whose financial position seems to be deteriorating at the time of the share valuation. The contingency for unpaid calls may be not only imminent but there is, in addition, a greatly diminished chance of benefit accruing to the shareholder. An estimated proportion of the share valuation must be eliminated to meet this contingent loss and the only principle which can be given for making the estimate is for the accountant to veer towards the side of pessimism.

Recent transfers

In the event of an arm's-length transfer of shares of the class to be valued having recently occurred prior to the date of valuation, the share value represented by the consideration paid must not be overlooked. The valuer's estimate may require revision if there has been no material alterations in the trends of the business or outside influences. In all cases, if the transfer records a bona fide sale, it will probably be a better indication of 'market value' than any valuation based on empirical principles.

Example 1

Valuation of shares

The balance sheet of the XY Co Ltd, as on March 31st, was as follows:

	£			£
Capital – Authorized and Issued:		Freehold property ..		50,000
		Plant and machinery ..		22,000
30,000 7½ per cent Cum.		Loose plant		8,190
Pref. shares	30,000	Fixtures and fittings ..		8,000
50,000 Ordinary shares	50,000	Stock and work in progress		10,606
6 per cent Debenture Stock	15,000	Sundry debtors		20,500
General reserve	12,000	Cash		16,700
Reserve for future tax ..	6,000			
Sundry creditors	4,496			
Provision for taxation ..	6,000			
Profit and loss account (balance)	12,500			
	£135,996			£135,996

The preference shares are entitled on a winding-up to repayment in full and to 25 per cent of the residue remaining after repayment of the amounts paid up on the ordinary shares.

The results and dividends of the preceding four years are as follows:

		Dividends		
Year to March 31st	*Net profit*	*Ordinary*	*Preference*	*Reserve transfers*
	£	%	%	
Year 1	6,023	10	7½	Nil
Year 2	362	Nil	5	£1,500 from Reserve
Year 3	1,496	Nil	5	Nil
Year 4	10,750	5	12½	£2,500 to Reserve

The profit for the current year before providing for taxation is £9,796, out of which it is proposed to pay the full preference dividend and 10 per cent on the ordinary shares.

VALUATION OF SHARES

The 'cover' for the capital is as follows:

	£	£
Total assets as per balance sheet (excluding goodwill) ..		135,996
Less Debenture stock	15,000	
Sundry creditors and provision for taxation ..	10,496	
Proposed dividends (gross):		
Preference £2,250		
Ordinary 5,000		
	7,250	
		32,746
Net assets		£103,250

The preference capital of £30,000 is thus covered more than three times, whilst the remaining net assets available as cover for the £50,000 ordinary capital are over £73,000. The cover must therefore be considered as reasonably adequate.

(*Note.* – Insufficient cover would increase the element of risk, and this would cause a higher yield to be expected on the shares than where the cover was adequate.)

The results of trading for the past four years indicate that the profits of the company are subject to considerable fluctuation, and this would justify the expectation of higher dividend yields than could be obtained upon investments in businesses of a more stable character.

Assuming that the prospects for the future indicate that profits will be maintained at something in the region of £10,000 per annum before deduction of income tax, and that reasonable expected yields are 8 per cent in the case of the preference shares and 12 per cent on the ordinary shares, the ex div. values are as follows:

Preference shares:

Value per share: $\frac{7\frac{1}{2}}{8} \times £1$ 94p

Ordinary shares:	£	£
Estimated profits:..		10,000
Less Normal transfer to reserve, say ..	2,750	
Year's preference dividend ..	2,250	
		5,000

Profits available for distribution as ordinary dividend £5,000 = 10% on capital

Value per share $\frac{10}{12} \times £1 = 83\frac{1}{2}p$

To the above figures should be added an allowance for accrued dividends, the figure being adjusted from time to time as the year progresses.

(*Note.* – The fact that the preference shareholders are entitled on a winding-up to 25 per cent of the residue remaining after repayment of the amounts paid up on the ordinary shares would not influence the valuations unless actual winding-up is contemplated.)

Example 2
Amalgamation scheme

The following are the respective balance sheets at July 31st, of Take-over Ltd and Bid Ltd:

TAKE-OVER LTD

	£		£
Authorized and issued share capital:		Freehold property, *at cost* ..	270,000
240,000 ordinary shares of £1 each fully paid ..	240,000	Plant and machinery, *at cost, less depreciation*	60,000
6 per cent Debenture stock	190,000	Stock..	90,000
Reserves	50,000	Sundry debtors	80,000
Sundry creditors and provisions: £		Investments	30,000
Trade 25,000		Cash at bank	10,000
Expenses .. 1,000			
Taxation .. 24,000			
	50,000		
Profit and loss account ..	10,000		
	£540,000		£540,000

BID LTD

	£		£
Authorized and issued share capital:		Goodwill, *at cost*	30,000
200,000 8 per cent preference shares of £1 each fully paid	200,000	Freehold property, *at cost* ..	160,000
150,000 ordinary shares of £1 each fully paid ..	150,000	Plant and machinery, *at cost, less depreciation*	60,000
	350,000	Stock..	120,000
Reserve for future taxation	50,000	Sundry debtors	60,000
Sundry creditors and provisions: £		Cash at bank	30,000
Trade 26,500			
Expenses .. 500			
Taxation .. 13,000			
	40,000		
Profit and loss account ..	20,000		
	£460,000		£460,000

Other relevant particulars are as follows:

Take-over Ltd:

(i) Dividends paid for the two preceding years, 10 per cent and 11 per cent, respectively. For the year just ended it is proposed to pay a dividend of $12\frac{1}{2}$ per cent.

(ii) The investments have been held for some years and yield 5 per cent on their book value.

(iii) An independent valuation of the property and plant discloses the following values:

					£
Property	..	..	..	..	395,000
Plant ..	..	..	..	..	95,000

(iv) Adjusted profits after recalculating depreciation on plant and providing for directors' fees, and before charging interest on debentures, for the three years to July 31st, have been £62,000, £65,000 and £68,000.

Bid Ltd:

(i) A dividend of 14 per cent has been paid on the ordinary shares for each of the two preceding years. A similar dividend is proposed for the year just ended. The preference dividend for the year is still due.

(ii) An independent valuation of the property and plant discloses the following values:

					£
Property	..	..	..	..	290,000
Plant ..	..	..	..	..	80,000

(iii) Depreciation was recalculated on the same basis as that of Take-over Ltd, and after making provision for depreciation and directors' fees, but before allowing for dividends on the preference shares, the adjusted profits for the three years to July 31st were £60,000, £57,000 and £54,000.

Suggest a scheme for amalgamating the two companies in the manner best suited to their financial status.

SOLUTION. – For the purpose of evolving a scheme of amalgamation of the two companies it will be necessary to take into account the revised values placed upon the assets on revaluation, and to compute the values of the goodwills of the two businesses.

In view of the fact that the profits of Take-over Ltd show an increasing trend, and those of Bid Ltd a decreasing one, it is considered that the businesses should be valued by reference to a 'weighted' average of the profits of the past three years, in order that the greater weight may be given to the more recent results.

Profits of Take-over Ltd			*Profits of Bid Ltd*		
£	£		£	£	
62,000 × 1	62,000		60,000 × 1	60,000	
65,000 × 2	130,000		57,000 × 2	114,000	
68,000 × 3	204,000		54,000 × 3	162,000	
6)	396,000		6)	336,000	
Average	£66,000		Average	£56,000	

Assuming that in both businesses 10 per cent would be a fai return upon the capital employed, the valuation will be as follows:

	£	Take-over Ltd £	£	Bid Lt £
Total assets as per balance sheet ..		540,000		460,00
Less Investments		30,000		30,00
				(Goodwil
		510,000		430,00
Add Increase on revaluation of assets:				
Property	125,000		130,000	
Plant	35,000		20,000	
		160,000		150,00
		670,000		580,00
Less Liabilities	50,000		40,000	
Proposed dividends (less tax)	17,250		21,275	
		67,250		61,27
Net capital employed in trading operations		£602,750		£518,72
		£		£
Net average profits		66,000		56,00
Less Income from investments		1,500		—
Net trading profits		£64,500		£56,00
Capital value of net assets which would give above return on a 10 per cent basis		£ 645,000		£ 560,00
Less Tangible net assets (above) ..		602,750		518,72
Residual value attributable to goodwill		£42,250		£41,27

The total values of the two undertakings for the purposes of th amalgamation can now be computed as follows:

	Take-over Ltd £	Bid L £
Tangible net assets	602,750	518,72
Add Goodwill as computed	42,250	41,2
	645,000	560,00
Investments	30,000	—
TOTAL VALUE OF UNDERTAKINGS..	£675,000	£560,00

These values are apportionable between the various interests i the companies according to the values of their respective holding

In the case of Take-over Ltd the above figure of £675,000 repr sents the value of 240,000 ordinary shares and £190,000 6 per ce debentures. Assuming debentures carrying this rate of interest be worth par, the value of the 240,000 ordinary shares may be take as £675,000 less £190,000=£485,000 or, say, £2 per share.

The share capital of Bid Ltd consists of 200,000 8 per cent preference shares and 150,000 ordinary shares. Assuming 8 per cent to be a fair market yield on preference capital in this type of company the preference shares may be considered to be worth par. The value of the ordinary capital will thus be £560,000 less £200,000= £360,000, or £2·40 per share.

SCHEME FOR AMALGAMATION

Having valued the undertakings it must now be decided what is the most suitable scheme for merging their interests.

The merger may take one of the following forms:

(*a*) the absorption of one of the companies by the other;

(*b*) the purchase of the two undertakings by a newly-formed company; or

(*c*) a holding company scheme.

(*a*) If this method is decided upon it is suggested that Take-over Ltd should purchase the undertaking of Bid Ltd, the purchase consideration being the assumption of the liabilities, the allotment to the preference shareholders of 200,000 8 per cent preference shares in Take-over Ltd and the issue to the ordinary shareholders of six shares in Take-over Ltd for every five held in Bid Ltd, i.e., in proportion to the relative values of the ordinary shares. (Take-over Ltd £2 and Bid Ltd £2·40.) This scheme would entail an increase of £380,000 in the authorized capital of Take-over Ltd, and relief from stamp duty, under section 55, Finance Act 1927, would only be obtained on £350,000, the amount of the present authorized capital of Bid Ltd.

(*b*) If a new company is formed it should be registered with an authorized capital of £590,000, which is equal to the combined authorized capitals of the two companies, so that no additional stamp duty will be payable.

The new company should purchase the assets of both companies in consideration of:

(1) the assumption of the liabilities;

(2) the issue to the debenture-holders of Take-over Ltd of £190,000 6 per cent mortgage debentures;

(3) the allotment to the preference shareholders of Bid Ltd of 200,000 8 per cent preference shares in the new company at par, being one new share for every one already held in the old company;

(4) the allotment to the ordinary shareholders of 390,000 ordinary

shares in the new company, at a premium of £1·15½ per share allocated in the following proportions:

To the shareholders of Take-over Ltd $\frac{480,000}{480,000}$ of 390,000 = 222,857

shares, or just under one new share for every one share now held;

To the shareholders of Bid Ltd $\frac{360,000}{840,000}$ of 390,000 = 167,143 shares, or

just over one new share for every one now held.

By issuing the shares at a premium the ordinary shareholders of each company will receive their proper proportion of the total ordinary capital of the new company, and the equivalent of the value of their present holdings, without the necessity of increasing the capital above the combined capitals of the two companies.

(c) If a holding company scheme is preferred, a new company, with an authorized capital of £420,000 in £1 ordinary shares, should be registered for the purpose of acquiring the whole of the ordinary capitals of Take-over Ltd and Bid Ltd. The consideration should be £480,000 for the ordinary shares of Take-over Ltd and £360,000 for those of Bid Ltd, and the shares of the holding company should be issued at a premium of £1 per share, and in the same proportions as in (b) *supra*. The debentures and preference shares need not be acquired.

This scheme would avoid capital duty on the whole of the shares allotted in consideration of the shares in Take-over Ltd, since not less than 90 per cent of such shares would be acquired, and not less than 90 per cent of the consideration would consist of shares in the transferee company. No saving of stamp duty would, however, be effected in respect of the purchase of Bid's ordinary capital, since the shares acquired represent less than 90 per cent of the total issued capital of Bid Ltd. In order that the saving in capital duty may be effected, the authorized capital of the holding company would have to be at least £585,000 and at least 165,000 of the preference shares of Bid Ltd would have to be acquired, as well as the whole of that company's ordinary capital.

In view of the fact that the adoption of either scheme (a) or (b) would have the effect of enlarging the security of the debenture-holders of Take-over Ltd and of the preference shareholders of Bid Ltd, it would seem that the holding company scheme would be preferable from the point of view of the ordinary shareholders of both companies.

From the taxation viewpoint there would be little to choose between schemes (b) and (c), since in (b) the increase in the assessments on the profits of Take-over Ltd would be offset by the reduction in the assessments on those of Bid Ltd, whilst in (c) the taxation liability would not be affected at all. If scheme (a) is adopted, however, there will be a slight saving of tax by reason of the fact that on the winding-up of Bid Ltd that company will be assessed as having discontinued its business, which would result in a reduction in its current assessment.

CHAPTER VI

VALUATION – PUBLIC LIMITED COMPANIES

The valuation of shares in public limited companies raises far fewer problems than is involved in the valuation of shares in private companies, for the simple reason that the price officially quoted on the Stock Exchange forms a ready-made valuation of the shares as ascertained between a willing buyer and a willing seller for all practical purposes. Providing that the public company shares enjoy an active market and are not unduly depressed for any reason (e.g., liquidation of a deceased holding), the quoted price gives as good and as accurate a guide as any to the approximate worth of the business though based largely on its earning power. Consequently, where valuable assets appear in the balance sheet at a written-down pre-war cost – freehold land and buildings for example – it might be appropriate for these assets alone to be revalued by a qualified valuer so as to ascertain their current market value. In recent years, most business mergers have been based on the above principles, i.e., an exchange of shares by which one public company makes an offer for the whole (or some smaller proportion) of the share capital of another public company at a price which is somewhat in excess of the current Stock Exchange quotation, otherwise the shareholders in the latter company would have little or no incentive to accept the offer.

Example 1
As an illustration of the manifold problems involved in trying to hold the balance, fairly, between two companies, one of which has a rather complicated capital structure, the following résumé of the final version of the Morris-Austin merger (into the British Motor Corporation Ltd) may be of interest. By extending the merger offer to holders of the preference shares, the new company secured a simpler capital structure in addition to saving an estimated £650,000 in stamp duties.

With an institutional seal of approval on it, the offer was accepted and the issued capital of the new corporation then consisted of £9,241,126 in 5 per cent £1 preference shares and £4,826,359 in 25p ordinary shares. Highly geared though the capital structure was, the additional cost of dividend payments on the new preference shares was slight; the combined net profits of Morris Motors Ltd and the Austin Motor Co Ltd, for their previous financial year, covered a year's dividend on the new preference capital more than

96

TABLBE VI
MORRIS-AUSTIN MERGER

Class of Stock or Share	Nominal holding	Market value of January 29th, 1952	Gross income	THE BRITISH MOTOR CORPORATION		
				Holding after Exchange	Estimated market value[1]	Gross income
	£	£	£		£	£
AUSTIN MOTOR						
4½% Cumulative Redeemable Preference £1	100	93·75	4·50	£100 5% Preference	107·25	5·50
7% Cumulative Preference £1	100	137·50	7·00	£150 5% Preference	146·25	7·50
% 'B' Cumulative Preference £1[2]	100	150·00	9·43	£190 5% Preference	185·25	9·50
20% Non-Cumulative Preference Ordinary 50p	100	290·62½	20·00	{ £160 5% Preference / £25 Ordinary	156·00 / 150·00 }	21·00[3]
MORRIS MOTORS						
7½% Cumulative Preference £1	100	139·06	7·50	£160 5% Preference	156·00	8·00

[1] Assuming a market value of 97½p for the 5% £1 preference shares and of £1·50 for the 25p ordinary shares.   [2] Free of income tax up to 30p in the £.   [3] Based on an expected ordinary dividend of 52% per annum.

nineteen times. The attraction for preference shareholders lay partly in the improved marketability of a B.M.C. preference share over that of constituent companies' shares, partly in the fact that the revised offer allayed any possible suspicion of losses on liquidation; but chiefly in the knowledge that preference shareholders all received a slight increase in income without any sacrifice of capital rights.

On the basis of market valuations at the time, however, the holders of Austin 7 per cent preference shares appeared to gain the least, and these were the only preference shares to be marked down after the offer was made public in March 1952. It will be seen that the element of equity in the dividends paid on the Austin 20 per cent non-cumulative preferred ordinary shares was recognized by an offer of a judicious mixture of preference and ordinary shares in B.M.C.

Example 2

Elliott Brothers (London) – Associated Automation merger
Purpose: The linking of Elliott Brothers (London) and Associated Automation and their subsidiaries forms the largest automation and instrumentation organization in Europe.

In many of the fields in which the Elliott-Automation group specializes it has established important connections with leading companies throughout the world engaged in similar activities (among whom are Bendix Aviation Corporation, the Bristol Co, Fisher Governor Co, G. M. Giannini & Co, Industrial Instrument Corporation (of Odessa, Texas), Panelli Inc, Fr. Sauter A.-G. (of Basle), the Swartwout Co, and Jarvis B. Webb Inc.).

The merger thus brings together the wide variety of techniques, apparatus, and manufacturing facilities possessed by the two companies and, being largely complementary to each other, they now give the group the means to serve industries requiring equipment for automating their operations on the necessary scale. At a time when the quality and the size of the scientific research effort available can be decisive, one of the more important aspects of the merger is that the group now possesses extensive research facilities able to serve the whole organization and which are on a scale and of a character perhaps unique in this country.[1]

Details of scheme: Elliott-Automation formed in 1950 has been reorganized to effect the merger and will allot its shares in exchange for the shares in the two companies on the basis of one $5\frac{1}{2}$ per cent preference £1 share for each £1 preference share of Elliotts, eight ordinary 25p shares for four ordinary 25p shares in Elliotts, and eight ordinary 25p shares for five ordinary 50p shares in Associated Automation. The directors recommended acceptance.

[1] *The Times*, October 8th, 1957.

Elliotts would pay a dividend of $11\frac{2}{3}$ per cent and Associated one of $4\frac{2}{3}$ per cent for the seven months to August 1st, 1957. It was expected that combined profits for 1957 attributable to ordinary holders would not be less than the £803,000 returned for 1956, when Elliotts earned 62·5 per cent of this figure and Associated 37·5 per cent.

Elliott-Automation foreshadowed an ordinary dividend of $4\frac{1}{6}$ per cent for the period to December 31st, 1957. This is equivalent to a dividend of 10 per cent for a full year which is in turn equivalent to 20 per cent on the Elliott ordinary and 8 per cent on the Associated ordinary. Associated shareholders would thus receive a slight increase in dividend reflecting to some degree that in relation to the adjusted profits the Associated ordinary dividend of $7\frac{1}{2}$ per cent for 1956 represented a lower rate than an ordinary dividend of 20 per cent by Elliotts.

Outcome: The offers made by Elliott-Automation to acquire the capital of Elliott Brothers (London) and of Associated Automation have been accepted in respect of 99·9 per cent of the preference shares and 88·9 per cent of the ordinary shares of Elliotts and of 93·16 per cent of the ordinary shares of Associated Automation.

The offers have been declared unconditional and acceptances will continue to be received under the terms of the offer.

In accordance with the terms of the offers, Elliott Brothers (London) have declared an interim dividend on the ordinary shares of $11\frac{2}{3}$ per cent, or 3p a share. Associated Automation have declared an interim ordinary dividend of $4\frac{2}{3}$ per cent, or $2\frac{1}{2}$p per share.[1]

Example 3
Amalgamated Asphalte Merger

Purpose: The news that arrangements are being made by Highways Construction, the Neuchatel Asphalte Co, and Ragusa to place their principal interests in the United Kingdom under common management needs to be read in conjunction with the review by Mr William Cash, the Neuchatel chairman, of current conditions in the road-making and allied trades. At the present time, he said, the amount of work offering in the United Kingdom was grossly insufficient to employ the road-making and similar facilities of the various companies equipped for the purpose. Intense competition and shrinking profit margins had become the inevitable result, as always, of too much plant chasing too little work.

A new company is to be formed to give effect to the new management arrangements. This will take over Highways Construction – whose capital is not quoted in London – as a whole, along with all the subsidiary companies of Ragusa (including John Hadfield & Sons, one of several businesses acquired by Ragusa in 1955 in order

The Times, October 2nd, 1957.

to provide sources of profit-making outside the original business), and most of the subsidiary companies of Neuchatel in the United Kingdom through the medium of a new Neuchatel company to be formed for the purpose. The overseas interests of Neuchatel on the Continent and in Australia and New Zealand, which maintained their profits generally speaking in 1956, remain outside the proposed arrangements. These are subject in any case to the consent of the holders of the Neuchatel 4½ per cent debenture stock, 1974–79, and the Ragusa 6 per cent unsecured loan stock 1959–64, as well as of the shareholders of those companies.

If the necessary consents are obtained the new company will begin business on October 1st, with Mr William Cash as chairman and Mr Eric Vigor, now the Neuchatel managing director, occupying the same post with the new company. Mr B. W. Hadfield, a director of Ragusa, Mr John Hadfield, the chairman of John Hadfield & Sons, Mr Oliver Poole, the chairman of Highways Construction, and Mr G. M. Fotheringham, of the Lawley Group, make up the rest of the board. It is confidently expected that the arrangements will result in greater efficiency, considerable economies, and a better service to customers.[1]

Details of scheme: the plan to place under common management the principal interests in the United Kingdom of Highways Construction, Neuchatel Asphalte, and Ragusa will be effected by a new private company, Amalgamated Asphalte Companies, which has been formed with an authorized capital of £2½ million.

Neuchatel are retaining the shares in Cray River Sand & Gravel, Campbell & McGill, Mendip Stone & Concrete, and Neuchatel Anti-Corrosion.

Before the assets are transferred to Amalgamated Asphalte a substantial proportion of the United Kingdom contracting assets of Neuchatel will first be transferred to a new subsidiary. Neuchatel Asphalte (Contracting), in exchange for shares in the new subsidiary. The shares in the new subsidiary will then be transferred, together with the shares in three other subsidiaries, to the holding company.

In return for the total number of shares to be acquired the holding company will issue 2,255,000 ordinary £1 shares, 720,000 to Highways and French Asphalte (which holds shares in Highways), 805,000 to Neuchatel, and 730,000 to Ragusa. The vendors of Highways have exercised an option to subscribe in cash at par for 10,000 ordinary £1 shares in the holding company.

It is estimated that book values of the total net assets of the holding company and its subsidiaries, based on the book values as at December 31st, 1956, will amount to £2,165,000. The directors are satisfied that the current replacement value is greater than the

[1] *The Times*, August 20th, 1957.

book values. Turnover in 1956 was about £6½ million. The turnover of the business to be transferred by Neuchatel was about £2,180,000. The directors consider the terms as fair and reasonable.[1]

Example 4
Clan Line – Union-Castle Scheme
Purpose: Both concerns had worked side by side in the South African trade for a long time. Accordingly, it was felt that a merger would bring to Union-Castle the ample resources which the more conservative management of Clan Line had built up over the years, besides giving a wider spread of trade routes (including Australia) and throwing into the common pool the expert management which had been responsible for the flourishing state of the Clan Line concern.

Details of scheme: Clan Line Steamers and Union-Castle Mail Steamship proposed a scheme for the amalgamation of the shareholdings in the two companies by means of an exchange of shares into a new holding company. On the assumption that all shareholders accept the scheme its share capital will consist of 4,285,000 5½ per cent cumulative preference £1 shares, 1,646,000 6 per cent cumulative preference £1 shares (redeemable on December 31st, 1965) and 5,552,000 ordinary £1 shares.

The basis of the original share exchange offer is shown on the next page.

The debenture stock of Union-Castle was not acquired by the holding company. The offer became effective on acceptance by the holders of 90 per cent of the shares or stock of each class or such lesser percentage as the board of the holding company deemed sufficient.

DIVIDEND FORECAST

Preference dividends of both companies for the six months to December 31st, 1955, were paid on that date. Interim ordinary dividends for 1955 totalling 25 per cent of Clan Line and 7½ per cent of Union-Castle were paid in due course. No further dividends for 1955 were recommended by either company. The holding company's shares would rank for dividend as from January 1st, 1956. Given satisfactory trading conditions in 1956 the holding company hoped to pay dividends totalling 16 per cent on its ordinary capital in respect of that year.

In formulating the scheme, account had to be taken of the fact that Clan Line had been paying in ordinary dividend a much smaller percentage of its profits than Union-Castle.

The boards of the two companies considered the scheme to be fair and equitable and that it would be beneficial to shareholders, giving

[1] *The Times*, October 5th, 1957.

greater diversification of interests with advantages in operation and administration. They strongly recommended its acceptance.[1]

Basis of exchange

It is important in judging these terms to note than in the case of Clan Line ordinary dividends have hitherto been very moderate in relation to earnings; for 1954 the cash distribution was 20 per cent out of earnings of nearly 200 per cent and the stock, therefore, offered a dividend yield at its market value of $7\frac{1}{16}$ of £1 unit for only 2·86 per cent. Union-Castle dividends have been relatively more liberal; that for last year was $7\frac{1}{2}$ per cent out of earnings of 19·4 per cent which would put the £1 shares priced in the market at £1·$32\frac{1}{2}$ on a $5\frac{1}{2}$ per cent yield basis.

The ordinary capital of the holding company would be distributed as to 60·5 per cent to Clan Line and 39·5 per cent to Union-Castle, but on the basis of dividends the proportions (thanks to the offer to Union-Castle ordinary of 6 per cent cumulative redeemable preference shares as well as ordinary shares in the holding company)

Present capital	Exchange basis	Holding company	
		Class of share £1 nominal	Amount
CLAN LINE			£
£700,000 $5\frac{1}{2}$ per cent Cumulative 'A' Preference Stock	11 new shares for 10 existing £1 stock units	$5\frac{1}{2}$ per cent Preference	770,000
£500,000 $5\frac{1}{2}$ per cent Cumulative Redeemable 'B' Preference Stock	do.	6 per cent Preference	550,000
£250,000 $5\frac{1}{2}$ per cent Cumulative 2nd Preference Stock	do.	$5\frac{1}{2}$ per cent Preference	275,000
£1,260,000 Ordinary Stock	8 new shares for 3 existing £1 stock units	Ordinary	3,360,000
UNION-CASTLE			
24,000 $4\frac{1}{2}$ per cent Cumulative Preference £10 shares	10 new shares for each £10 existing share	$5\frac{1}{2}$ per cent Preference	240,000
2,500,000 6 per cent 'A' Cumulative Preference £1 shares	6 new shares for 5 existing shares	$5\frac{1}{2}$ per cent Preference	3,000,000
£5,480,000 Ordinary stock	1 new share for every 5 existing £1 stock units and	6 per cent Preference	1,096,000
	2 new shares for every 5 existing £1 stock units	Ordinary	2,192,000

[1] *The Times*, October 4th, 1955.

would be rather closer – Clan Line 56·5 per cent and Union-Castle 43·5 per cent. Clan stockholders get a sharp increase in dividend income, though one less well covered by earnings than now. Union-Castle shareholders get a much smaller increase in income but a greater earnings cover for it – a 16 per cent. Holding company ordinary dividend would be covered about three times by the combined constituent earnings.

Clash on terms
The new holding company (named British Commonwealth Shipping) was clearly, and it would seem, justifiably dominated by Clan Line. In consequence, the scheme soon came under fire from the Union-Castle end, on the ground that Clan Line would be so much the dominant partner that the whole scheme amounted to nothing more than a straight take-over by Clan Line, on terms that were held to be anything but generous.[1]

The sponsors of the scheme, however, took an opposite view. They contended that Union-Castle was merely being asked to accept a minority status, so recognizing the fact that that company no longer dominated the trade in which it had lived for 100 years. Moreover, the sponsors must have been influenced by the fact that Clan Line's earnings over a period of years had been rising while Union-Castle's had been heading the other way.

On the opposite side, much play was made with wild guesses at the replacement value of the two fleets, but as yet little concrete evidence had emerged. Apart from all this skirmishing, the whole affair was given an unusual twist by the existence of *full voting rights* attaching to the two classes of preference capital in Union-Castle.

Early in November 1955, the terms of the offer were slightly modified. The new offer consisted of 50p nominal of ordinary capital in the new holding company for each £1 of Union-Castle ordinary capital in place of 40p nominal of ordinary capital plus the 20p nominal of 6 per cent preference capital originally offered. At the same time the offer to Clan Line shareholders was also increased from eight £1 shares in the new holding company for each three £1 Clan Line shares to forty-one 50p ordinary shares in exchange for every seven £1 Clan Line shares (equal to about £2·92½ nominal of the new capital in place of the £2·66½ previously awarded). At this stage, the new holding company had an ordinary capital of £6,430,000 in place of £5,552,000 and still anticipated paying a 16 per cent dividend. In terms of prospective income, Union-Castle ordinary shareholders were offered a small improvement and in terms of control their proportion of the new company's equity rose from 40 per cent to 42½ per cent.

[1] *The Economist*, October 8th, 1955, page 147.

The formal offer on these lines was sent to shareholders along with a wealth of supporting information.

Table VII shows the new offers (disregarding fractions) for £100 nominal of each class of capital and the rise in income that each class would enjoy assuming a 16 per cent dividend from the new holding company.

TABLE VII

Holding before scheme	Income	Holding after scheme	Income
CLAN LINE STEAMERS	£p		£p
£100 5½% 'A' Pref.	5·50	£110 5½% Pref.	6·05
£100 5½% 'B' Pref.	5·50	£110 6% Pref.	6·60
£100 5½% 2nd Pref.	5·50	£110 5½% Pref.	6·05
£100 ordinary (on basis of latest dividend)	25·00	585 50p Ordinary	46·80
UNION-CASTLE			
10 4½% £10 Pref.	4·50	£100 5½% Pref.	5·50
100 5% £1 Pref.	6·00	£120 5½% Pref.	6·60
£100 Ordinary (on basis of 7½% dividend)	7·50	100 50p Ordinary	8·00

A comparison of earnings since 1951 (free from, hitherto undisclosed, transfers to hidden reserves allowed to shipping companies) is given in Table VIII.

TABLE VIII
Equity Earnings Compared[1]
(£000s)

Year	Clan	Union-Castle	Combined Profit	Clan	Union-Castle
	£	£	£	%	%
1951	2,631	3,440	6,071	43·3	56·7
1952	3,652	2,767	6,419	56·9	43·1
1953	3,116	2,012	5,128	60·8	39·2
1954	2,778	798	3,576	77·7	22·3
1955	3,425	1,800	5,225	65·6	34·4

This brings out the fact that Union-Castle's proportion of the combined earnings of the two groups fell from 56·7 per cent in 1951 to a low point of 22·3 per cent in 1954, though recovering slightly in 1955. But if depreciation had been measured on a replacement cost basis instead of on original cost, Union-Castle would not have shown any profit at all in 1955, whereas Clan Line still came out on the right side, viz.:

[1] Before taxation, but after preference dividends.

TABLE IX
Current Depreciation
(£000s)

	Clan Line	Union-Castle
	£	£
Twenty years on actual cost	1,230	1,795
Twenty years on repalcement cost	3,050	5,000
Profit (+) or loss (—) if depreciation on replacement is substituted	+1,605	—1,405

When it came to asset values (Table X), shareholders found that the picture was reversed.

Union-Castle with 42½ per cent of the equity puts in the majority of the assets. At balance sheet values Union-Castle contributed £22¼ million of net assets attributable to the equity against Clan Line's £17½ million. At the then current replacement costs, the figures still point in the same direction: for Union-Castle put in £39 million against Clan Line's £32¼ million.

TABLE X
The Two Fleets
(£000s)

	Clan Line	Union-Castle	Combined
	£	£	£
Replacement cost	60,750	100,250	161,000
Less provision for depreciation[1]	31,900	63,900	95,800
Net value	28,850	36,350	65,200
Net tangible assets (at end 1954 book value)[2]	17,679	22,285	39,964
Replacement value	32,210	39,193	71,403

The problem confronting Union-Castle shareholders could be summed up as follows: On an earning basis the offer seemed fair without being over-generous, but on an asset basis (which admittedly the shareholder cannot realize and which exhibits a poor yield anyway) it seemed meagre to say the least.

A few further relevant facts had to be weighed in the balance. First, Union-Castle, for all its valuable assets, had a big bill in prospect for replacing them. By December 1964, Union-Castle will have ships worth at replacement cost £51 million but over twenty-five years old and urgently in need of replacement; Clan Line will have only £8·6 million worth in that condition. In foreshadowing

[1] At 5 per cent per annum from completion.
[2] Depreciation over twenty years on actual cost.

a dividend of 16 per cent, the directors expressed an intention, granted reasonably prosperous trading conditions, gradually to increase the amount.

The merger plan had the support of Morgan Grenfell & Co and Baring Brothers, and both firms of auditors expressed the view that the terms were fair. Even so, the opposition were not satisfied and requisitioned a meeting of shareholders for January 5th, 1956. By this time, the requisitionists could muster £1,418,651 stock – though still far from a majority of the 8,220,000 votes that could be cast at the meeting.

Outcome: On the eve of what promised to be one of the bitterest of struggles for the control of a big company, the two sides in the Union-Castle–Clan Line dispute finally came to terms.[1]

The opposition, led by Mr M. C. Drayton and Mr Jack Billmeir, managed to win a substantial concession, all the more praiseworthy because Mr Drayton disclosed the fact that had the opposition fought the issue to a vote it was most unlikely that it could have mustered a majority.

The concession represented a 10 per cent advance on previous offers for Union-Castle ordinary shareholders. Thus the holder of 100 £1 ordinary shares of Union-Castle who, under the original offer, would have received 100 50p ordinary shares of British Commonwealth Shipping (the new holding company) in exchange, now received 110 shares, and the proportion of the equity of British Commonwealth Shipping, first proposed early in November 1955, at 40 per cent Union-Castle and 60 per cent Clan Line, had been screwed-up in two stages to 47 per cent for Union-Castle. The new offer did not apply, however, to such of the Union-Castle shares as were already held by the Cayzer family which controlled Clan Line (and their holdings were thought to be greater than the £800,000 slice disclosed at the beginning of December 1955). The Cayzer family alone bore the whole cost of the concession, thus rigidly adhering to their view that it could not ask Clan Line shareholders to make a more generous offer. Consequently, it was not proposed either to enlarge the capital of British Commonwealth Shipping or to ask the shareholders of Clan Line – other than the Cayzer family – to share in the sacrifice.

Four conclusions can be drawn from the battle. First, the opposition won a useful concession, but the cost of it was much reduced by the fact that the controlling interest in Clan Lines was itself a big shareholder in Union-Castle. Secondly, the real issue at stake – whether earnings or asset values should be the basis of the merger – was compromised, though leaning slightly towards the direction of earnings. Thirdly, the terms of the merger were under fire – not the

[1] *The Economist*, January 7th, 1956, page 63.

intentions of the merger. Lastly, two big groups were both pitch-forked into heavy buying of Union-Castle ordinary shares.

Example 5
Courtaulds – British Celanese
The explanation for the merger given by the two boards[1] reads thus:

> 'It would greatly strengthen the ability of both companies to meet competition from imported textiles in the home market, and would also enable them to improve their position in the export markets having regard particularly to the problems and opportunities which are certain to arise if the proposals for the European Common Market and Free Trade Area are completed.'

Even so, one might add that the first tentative moves to arrange a merger date from before the Second World War.

The terms of the offer by Courtaulds for British Celanese were most attractive. The basis of exchange into Courtaulds ordinary and preference stocks shown in the following table gave each class of stockholder a prospective rise in income with the exception of the participating second preference holders, and they got cash compensation.

TERMS OF EXCHANGE

Holdings in British Celanese	Existing Income Gross	Exchange offer by Courtaulds	Prospective Income Gross[2]
	p		p
£3 of ordinary	14	£2 of ordinary ..	20
£5 of 7% preference ..	35	£6 of 6% preference	36
£4 of 7½% participating Preference	40	£5 of 6% preference (plus £1 in cash) ..	30

The immediate effect of the scheme was to give British Celanese ordinary at 76p an immediate rise of 37½p; in addition to which the two classes of preference stockholders also benefited through the acquisition of a much better covered security. It should be observed that the offer excluded final ordinary dividends by both companies (a promised total of 10 per cent for Courtaulds and 4½ per cent for British Celanese). On the basis of a possible mainten-ance of a 10 per cent dividend after the merger, the then quoted price of £1·77½ for Courtaulds ordinary was justified – and, inci-dentally, made British Celanese ordinary worth £1·19 on that basis.

The ultimate result of this merger was the creation of a single vast combine controlling over 85 per cent of the British rayon industry.

[1] *The Economist*, April 20th, 1957.
[2] Based on a future dividend of 10 per cent.

But what caused Courtaulds to swallow its much smaller rival and, in so doing, make a high bid?

British Celanese was unmistakeably the weaker of the two, as the announcement of the bid showed. For British Celanese profits were forecast as being about two-thirds of the £2·4 million achieved in the previous year, while Courtaulds profits for the same period had only slipped to about four-fifths of the previous year's £18·1 million. It certainly looked as though British Celanese ordinary stockholders were about to leave a company in which earnings per stock unit were about 6 per cent, and going into one which could show earnings in the region of 22 per cent. Thus, they were noticeably leaving a highly-geared company, where the fortunes of management had swayed backwards and forwards at intervals over the years, and where the vulnerability to trade fluctuations is high for one which has low capital gearing, a conservative record in dividend, and a dominating position in the industry.

On Courtaulds side, the buying was probably actuated by asset values – as much as any other factor – particularly the excellent manufacturing capacity on the more expensive acetate side of the industry which British Celanese possessed. The terms certainly seem to have been inspired by asset values, because Courtaulds net tangible assets (based on the balance sheet to March 31st, 1956) would have shown a rise from £124 million to about £146 million and its issued share capital from £56 million to £70·6 million.

The combined firm probably inherited well over 80 per cent (and maybe nearer 90 per cent if Courtaulds half-interest in British Nylon Spinners is included) of the home market production of man-made fibres. It is nothing like so dominating, however, in the newer synthetics such as acrylic fibre and nylon. The chemical sides of the two firms should also fit in well together. But at the places where the two companies overlap – in acetate, in triacetate, in warp knitting, in development overseas in the United States and in Australia, and in the large staffs, centred in London and Manchester – opportunities existed for large scale and, doubtless, painful measures of economy.

This merger soon led to 'rationalization' in more than one direction. The rapid development of warp knitting has enabled knitted goods to replace (and to look like) many conventional woven fabrics, and similar inroads on lace are also reported. F.N.F. Machinery Manufacturing Co, a Courtauld subsidiary with Morton Sundour as a minority holder, makes a large share of the warp knitting machinery in this country. Its issued capital is £518,000, divided into £144,000 redeemable preference shares, all held by Courtaulds, and £374,000 ordinary shares, of which Courtaulds holds £355,000 and Morton Sundour £18,500. In the first week of

CAPITAL STRUCTURE AND GEARING

Type of capital	British Celanese			Courtaulds (pre-offer)			Courtaulds (post-offer)		
	Description	Amount	Gearing	Description	Amount	Gearing	Description	Amount	Gearing
		£	%		£	%		£	%
Debenture	4% 1st	1,989,060	11	—	—	—	4% 1st	1,989,060	2½
	3½% 2nd	868,586	5	—	—	—	3½% 2nd	868,586	1½
		£2,857,646	16	—	—	—		£2,857,646	4
Preference	7% 1st	3,500,000	19	5% Cum.	8,000,000	14	5% 1st Cum.	8,000,000	11
	7% partg. 2nd	4,250,000	23¼				6% 2nd Cum.	9,512,500	13
		£7,750,000	42¼		£8,000,000	14		£17,512,500	24
Ordinary	£1	7,518,534	41½	£1	48,079,453	86	£1	53,088,476	72
Total		£18,126,180	100		£56,079,453	100		£73,458,622	100

Note. – Over 90% of British Celanese stockholders accepted the offer and Courtaulds' stockholders duly approved the necessary increases in capital.

March 1958 came an announcement that Holbourn Aero Components – a member of the Thomas Tilling group – had bought half the preference and half of each holding of ordinary shares.

The explanation of the deal lies in the work other than knitting machinery that F.N.F. Machinery Manufacturing had been doing. Its Government contracts had come to an end with the defence cuts announced in August 1957, and it was hoped that Holbourn Aero Components, which had apparently been successful in obtaining new engineering business, would be able fully to occupy F.N.F.'s existing factory space.

CHAPTER VII

DEBATE ON TAKE-OVER BIDS

The wave of take-over bids that took place during 1953 and early in 1954 caused some concern in business circles as well as in the political world.

Among the wealth of good advice which the bankers annually bestow upon their shareholders in particular and the public in general, the following statement by Mr Bibby in the 1953 report of Martins Bank dealt with the vexed issue of bids:

'During the year there has been an epidemic of "take-over bids": some of them are obviously economically sound propositions but too often the victims of these take-overs bid are those companies which, by good and careful management, have ploughed back their earnings in to their business and carried out their expansion without calling for additional outside capital.

'By adhering to successive Chancellors' exhortations to conserve resources and exercise restraint in dividend increases, they have directly laid themselves open to exploitation.

'Too often the bidder merely wishes to take possession of the assets and liquidate a perfectly sound unit in our commercial or industrial structure.

'The profit to the bidder is clear, and the shareholder in the company who receives the bid sees a chance for a tax-free capital profit out of all proportion to his taxed dividends. This ultimately means the disappearance of many of the smaller firms who make so large a contribution to the virility of the country's economy.'

Commenting on these views, *The Economist* pointed out that if resources are successfully employed to yield their best economic return, the companies in question never need be 'victims' at all, for the bidder will be defeated. But if the assets are not yielding a proper return, then a bidder will generally be performing an economic service to the community.[1]

A few weeks later, Mr Roy Jenkins initiated a debate in the House of Commons on the subject, by moving the following motion:

'That this House deplores recent manifestations of the technique of take-over bids in so far as they have put large, untaxed capital profits into the hands of certain individuals and seriously undermined the policy of dividend restraint. It therefore calls upon the Government to appoint a committee of inquiry into all aspects of these activities, including the effect upon dividends, share prices, and company savings, the sources of the finance used, the capital profits obtained, and the counter measures taken by the directors of the companies concerned; such a committee to be empowered to suggest remedies as well as to investigate facts.'[2]

[1] *The Economist*, January 23rd, 1954, page 254.
[2] *Hansard*, February 11th, 1954 (Volume 523, No. 52).

Mr Jenkins had evidently given a good deal of thought to the causes of the present spate of take-over bids for he listed two main factors.

First and foremost the policy of conservative dividend distribution in recent years had given rise to these special situations. While company profits had increased steadily, there had been no corresponding increase in dividend payments, largely as a result of appeals for restraint from successive Chancellors of the Exchequer. In consequence, an increasing proportion of profits were ploughed back, thereby providing the most important source of savings in the country. Although these amounts were put to reserve and increased the assets of the company, they belonged legally to the ordinary shareholders. But the Stock Exchange, for its part, is always primarily interested in questions of current yield, so that the growth in the assets of the companies concerned was not fully reflected in the prices at which their shares stood in the market.

The second factor was that prices had been rising in this country for more than a decade. As a result the real value of the assets of many companies – real property in particular – was very much higher than the balance sheet value. Side by side with this situation, it was perfectly possible to imagine a company which was earning a reasonable rate of profit on the balance sheet value of its assets, but on another approach was seen to be earning a very low rate of profit on the real value of its assets. In that perplexing clash of values lies a temptation to certain people from outside to bid high prices in order to gain control of the company. Clearly, trading profits are not the real attraction; on the contrary they are usually poor. The main purpose is to gain control over the assets, either to put them to more profitable use (including adaptation to an entirely new use) or to sell them off at a substantial capital profit.

In the course of the debate, the gap between the views of the Opposition and those of the Government proved quite narrow. Mr Jenkins, for example, conceded that there was 'something' to be said for the activities of bidders. Indeed, he was at pains to point out that 'there is nothing new or objectionable about one company taking over another and that it has happened very often in the past. It can be said that it is in many ways quite habitual and serves the interests of economic progress. Many of our biggest and most successful businesses have been built up by a process of amalgamation. I do not dispute that such developments may be entirely reasonable, even when they involve take-over bids'.

As an instance of what he regarded as a reasonable take-over bid, he cited the case of Wiggins Teape, the paper manufacturers, who had just taken over Thomas Owen & Co, another firm of paper makers. His attitude was clearly influenced by the fact that no cash passed; it was merely an exchange of shares between two companies in the same line of business. Apart from this, however, the really undesirable consequence, in his view, was that 'the whole technique of take-over bids drives a coach and four through the policy of dividend restraint'.

Supporting the motion, Mr Eric Fletcher mentioned six evils which result from the abuse of take-over bids.

First, it would appear that 'very large capital gains have been made by certain individuals which are not subject to taxation'.

Second, the fact that these tax-free gains occur 'produces a considerable psychological effect on all workers in industry'.

Third, take-over bids give rise to rumours with the result that there is excessive and undesirable speculation.

Fourthly, excessive dividend distribution is apt to be practised by all companies – not just those threatened by bids.

While the fifth evil that was revealed was the counter-measures taken to try to defeat the bid.

Lastly, the duty of the directors where a conflict occurs between the interests of the shareholders and the employees of a company when a bid is announced.

For the Government side, Colonel Crosthwaite-Eyre introduced a note of realism by asserting that: 'No one would make a take-over bid unless, in his prudence and with the consent of his colleagues, he knew he could use the assets of a company more appropriately and more efficiently.'

In winding-up the debate, the Chancellor of the Exchequer (Mr R. A. Butler) showed that a great variety of transactions is covered by the phrase 'take-over bid'. Not all are anti-national or abnormal. Furthermore, if industry and commercial activity was to avoid stagnation, there must be a sense of adventure, a sense of risk, and at times, a sense of acquisition.

Nevertheless, there was one type of take-over bid which he disliked. Where, for instance, 'it is the sole intention of the purchaser to make a capital gain; and that he cares little whether he destroys some long-established business, or whether he saps the financial strength of the business by distributing profits which ought, in fact to be ploughed back'.

However, he made it plain that after a very wide examination of this matter, there was no evidence that any business had, in fact, been destroyed or had its resources plundered in order solely to realize capital gains, though there was evidence of abuse. He thought that this was taken care of by guidance given by the Bank of England to banks and other financial institutions for special care in dealing with requests for facilities for take-over transactions in cases where there appeared to be a speculative element. Moreover, Mr Butler was able to refute the allegations that take-over bids had driven a coach and four through the policy of dividend limitation, pointing out that rises in dividends began in the early part of 1951 long before take-over operations were thought of or noted. Figures were produced for 1952 and 1953 which clearly indicated that there was not the runaway lack of restraint in dividend distribution which the Opposition had suggested. In fact, when dividends were compared with capital employed there had been a steady drop. As Mr Butler remarked: 'It seems very often that it is the absolute or total amount paid in dividends which is mentioned, and the reason why they have increased is the quite simple, natural and common-sense reason that the amount of capital employed has increased more than *pro tanto*.'

As to counter-measures, Mr Butler dealt with some of the ways and means open to companies defending themselves from the unwelcome attentions of a bidder. First, the company or the management of the company can advise the shareholders not to sell to the bidder because the shares are worth more than the bid, or will be worth more if the company continues to be managed by the present board. Or they could retain the shareholders' confidence by disclosing the board's plans for future development so as to make full use of the company's assets. Alternatively, they could take such action as is open to them under the Companies Act, to make the company unattractive to a potential bidder by placing restrictions on the use or disposal of the company's property.

Since then, the subject of take-over bids has come up for further debate from time to time. The House of Lords, for instance, considered the matter in March 1959 when Lord Meston asked the Government whether they would consider introducing legislation to deal with take-over bids.[1] He suggested that the appropriate Government Department, the Treasury or the Board of Trade, should be entitled on application made to them by an interested party, to suspend transactions in the voting shares of a company for three months. In his view a suspension of three months would enable shareholders to find out who really was the take-over bidder. The shareholders would have time to form a proper opinion whether the bid was really in their interest.

Replying for the Government, the Earl of Dundee, Minister without Portfolio, said that the Government were not contemplating the assumption of any further powers which would enable them to discourage or restrain the process of take-over bids. The great majority of them, he had no doubt, were socially and economically beneficial, although there might be some which while perfectly legal, might incidently involve some practice or procedure which some people did not happen to like.

[1] *Hansard*, Vol. 214, 50.

One method by which take-over bids of any kind could be discouraged at the moment were under the Exchange Control Act, relating to foreign bids. Permission would be refused where security interests were involved. The Earl of Dundee went on to say that if the shareholders had made their decision they were responsible for seeing whether they were getting a fair deal. He did not know how fat it would be equitable for the Government to interfere in order to protect shareholders against themselves. He would not like to see officials of the Treasury or Board of Trade trying to decide whether a certain bid had been in accordance with certain standards of conduct which did not seem to be clearly defined.

A few months later, the House of Commons became the centre of further inquiry, when Mr Sidney Irving asked the President of the Board of Trade whether, owing to growing public concern, he would set up a departmental committee to investigate the operation of take-over bids, with a view to recommending such appropriate amendments to the Companies Act as might be necessary in the public interest. In turning down the idea, Mr Rodgers, Parliamentary Secretary, Board of Trade, thought that the great majority of take-over bids were of great benefit, both economically and socially, to the country. The possibility of such bids kept directors on their toes and ensured that assets were fully utilized. On the whole this operated in the interests of workers, industry, and the country.[1]

Later on in the same month, Mr Cyril Osborne asked the President of the Board of Trade if he would move to appoint a select committee to investigate the economic consequences of the growing movement towards greater industrial and commercial amalgamations.

Once again, the task of replying fell to Mr Rodgers, who delcared that he was satisfied that the growing movement towards industrial amalgamations did not operate against the interests of consumers or the economy as a whole – reminding the House that the Monopolies Commission was ever watchful in this direction.[2]

Finally, at the end of June 1959, Mr Harold Wilson initiated another debate on what he described as 'these undesirable developments in private industry', though taking care not to condemn all take-over bids out of hand. A most undesirable feature of these activities, he asserted, was the fantastic profits made in tax-free compensation for loss of office; the so-called 'golden handshake' for the benefit of the displaced directors and executives. It was also the Labour Party's view that a capital gains tax would take some of the gilt off the gingerbread for the less justifiable form of take-over bid and financial speculations. In reply, Mr Heathcoat Amory,

---

[1] *The Times*, June 3rd, 1959.
[2] *The Times*, June 17th, 1959.

the Chancellor of the Exchequer, said that there was a good deal of evidence that to date take-over bids had been beneficial rather than harmful from the points of view of the efficiency of industry, of the interest of the employees concerned, and of the economy at large. Moreover, he did not believe that there were grounds for important legislative action by Parliament. An examination of some of the best-known take-overs of recent years indicated that the businesses concerned had prospered and developed still more favourably than before they were taken over. In cases where take-overs produced bad results, the fault would most likely be due to inertia on the part of shareholders in looking after their interests. That by itself would hardly justify major alteration of the law.

As to the question whether capital gains should be subject to tax, Mr Amory said there were two important considerations at stake. Would such a tax be to the advantage of the economy? The majority of the Royal Commission on Taxation thought not. Furthermore, the Opposition were seldom very clear whether in advocating a capital gains tax they also envisaged tax relief at an equivalent rate on capital losses.

Speaking in a debate on the proposals contained in a White Paper (Cmd 2299) on monopolies, mergers and restrictive practices in July 1964, Mr Heath, the then Secretary of State for Industry, Trade and Regional Development, said:

> 'There was clearly today a trend towards concentration of industry. Many mergers were highly desirable. They ensured that capital was more profitably employed or secured economies of scale. But it should be possible for a Government to inform itself and take appropriate action when it suspected a merger might have undesirable conclusions. The investigation proposed in the White Paper could begin as soon as a merger was proposed and came to the notice of the Board of Trade.
> 'It was true that normally an investigation would take place after the event, and many interesting suggestions had been made about how potentially harmful mergers could be prevented in the meantime. This form of proposal could only work if all mergers were brought into it. There would be bound to be delays. It was wrong to assume that the only answer to an undesirable merger was to break the companies apart. It might well be possible to safeguard the public interest by less drastic requirements or undertakings on how the merged firms would conduct their business.'

During the 1964 General Election campaign, all three major political party manifestos contained proposals for dealing with mergers and take-over bids. All the parties were agreed that practices in restraint of competition, and abuse of monopoly power in industry, should be subject to more effective procedures. On the restrictive practices side, powers were taken under the Resale Prices Act 1964 to encourage more competition in the distributive trades. But the culminating point of this long drawn out public debate – stretching right back to the early 1950s – was the introduction of new legislation under the title of the Monopolies and Mergers Act 1965.

In many respects, this was bi-partisan legislation in the sense that it was fathered by a Conservative Government and inherited by a Labour Government which saw it safely on to the Statute Book in 1965.

The typical take-over bids of the 1950s which thrived on the under-valuation of fixed assets, particularly freehold land and buildings, have slowly given way to the 1960-style mergers and take-overs where the accent is on rationalization.

This subtle change has come about through the gradual re-organization and regrouping of one industry after another into larger and more viable units. Only in this way can scarce economic resources be deployed to the best advantage.

Then in 1966, the Government set up its own agency to promote industrial reorganization. The Industrial Reorganization Corporation, as it was called, was established by Act of Parliament on December 21st, 1966. Its functions were as follows:

'The Corporation may, for the purpose of promoting industrial efficiency and profitability and assisting the economy of the United Kingdom or any part of the United Kingdom:

'(a) promote or assist the reorganization or development of any industry; or

'(b) if requested so to do by the Minister of Technology, establish or develop or promote or assist the establishment or development of, any industrial enterprise.'

In order to carry out these functions the I.R.C. was given powers to draw on financial resources of up to £150 million. Thus in some cases the I.R.C. took the initiative in exploring the scope for rationalization in a particular sector of industry, sounding out the leading companies, assessing the practical case for rationalization and examining the form it might take. In other cases, there was no need for direct financial support – the corporation simply acted as a catalyst and in that way did little more than set the wheels in motion.

It is possible to identify three main fields of activity in its work at the micro level with individual companies and at the difficult interface between the public and private sectors of the economy:

(1) Reorganization – the bulk of I.R.C.'s work was devoted to the task of effecting reorganization through company mergers.

(2) Stimulation – the I.R.C. used its influence to stimulate British industrial companies to effective and profitable reform, without recourse to merger or take-over by others.

(3) Selective Investment – the sectors of industry to which I.R.C. give priority for selective investment are typically those of high

growth, key exporters, capital goods and component suppliers. But before providing development finance I.R.C. had to satisfy itself that the money was not available from other resources, that the project was a viable proposition and that I.R.C.'s contribution would show a commercial return.

The completion of a three-way merger in the summer of 1969 between Ransome & Marles Bearing Co, the Hoffmann Manufacturing Co and Pollard Ball and Roller Bearing Co laid the basis for a viable British-owned ball bearing industry.

Other quoted investments held include a stake in Brown Bayley Steels, and George Kent, where nearly 25 per cent of the equity is owned. Substantial loans have also been made to G.E.C. – English Electric, British Oxygen, Whessoe, Qualitex, Joseph Lucas and Plessey among others. And then towards the end of its short reign, I.R.C. made commitments of £6 million to the Cammell Laird group and a £20 million promise to Rolls-Royce.

Much of the criticism of the I.R.C. has been directed against its interventionist role in the market. Indeed, concern has been expressed in many quarters about the opportunities for distorting market forces in certain take-over bid situations.

The I.R.C. was, therefore, bound to be in the forefront of political and industrial debate when the Conservative Government took over after the General Election of June 1970. It was then only a question of time before the new Government unwound the commitments entered into by I.R.C. and sold off its investments in equity shares. Mr John Davies, Secretary for Trade and Industry, served notice of the Government's intentions when he announced that legislation would be introduced in due course – probably early in 1971 – to carry out the Government's decision, and would provide for the transfer to the Government of the I.R.C.'s assets and liabilities. So ends an interesting, yet in some ways an unsatisfactory, phase in the continuing search for industrial efficiency throughout the length and breadth of the economy.

Private enterprise is also very much to the fore in furthering rationalization. The merchant banking firm, Singer and Friedlander, have opened a 'mergers and amalgamations register'. Though they have put a bottom limit of £50,000 on the valuation of companies that can be registered, this method of finding a partner is clearly of greatest importance for the small and medium-sized firms. The register will be kept in Birmingham, with Singer's other offices in Nottingham and Leeds feeding in potential clients initially. A number of business brokers are said to be active in the same field. Early in 1967, the Industrial and Commercial Finance Corporation also formed a subsidiary called Industrial Mergers Limited which offers a service in the merger field to I.C.F.C.'s existing client firms and indeed to all-comers in the small and medium-sized field which the corporation serves.

The social dislocation caused by mergers is part of the price which has to be paid for industrial change.

The G.E.C. decision to close down the A.E.I. Woolwich factory (announced early in 1968) and other similar closures created some discord among unions and employees at the time.

The threat of redundancy led to a Commons motion, signed by seventy-six Labour M.P.s expressing grave concern about 'the lack of social responsibility evident in recent company mergers with their subsequent effect on factory closures and unemployment'. The motion called for the Government to start talks with the Trades Union Congress and the Confederation of British Industries 'to prepare a code of conduct applicable to all private firms in receipt of public funds'.

The Government's point of view was put by Mr Edmund Dell, Parliamentary Under-Secretary of State at the Department of Economic Affairs, in a written answer:

> 'The employment effects of mergers often cannot be forecast in advance but the Government expects companies to co-operate closely with it and the trade unions so as to ensure that any necessary redeployment of labour is orderly and planned.'[1]

Quite apart from the social consequences, the Government also decided to make a special study of the whole area of its monopoly, merger and restrictive practice policy.

A general reassessment and clarification of existing laws is somewhat overdue because there is some confusion in the public mind about the apparent rival activities of the Industrial Reorganization Corporation on the one hand and the Monopolies Commission and Restrictive Practices Court on the other. Moreover, the Prices and Incomes Board sometimes take a different view from these other bodies. The object of the study is to seek ways of avoiding a conflict of policy.

On the positive side, the I.R.C. was busily engaged in promoting mergers, while on the negative side the Monopolies Commission was sifting the evidence presented in favour of proposed mergers which had been referred to them by the Board of Trade. At the same time, the Government for its part, was concerned that existing mergers should also come under the same kind of scrutiny. This post-merger study was seen as a check on performance and a test of how far, if at all, mergers had fulfilled their stated intentions.

Outlining Government policy on mergers, Mr Anthony Crosland (the then President of the Board of Trade) said:

---

[1] *Financial Times*, February 20th, 1968.

'But because the general presumption is at present in favour of mergers, and because the Government itself takes energetic steps to bring particular mergers about, it does not follow that we should view all mergers uncritically and (apart from those cases where we take positive action) adopt a passive or *laissez-faire* approach. This is not a field which can be left solely to the market and to the judgement of shareholders and boards of directors, and I would like to explain why.

'First, large-scale mergers, especially where they involve factory closures, may have profound social consequences for the workers concerned, and indeed, for the life of a town or region; in such cases the private costs of a large firm's actions may diverge from the social, or in its widest sense the economic costs. Moreover, the merger movement as a whole may have implications for the distribution of wealth or the concentration of power; no Government can neglect these wider social and even political considerations.

'These are the most important reasons why the Government must hold a watching brief over significant mergers. But there are also reasons of economic efficiency. Because we judge the recent merger movement to have been on balance beneficial to the economy, it does not follow that all mergers without exception are beneficial.'[1]

All this time though, industry was increasingly disturbed about the lack of guidance available to them when contemplating a merger. How could they judge whether merger proposals would be accepted or not? What public criteria or guidelines did the Board of Trade follow in deciding whether or not to refer a proposed merger to the Monopolies Commission? This was a very real criticism which the Board of Trade finally met by publishing its policy guidelines in 1969.[2]

Meanwhile, the Government had transferred overall responsibility for mergers and monopolies policy from the Board of Trade to the Department of Employment and Productivity (D.E.P.) preparatory to the setting up of a so-called 'Superboard' or Commission on Industry and Manpower (C.I.M.).

But before all this could be put into effect, the General Election of June 1970 intervened and a new Government was voted into power with very different ideas. In announcing their policy in the autumn of 1970, the new Government's intentions soon became clear.

A new Department of Trade and Industry was formed (taking over the Board of Trade and Ministry of Technology) which inherited the vetting procedure for mergers, the investigatory powers of the Monopolies Commission were strengthened while both the I.R.C. and P.I.B., were dissolved early in 1971.

The revival of merger activity during 1972 came under Parliamentary scrutiny and the Government decided to step up its own

---

[1] Extract from a speech given to the Association of British Chambers of Commerce, London, June 25th, 1969.
[2] *Mergers – a guide to Board of Trade practice*. H.M.S.O.

monitoring role – particularly in the case of some conglomerate mergers.

In the course of a House of Commons debate in November, 1973, the activities of the Barclay Securities Group[1] under its then Chairman, Mr John Bentley, were strongly criticized by Miss Janet Foukes, the Conservative member for Merton and Morden. The closure of a large factory which Barclay Securities had bought from the former Lines Bros toy firm when it went into liquidation had resulted in considerable unemployment in her constituency. She was joined in protest by Mr Maurice Edelman, Labour member for Coventry North, who spoke on the decision by the Barclay Securities directors to close a large part of the Shepperton Film Studios (which came into the ownership of the company when it took over British Lion) and to redevelop the site.

Speaking at the end of the debate, Mr Anthony Grant, Under-Secretary for Industrial Development, announced that the Government is to tighten its control over take-overs and mergers by making increased use of the Monopolies Commission. Special attention will be given to merger proposals of a conglomerate nature and those where asset stripping appears to be a major consideration. The potential effect on jobs and the likelihood of redundancies will also weigh in the balance when the D.T.I. considers whether to refer a bid to the Commission for further inquiry.

However, even before this Parliamentary debate there had been indications of Government concern over possible monopoly situations and it had already referred the Beecham Group and Boots bids for Glaxo to the Commission (the Commission's recommendation that both bids should be vetoed was accepted and acted on by the Government). It had also requested the Commission to examine the bid by Sir Charles Clore's Sears Holdings Group for control of the William Timpson Shoe retailing chain – although deciding against similar action in the case of the competing bid put in by United Drapery Stores.

Addressing a seminar on mergers and take-overs organized by the Institute of Economic Affairs, Sir Anthony Burney, Chairman of Debenhams, who had himself been involved in resisting a bid by United Drapery Stores to gain control of Debenhams, referred to take-over bids as almost becoming a 'city game' and he went on to suggest that the city should sit down and work out whether or not it approved of the present situation.

Although some mergers can be fully justified by subsequent performance (the G.E.C./A.E.I. merger is one such case), it is likely that the present 'anti-merger' sentiments will result in a dampening down of bids for the time being. It may be, of course,

[1]The company was, in its turn, taken over by Vavasseur in 1973.

that some of the larger U.K. companies will decide to look for possible take-over opportunities in Europe now that they can operate within the E.E.C.

And there, for the moment, the long drawn out clash of views comes to a halt.

CHAPTER VIII

THE TAKE-OVER BID TECHNIQUE

Any person or group of people wishing to obtain control of a company may accomplish their aim in one of four ways:

(i) purchase the company's undertaking;

(ii) make a general offer to the shareholders to purchase their shares or sufficient of them to give control;

(iii) do a deal with the existing board of directors, whereby they undertake to sell all their shares and resign their offices; the casual vacancies thus created being filled by the purchaser(s) nominees; or

(iv) acquire sufficient shares by purchase on the Stock Exchange or otherwise, to wage a successful battle of proxies with the existing management so that they are dismissed and replaced by the purchaser(s) nominees.

In all but the last case it will be necessary (or, at any rate, highly desirable) to have the concurrence of the existing directors.

Any one of the procedures outlined above is commonly referred to as a 'take-over' bid. Although on the surface they have much in common with mergers, the motives are different. Apart from (i) the situation is one in which, from the legal aspect at any rate, the company itself does not participate. The company's existence is not affected, nor need its constitution be altered: all that occurs is that its shareholders change. From the legal point of view this distinction is perhaps impressive, but commercially the two things may be almost identical. If, as is normally the case, a controlling interest is acquired, the company (or companies; for there may well be more than one) will become a subsidiary of the acquiring company with a different management, and cease, in fact though not in law, to be an independent entity. Looked at from the viewpoint of the members, the results are virtually identical with a reconstruction under section 287, Companies Act 1948. Under both methods the former members may be left with shares in the transferee company in place of their original holdings (or acquisition of a controlling interest might be the preliminary to an acquisition of the undertaking under section 287).[1]

In fact, the difference is neither more nor less than that between

[1] If this is the intention, the acquiring company may be satisfied with something less than a 100 per cent interest and may choose not to invoke the section 209 procedure outlined later on.

the two methods employed in taking over firms or industries of nationalization.[1]

Although a take-over bid seldom takes the form described in (i), the Royal Dutch-Shell group made an offer for the entire assets and business of the Canadian Eagle Oil Company for the express purpose of effecting a complete amalgamation of interests.[2] At the time, this ranked as one of the largest take-over bids ever made, since at the ruling stock-market prices, Shell were offering the equivalent of some £95 million (in a share exchange) for the 23,826,071 Canadian Eagle shares held by the public.

The term 'take-over' bid strictly refers to an offer which may be made either to the whole of the shareholders or to those owning the equity of a company to purchase their existing holdings at a price which is sufficiently above the current Stock Exchange quotation for the shares, as to induce them to sell out – either in exchange for quoted shares in the company making the bid or wholly for cash or partly cash and exchange of shares. In some respects there is little to distinguish many of them from the kind of mergers which have been taking place in British industry for several decades. Such an offer may be made by persons who wish to obtain complete control of the company for one reason or another. Companies may find themselves in a take-over position if full use is not being made of their resources. Such inadequate use is generally to be found in relation to current values of their freehold properties and to the amount of their liquid resources. If a company is earning, say, 9 per cent on the cost price of its fixed assets, but these are worth today, perhaps, three times the original cost, its earnings are only a meagre 3 per cent on the true value.

An excessive amount of cash, in relation to possible needs, held by the company makes the cost of the take-over to the purchaser that much the less. Furthermore, excess liquid resources generally indicates a niggardly dividend policy by the directors in the past and the result of this is that the shares stand in the market at a price which is low if considered in relation to actual earnings, and, of course, still lower in relation to potential earnings. Companies which are not making full use of their assets, and which happen to have excessive liquid resources, may still not be in a 'take-over position' if they are controlled by a family. If more than 50 per cent

[1] (a) Where existing company, chartered or registered, was kept in existence but nationalized by the acquisition of the whole of its share capital, viz., the Bank of England, Cable & Wireless, Short Bros Ltd.

(b) The customary method, where one or more special *ad hoc* statutory corporations were formed, e.g., National Coal Board, Gas Council, British Transport Commission, etc.

[2] *The Times*, March 23rd, 1959.

of the equity is held by a group which does not welcome a take-over, other interests who otherwise might wish to make a more profitable use of the company's assets will be defeated.

The reasons vary, of course, from one bid to another but in general arise from the following motives:

(1) the existing management is regarded as unenterprising causing the assets to be under-employed or earning a below-the-average return;[1]

(2) valuable freehold land and properties owned by the company may be sold and taken back again on lease, thus not only gaining a capital profit but acquiring a substantial holding of cash which can be reinvested in more remunerative assets;

(3) a company may have built up large liquid assets (either cash or realizable investments) for which it has no immediate use and on which, in its present form, the company can only earn an inadequate return. In the hands of the bidding company these liquid assets could be put to active use besides giving it the chance of getting hold of fresh capital cheaply.

These opportunities present themselves because, as already explained, Stock Exchange quotations for shares are determined to a great extent by the dividends which have actually been paid on them in the immediate past and on future prospects. Owing to frequent Government appeals in the past for restraint in the distribution of profits coupled with the restrictive impact of profits tax (especially the higher rate on distributions), many boards of directors have seen fit to follow a policy of paying a consistently lower rate of dividend than would have been justified by the company's earnings record. This cautious dividend policy has, moreover, been reinforced by the knowledge that the increased replacement cost of fixed assets attributable to inflation may cause serious inroads into the company's resources at some future time.

However well-intentioned this ultra-conservative dividend policy may have been, judged from the long-term interests of the shareholders, the fact remains that it has tended to depress the market prices of the shares and thus prevent members from participating fully (either in increased income or enhanced capital) in the prosperity which the companies have been enjoying. Given the opportunity, therefore, many shareholders have welcomed the chance of selling their shares at prices which are much higher than those warranted by dividend yield alone, and at the same time realize a capital profit.

---

[1] Though public policy might have prevented the most profitable use of the assets, viz. planning permission could have been refused.

Again, some boards of directors have pursued a policy of plough-ing back profits into the business in excess of the sums strictly needed for the maintenance and foreseeable development of the business, and have neglected to use the funds so retained to the best advantage (i.e., the money may merely have been placed on deposit with a bank, building societies, hire-purchase finance house, or temporarily invested in gilt-edged securities, all of which the share-holders could have done quite well – and perhaps better – for them-selves had they been free to dispose of the money). As a result of these and other factors (mainly post-war inflation), the break-up value of some shares may well be worth much more than their value on a going-concern basis. This is particularly the case where land and buildings appear in the balance sheet at a pre-war cost or valuation, which bears little or no resemblance to the price they would now fetch if sold on the open market (i.e., property market). A somewhat unsatisfactory feature of take-over bids, however, is the wave of speculative dealings on the Stock Exchange that is engendered by rumours and then counter-rumours of forthcoming bids or pre-liminary discussions between boards of directors prior to a formal bid. Again, the take-over bid has not always been used for the legitimate purpose of effecting a lasting business merger. Thus, con-trol of a company may be acquired simply to enforce the declaration of larger dividends, causing the quoted price of the shares to rise on the one hand, but, in the process perhaps, stripping the company of accumulated liquid resources earmarked for capital commitments or development schemes. Another aspect of this speculative bid occurs where control is obtained merely for the purpose of making a quick capital profit, without regard to the company's future, by disposing of some or all of its assets at an advantageous price, and then distri-buting the assets by placing the company in liquidation. In either case there is evidently no intention whatsoever to reorganize, re-group or develop the assets for the purpose of the company's business. Furthermore, it can be argued that although there is much to be said for bids which substitute economic progress for economic stagnation, their social impact, their effect on morale inside the firm, on labour relations in the concern, and on class feelings generally may not be so beneficial. From this point of view, the economic argument, which is based on making the best use of physical assets, is a narrow one; it tends to ignore that the process of bidding for and taking over a concern in the manner in which it has frequently been done since the war, leads to large tax-free capital gains, defeats the tenets of voluntary dividend restraint and so many inhibit effort to encourage restraint in wage claims.

At the same time, it should be borne in mind that these arguments are not really arguments against take-over bids as such. They are arguments against some of the possible adverse effects of these bids. In any event, the improvement in earning power brought about is beneficial both to those who are employed in the company as well as to those who own it. What is more, the economy as a whole benefits in the process. In spite of these drawbacks, however, it is only fair to place on record the view that the majority of take-over bids are genuine, and deemed to be for the ultimate good of the company, as well as for those shareholders who choose to accept the bid. Naturally, from time to time take-over bids are announced which excite intense and heated opposition. That is only to be expected. For like most other people, company directors are loath to be deprived of a livelihood (even if some compensation for loss of office is promised) which often confers upon them added status and influence outside the company itself. It is sometimes difficult for them to realize that the assets under their management are capable of being put to better use in their existing state or of earning more in an alternative use, viz., an hotel converted into a block of offices. At this turning-point in a company's fortunes, it is almost too much to expect an elected board of directors to impartially assess the merits of a bid which threatens their own position and future.

Indeed, the methods which have sometimes been employed to ward off take-over bids leave one with the impression of improvised moves which are doomed to failure because they are too little and come too late. For example, directors have advised shareholders not to accept a bid on the grounds that it is far below the 'real worth' of the company's net assets. Then, rather belatedly, they adopt desperate measures in trying to force up the market price of the company's shares and bring them near the bid price, by immediately declaring a bonus issue of shares out of reserves (so bringing the issued share capital more into line with the capital employed in the business) and either increasing the interim dividend far beyond all expectations or raising the final dividend to a level where earnings are distributed up to the hilt. Even so, these last-minute skirmishes seldom succeed in their aim.

If boards of directors *in situ* had only seen fit to deploy the assets under their command in the same way as the take-over bidder planned to do – if and when he gained control – most take-over bids would never have seen the light of day.

Legal standpoint

The divorce of management from ownership, which is an important by-product of the joint-stock system, has given rise to important conflicts of legal opinion on more than one occasion. In particular, the attempt on the part of a board of directors to 'freeze' an important part of the company's assets without fully consulting their shareholders, led to a report by a Board of Trade Inspector under section 165 (b) of the Companies Act 1948.[1] The investigation was made into the affairs of the Savoy Hotel Ltd, and the Berkeley Hotel Co Ltd, with special reference to the formation of Worcester Buildings Co (London) Ltd, and the transfer to that company of the freehold of the site of the Berkeley Hotel.

At this point it may be useful to recall the whole background scene to 'the Worcester scheme' especially the facts and events that led up to it and the motives and purposes which actuated the directors who were responsible for it.

In the early autumn of 1953, the £1 ordinary shares of the Savoy Hotel Co stood in the market at about £1·40. At that stage, two financiers became interested in the shares and each attempted to gain control of the company. Unknown to one another at the time, they both went into the market and started buying on a big scale. The board of Directors of the Savoy became perturbed as the price of the stock rose sharply from day to day, as they sensed that a bid was in the offing and by this time had a fairly good idea that the Berkeley Hotel was the immediate target of the interests then actively buying the shares. Unfortunately, the Savoy directors were unable to ascertain the buyers' identity, since the parties concerned operated largely through nominees. Accordingly, the directors called for an inquiry under the Companies Act 1948,[2] so as to establish their identity.

An inquiry was duly set up under Mr J. B. Lindon, Q.C.,[3] the subsequent report revealing that Mr Samuel, through his company Land Securities Investment Trust, owned rather more than 20 per cent of the equity, and that Mr Clore had managed to gain control of about 10 per cent. At that point, when the report was published, Mr Clore and Mr Samuel came together and the upshot was that Mr Clore sold out his entire holding of Savoy stock to Mr Samuel – netting a handsome profit into the bargain – and leaving the latter in undisputed possession of well over 30 per cent of the ordinary shares.

Whereupon the Savoy directors reacted in a most unexpected manner by devising the Worcester Buildings Scheme, as it became known. It had been recognized by the directors of the Savoy Co that, on a short-term view, a large and immediate profit might be made by directing attention primarily to the exploitation of the property and site values. For the very valuable hotel properties and sites owned by the Savoy company and its subsidiary companies

[1] Report of Mr E. Milner Holland, Q.C., on the Savoy Hotel Ltd, and the Berkeley Hotel Co Ltd, June 1954.
[2] Under section 172.
[3] See Report, H.M.S.O., 1953.

all stood in the books of those companies at cost and accordingly at figures considerably lower than their current values. Next, from 1945 up to the end of 1952, there had been a very substantial fall in the trading results of the Berkeley company, mainly accounted for, it was said, by a decline in the restaurant side of the business since the hotel profits remained substantially steady.

Thus, taking into consideration the great value of the Berkeley Hotel and site (incidentally valued by Messrs Knight, Frank & Rutley at just over £490,000), a case could clearly be made out on these figures for turning the property to account in some other manner than that for which it was being used. Indeed, the possibility of a substantial profit was particularly applicable to the Berkeley company, and the directors were very much alive to that fact. On the other hand, somewhat different considerations seemed to apply to the Savoy Hotel and Claridges Hotel in view of the satisfactory level of their trading results, and without knowing for sure the policy of the person who might gain control the directors came to the conclusion that the most probable aim was the exploitation of the valuable properties of the companies in preference to the continuance of the hotel and restaurant business. No doubt the Berkeley Hotel was the most likely target, at any rate in the first instance. In the opinion of the directors, however, the Savoy, Claridges and Berkeley hotels formed a suitably balanced group of hotels; and it was felt that the Berkeley ought not to be lost to the group as a hotel, in spite of the unsatisfactory trading results currently disclosed. It was thought that the best interest of the interrelated companies would be served by continuing, in the same general manner as before, the hotel and restaurant businesses then being carried on. The directors stressed the fact that they had had under consideration for some time a number of alternative schemes for development or redevelopment of the Berkeley Hotel all of which involved retaining the goodwill of the hotel. Although no final conclusion has been reached as to the best course to adopt, none of these alternative schemes, it was pointed out, involved the closing down of the Berkeley Hotel and the consequent loss of its goodwill, and the directors at all times viewed this possibility as representing a disastrous policy.

In these circumstances, the directors gave close thought, during October and November, to the question whether there were any means open to them of preventing such control being acquired by the purchaser or purchasers of Savoy stock. At once the question was mooted whether the unissued shares, of which there were then 96,301, might be subdivided so as to give them greater voting power, and then issued to trustees of a staff benevolent fund trust created for the purpose, who, it might be supposed, would not submit to the influence of the persons seeking to obtain control. However, the directors were emphatically advised by counsel that this could be instantly set aside as an inadmissible exercise of their powers to issue shares.

Finally, at the beginning of November 1953, a scheme very similar in content to that ultimately adopted was evolved and laid before a barrister of high standing and long experience in company matters. After consultations with the directors at which possible legal objections and difficulties were very fully ventilated, counsel gave a long and carefully reasoned opinion in writing, in which he advised the board that so long as they acted bona fide in what they believed to be the best interests of the company a sale of the character contemplated was within their powers. He advised that in the phrase 'the best interests of the company' the expression 'the company' did not mean the sectional interest of some (it may be a majority) of the present members, or even, in his opinion, of all the present members, but of present and future members of the company.[1]

The general nature and effect of 'the Worcester scheme' was, at long last, ready for disclosure to Savoy stockholders and a circular was sent out by the joint secretaries of the Savoy company dated December 5th, 1953. Meanwhile, Mr Harold Samuel had become aware of the incorporation of the Worcester (London) Co with an unusual capital structure and suspecting that a plan was afoot to put the Berkeley Hotel beyond the reach of the stockholders requested the Board of Trade to appoint an inspector. On December 7th, 1953, substantial amounts of Savoy stock were purchased in the market by directors of the Savoy, and on December 8th, Mr Harold Samuel made an offer through brokers to sell the holdings of Savoy stock in the hands of his company, and threatened legal proceedings with the object of setting aside the Worcester scheme. Finally, on December 11th, as the result of negotiations conducted between Sir Alan Rae Smith and Mr Russell Tillett an agreement was reached for the sale of the stock (at a price of £3·12½) held by Mr Harold Samuel's company. In the end, Worcester Buildings Co (London) Ltd was liquidated and the Savoy company resumed full control of its assets once more.

Thus, recapitulating for a moment, the essential circumstances were that the Savoy Hotel Ltd became the target of a sensational take-over bid because it owned extremely valuable properties – in particular, the Berkeley Hotel – which it was alleged could be exploited far more profitably as offices and showrooms than as an hotel. In order to discourage these unwelcome attentions, the Savoy directors sought ingeniously to rearrange the ownership of these

[1] Report of Mr E. Milner Holland, Q.C., in respect of a Board of Trade investigation into the Savoy Hotel Co Ltd, June 14th, 1954, page 16, paragraph 10.

properties, so that a departure from their existing user would be beyond the power even of a unanimous vote of their shareholders; and they acted in pursuance of articles of association giving the usual full powers of management and the disposition of assets.

The transaction involved two operations. The ownership of the properties concerned was transferred to Worcester Buildings Co (London) Ltd, which had been incorporated *ad hoc* with an ingenious, though unusual, capital structure. This company proceeded to lease them back, one of the conditions of the Berkeley lease being that it should not without the Worcester Co's consent be used otherwise than as an hotel. Worcester Co had a capital of £650,000 but the articles conferred two-thirds of the votes on the holders of 10,000 £1 ordinary shares, and these shares were allotted to the trustees of a benevolent fund for Savoy employees, which was also constituted *ad hoc*. Whereas prior to these moves, a simple majority of the Savoy stockholders could have forced a change of policy with regard to the use of these properties by voting the removal of the directors in accordance with their statutory right, after they had been concluded they would have needed the consent of the Worcester Co's directors, who were in no way amenable to their control.

The eminent counsel who advised the Savoy directors took the view that, provided the directors bona fide considered it in the interests of the company, the scheme was legally valid. Mr Milner Holland, while accepting their bona fides, did not regard that as concluding the matter. He held that it is both legitimate and relevant to look beyond, 'to the object or purpose behind an exercise of the directors' powers in order to determine its legal validity'. The powers conferred on the directors by the articles, he said, were used 'to render irrevocable for all time the policy view of the present board', and in his opinion, 'such a use of directors' powers is in principle not distinguishable from an issue of shares to affect voting power,[1] and, however proper the motive behind it, is not a purpose for which these powers were conferred on the board. Powers conferred by the shareholders on directors for the purpose of managing the business of the company cannot be used for the purpose of depriving those shareholders of such control as under the regulations of the company they may have over the company's assets'.

This opinion does not, unfortunately, have the binding force of a judgement of the Court and some element of doubt must still exist. As Mr Milner Holland so aptly observed:

'These are difficult questions which are not made easier by the apparent absence of any judicial decision which clearly bears directly

---

[1] Held to be an improper exercise of directors' powers. (See *Piercy v. S. Mills & Co Ltd* ([1920] 1 Ch. 77).)

upon them; and it need be a matter for little surprise that different minds reach different legal conclusions in answering them.'

In summing up one may venture to say that the plan devised by the Savoy directors and their advisers generated a good deal of hostile opinion in the City of London and elsewhere, and even before Mr Milner Holland's report was published there was a considerable body of legal opinion which openly declared that the scheme would have been defeated in the Courts anyhow. Moreover, it would be premature to call upon Parliament to amend the Companies Act until such time as it has been proved beyond all shadow of doubt that the present Act is wanting in this respect. In any event, it would be extremely difficult to draft such an amendment (as was pointed out in the House of Commons at the time) and it is possible to question its urgency.

The Savoy Hotel was in the headlines again in December 1970, this time over the relative voting power of the 'A' and 'B' ordinary shares when shareholders were asked to ratify the issue of shares in respect of the acquisition of the Headfort Hotel in Belgravia and the Lancaster Hotel in Paris. The bone of contention was the Lancaster deal because to buy this hotel the Savoy directors issued a very large proportion of 'B' shares (30,207 'B' against 92,000 'A') to the vendor. This had the effect of reducing the voting power of the 'A' from 53 per cent of the votes to 50 per cent. The Savoy board argued that it was only restoring the position to what it was when 'A' shares were issued to acquire the Connaught Hotel in 1956. But Trafalgar House Investments, which only began to acquire its holding of 'A' shares in 1968 wanted the voting power of the 'A' shares restored to the 53 per cent that ruled between 1956 and 1970, contending that the issue of an above average number of 'B' shares (which carried 40 times as much voting power per pound of nominal capital as the A" shares) would ensure that control of the group would remain with the board and its associates. However, the board's view on this occasion was endorsed at an extraordinary meeting of the company.

Another company battle which captured the headlines concerned the bid by Mr Charles Clore for Scottish Motor Traction – this time one which was successful in the end. As a leading weekly journal said at the time: 'The S.M.T. case will surely rank with the Sears and the Savoy Hotel disputes as one of the leading examples of the take-over bid.[1] All the ingredients were there. Rabid prejudice against the bidders, *ex parte* statements, counter bids, and counter moves by directors, were resorted to as much from national pride as from sentimental attachment to the concern.

[1] *The Economist*, June 30th, 1956

The opening moves were made in the following manner. Mr Clore's original bid was one 25p 'A' ordinary share in Sears Holdings for every 25p ordinary share in S.M.T. Mr Hugh Fraser countered with a similar offer in the shares of the House of Fraser, the relative attractiveness of the two bids turning on small variations in the market prices of the respective shares. Mr Clore then added a cash premium of 5p a share to his offer, and Mr Fraser immediately followed suit. On June 18th, 1956, Mr Clore announced that he had gained control, after owners of 53 per cent of S.M.T.'s ordinary capital had accepted his offer. Meanwhile, Mr Fraser had not withdrawn his offer and, on June 19th, 1956, the directors of S.M.T. (with one exception) assented to it in respect of their own holdings. Mr Clore, wanting something larger than a bare majority, left his offer, including the cash premium, open until the close of business on June 25th. On June 23rd, however, Mr Hugh Fraser had retired from the battle 'with great regret' following the revelation of the 'Atholl transactions' as they came to be known.

The Atholl transactions were very similar to the sort of subterfuges practised earlier in the Savoy Hotel case. The bare details of these transactions were first revealed in a statement issued on June 21st, 1956, by Sir Andrew Murray, who throughout the whole contretemps seems to have been at variance with his former colleagues on the S.M.T. board. The next step was a formal statement from the S.M.T. directors summarizing the transactions as follows:

(1) S.M.T. agreed to purchase from Mr R. N. Scott the whole of the issued capital of Atholl Houses, a private building and construction company, for £850,000. Of this, £250,000 was to be paid over at once and securities representing the balance were to be lodged with the Commercial Bank of Scotland, pending a confirmatory valuation by a firm of chartered accountants.

(2) S.M.T.'s wholly-owned subsidiary S.M.T. Sales and Service, granted an option for £14,000 to Atholl Developments, a private company with which Mr R. N. Scott was associated, to purchase properties owned by S.M.T. Sales and Service for £1·4 million. One clause of the option was that Atholl Developments should grant S.M.T. Sales and Service ninety-nine-year leases on the properties sold.

(3) In consequence of these arrangements, Mr R. N. Scott was appointed a director and the chairman of S.M.T.

The transactions between the 'Atholl' companies and S.M.T. seem to have been arranged with undue haste, as Mr Fraser, whose counter-offer the S.M.T. directors had supported, seems to have been taken by surprise. As it was, Sir Andrew Murray was summoned to the meeting only an hour before it took place and in commenting on the Atholl Houses purchase he is reliably reported as saying: 'This was the first time this matter had been mentioned to the board although there had been a meeting two days earlier and the board had no information or expert advice before them to give the matter proper consideration.'

On June 26th, 1956, Sir Andrew Murray sought and secured an injunction in the London Courts putting a restraint on the transfer of securities in connection with the Atholl Houses purchase (valid until June 29th). In the course of his argument, counsel read an affidavit from Sir Andrew in which he said that four of the S.M.T. directors had entered into the proposed transactions: 'with the object of causing loss to the company and the stockholders by disposing of, or purporting to dispose of, assets for a grossly inadequate consideration. They sought to put the assets beyond the control of the majority of stockholders and a future board of directors. They were in breach of their fiduciary duties to the stockholders'. It must be emphasized that these words were used by one of the combatants in an acrimonious struggle, and when the Court granted the injunction it did no more than find a prima facie case. While Sir Andrew sought an injunction in London, two petitions in connection with S.M.T. and the Atholl transactions were lodged in the Court of Sessions, Edinburgh. They were withdrawn on the same day, June 26th, for 'by mutual agreement' the Atholl transactions had been rescinded.

It was contended at the time that the Atholl transactions might have prevented Mr Clore from gathering the fruits of victory, but as they were subsequently withdrawn the opportunity of submitting them to legal test never arose. In many ways this is to be deprecated, because once again the transactions raised important issues about the responsibilities of directors towards the disposal of properties and the interests of shareholders.

Both the Savoy and S.M.T. cases raised difficult and still largely unresolved questions about the fiduciary responsibilities of directors towards shareholders. It is understandable that directors faced with aggressive buying of shares by 'outsiders' may be disinclined to put this responsibility first. Granted that it is quite legitimate for directors to resist a bid for shares within all proper bounds, but resistance must never be allowed to clash with their overriding duty to shareholders. It is as well to remember that bids are usually made because directors have not been doing as much for their company and the shareholders as the bidder promises to do in the future. In vying with the bidder, the directors only draw attention to their failures in the past. Moreover, the directors must surely expect to be challenged at every step in attempting to wriggle out of the dilemma by such doubtful artifices as changing the nature of the assets, or removing some of them from the custody of shareholders for all time.

A prospective take-over bid was also brought to the fore in a dispute over the interpretation of a clause in one of the articles of association of a private company, namely, Lyle & Scott Ltd, the Hawick knitwear firm. In the early part of 1957, an interim injunction was granted preventing eight investment trusts and five individual shareholders from voting at an extraordinary meeting of the company. At this meeting resolutions for the replacement of three directors by Mr Hugh Fraser and two of his associates failed. The firm, in the course of thirteen actions brought in the Court of Session, Edinburgh, asked the Court to decree that the defendants should implement the terms of one of the articles of association.

The article provided that no registered holder of more than 1 per cent of the ordinary share capital shall, without the consent of the directors, be entitled to transfer any ordinary shares for a nominal consideration or by way of security so long as any other shareholder is willing to buy them.

In finding against the company, Lord Strachan said he had reached that conclusion with reluctance, but he did not see how he could do otherwise. In none of the many Court cases dealing with restrictions on the transfer of shares had any such provision in a company's articles been held to be compulsory. Consequently, although he agreed that the sale of ordinary shares to an undisclosed offerer contravened the articles of Lyle & Scott Ltd, Lord Strachan held that this provision was not compulsory and binding.

Subsequently, the House of Lords, on appeal, reversed the decision of the Court of Session.[1] Giving judgment, Viscount Simonds said that once a shareholder was deemed to be desirous of transferring his shares, the machinery of Article 9 was put in motion; he must inform the secretary of the number he desired and had agreed to sell, the price would be fixed in the manner prescribed, and the matter would so proceed. What he could not be permitted to do was to adhere to his contract and in the same breath assert that he did not desire to transfer his shares.

The take-over procedure

A long run of take-over bids had exposed a number of detailed gaps and weaknesses in procedure which could have led to abuses if left unregulated. The idea of a code of procedure, however, had its origin in a suggestion made by the Governor of the Bank of England. Eventually, the City's considered views on take-over bids were first published in October 1959 under the title of *Notes on Amalgamation*

[1] Times Law Reports, June 19th, 1959.

of British Businesses. The actual report was prepared by the Executive Committee of the Issuing Houses Association in co-operation with the Accepting Houses Committee, the Association of Investment Trusts, the British Insurance Association, the Committee of London Clearing Bankers and the London Stock Exchange.

The authors of these notes fully endorsed the virtues of amalgamation and acquisition, pointing out that they have been a fairly common feature of the industrial scene from its earliest beginnings.

The working party met again in 1963 in order to prepare a revised version of the rules, taking into account the report of the Jenkins Committee on Company Law Amendment and the Board of Trade's new rules for licensed dealers.

Admirable as their notes were in range and content, they did not possess the ultimate power of sanction. These *ad hoc* arrangements were further strengthened in 1966 when the Stock Exchange's General Undertaking came into force, but even then it still did not insist that all quoted companies should sign the undertaking whether or not they were contemplating a new issue of shares.

It had been hoped that after the dust had settled on the British Aluminium affair in 1959 that such unseemly conduct would be a thing of the past, but as time went on the guide lines laid down under the so-called 'City code' began to be flouted, first by one company (or their financial advisers) then another until a series of bitterly contested take-over bids midway through 1967 brought matters to a head.

The more dramatic bids of those months may not have broken the letter of the old rules but they wittingly or unwittingly offended against the spirit of them and recalling some of the details of these episodes may help to clarify the issues at stake. For instance, in May 1967 Aberdare Holdings made an opening bid for Metal Industries worth about £10 million. This was rejected out of hand by the Metal Industries board and an improved offer of £11·8 million also suffered the same fate. Then, on July 1st, 1967, Thorn Electrical Industries entered the fight with an offer worth £15·3 million. At that time Aberdare claimed over 25 per cent of the Metal Industries' equity. Armed with these firm holdings and acceptances and fortified by aggressive buying in the market, the scales were tipped in favour of Aberdare who claimed control at this stage.

A new formal offer from Aberdare raised their mixture of convertible unsecured loan stock, Aberdare shares and cash above the all-cash alternative in Thorn's counter-offer and victory seemed in sight. Then came a questionable tactical manœuvre by which Thorn snatched control from under Aberdare's very nose. The deal involved the issue by Metal Industries of almost five million *previously unissued shares* as the price for acquiring Glover & Main Ltd – one of Thorn's subsidiaries. So, by devious means, Thorn ended up with a 39 per cent stake in Metal Industries while the erstwhile victors – Aberdare – were left stranded with only 32 per cent of the enlarged share capital of Metal Industries. The deal was accompanied by a new and higher offer from Thorn worth a total of £24 million.

What bore all the signs of an acrimonious fight to the finish finally fizzled out on July 19th, 1967, when Hambros Bank agreed to underwrite the Thorn shares offered for Metal Industries so as to give an effective cash alternative equal to the value of the share offer. Both Aberdare and their advisers, Morgan Grenfell, agreed to accept this offer in respect of their large – though as it turned out not large enough – holding in Metal Industries and withdrew from the battleground. All one can say in mitigation of the in-fighting which flared up between Aberdare and Thorn is that the highest bid triumphed in the end but not without a good deal of heart-searching in the City and beyond.

One curious point about this deal was referred to in one of Aberdare's statements, namely, that the shares which Metal Industries proposed to allot to Thorn had been created by the shareholders in general meeting way back in May 1960, when the directors apparently gave an undertaking that they would not issue any further share capital if it meant the passing of control. Yet when asked about this statement, Kleinworts – who were advising Metal Industries – were reported to have said that 'to suggest that an intention seven years ago is binding is to do the English language an injustice'. Does one infer from this that shareholders' rights are erased by the passage of time?

Another bid which aroused strong feelings on both sides concerned International Distillers and Vintners and Showerings. The former, faced with an unwelcome bid, resorted to the usual defensive tactics of forecasting higher profits and dividends. Showerings countered by adding 10p a share in cash to their existing offer but were thwarted in their purpose because an unnamed third party (identified later as Watney Mann) entered the market and bought heavily, pushing the market price above the increased bid price for a short time. This effectively blocked the Showerings offer for good.

A similar, but equally daunting, situation occurred in December 1966, when Thorn and Philips Electronics were locked in a battle for Pye. Here, Philips Electronics suddenly found themselves guaranteed over nine million Pye shares which had been bought in the market and had subsequently 'come into the possession' of Philip's Dutch parent company. The Dutch company stated at the time that 'In our experience the manner in which the whole situation arose is not unusual outside the United Kingdom, particularly in a case where large blocks of shares are involved.'

Finally, there was a hectic battle in June 1967 between Courtaulds and Rodo Investment Trust (acting for Macanie (London)) for control of Wilkinson & Riddell when last-minute buying in the market pushed up the share price to the dizzy height of £3·25 compared with a closing bid price of 76p; here was yet another warning that the rules required strengthening.

At the time these stratagems not only threw the City into a ferment but gave rise to critical comment in almost every section of the financial Press.

Conscious of the need for action to curb these abuses of the established code of conduct (and only too well aware of the strong possibility of Government legislation being imposed if they failed to put their own house in order) the Stock Exchange announced in July 1967, after consultation with the Governor of the Bank of England, that they had requested the Issuing Houses Association to reconvene the working party which prepared the 1959 and 1963 versions of the rules 'as a matter of urgency'. In addition to the original members of the working party, the Confederation of British Industries agreed to participate in the discussions.

Even before the working party had completed its deliberations, it was announced that a panel or watchdog committee would be set up, under the chairmanship of Sir Humphrey Mynors, former deputy governor of the Bank of England, to oversee take-over practice in accordance with the new set of rules.

The panel was drawn from the same institutional bodies as had supplied representatives to the working party.

The Panel's eventful first year in office – 1968 – was an unusually active time for mergers and take-overs and it was only to be expected that the Panel's rulings would at some stage bring it into conflict with the parties involved. It is entirely to the Panel's credit that this happened in only five bids out of some 500 cases when it felt obliged to issue formal statements for publication. Even then, three of the statements made related to matters of procedure rather than to the conduct of the parties. One may briefly recall the other two occasions. First, Courtauld's announcement of an offer – without terms – for International Paints in face of a rival bid from Dufay Bitumastic (held to be in conflict with Rule 14); secondly, Morgan Grenfell and Cazenove's handling of the partial bid made in May 1968, by American Tobacco for Gallaher was held to be in breach of the Code's general principal No. 7.

The new code – like its predecessors still lacked the power of sanctions and its fate hung in the balance little more than eight months after it came into effect.

First, the Panel's rather inept handling of the American Tobacco Company's partial bid for Gallaher closely followed by its long delayed reaction to the questionable methods employed in the struggle for control of the News of the World Organization Ltd, lent support to those whose voices had long pleaded for a statutory body. Here the tangled skein of events began in mid-October 1968, with a £26 million bid by the Pergamon Press. It reached its climax early in 1971 when shareholders voted for the deal with Mr Rupert Murdoch's Australian News Ltd, whereby certain of its magazine, newspaper and publishing interests were injected into News of the World against an allotment of shares equivalent to 35 per cent of the increased voting capital. The London Stock Exchange had banned dealings in the News of the World shares as far back as October 25th, 1968 (they were resumed on December 19th following the release of the terms of the agreement with News Ltd) in order to give shareholders time to assess the relative merits of the Pergamon bid and the News of the World blocking deal with News Ltd.

As soon as dealings were resumed, the Stock Exchange and the Take-over Panel announced that News Ltd, News of the World and Pergamon had agreed not to intervene in the reopened market (though all three parties, acting through their financial advisers had engaged in market operations long before dealings were banned). All the way through, the Panel had been unduly hesitant in its retaliatory moves.[1]

By all accounts, the voluntary system had been granted a temporary reprieve but only on two conditions – that the Panel was strengthened and the rules revised.

The revised version of the City Code, duly introduced at the end of April 1969, incorporated a limited number of revisions and additions made by the City working party in the light of experience gained in its operation since March 1968. Indeed, it was generally accepted that the choice before the City in its conduct of take-overs and mergers was either a system of voluntary self-discipline based upon the code and administered by the City's own representatives or regulation by law enforced by a Government Department.

What really counted, however, was the Panel's new power to impose penalties upon the code breaker. In future, the Panel will have recourse to private or to public censure or, in a more flagrant case, to further action designed to deprive the offender temporarily or permanently of his ability to practice in the field of take-overs or mergers. At long last, the introduction of powerful sanctions like these seems to have saved the day for the voluntary system.

The City Code was further revised in February 1972 and in June 1974 – when at the request of the Panel, the working Party reconsidered and revised the rules relating to the obligation to make a

---

[1] It acted in a more forthright manner later in the same year in its handling of the Leasco-Pergamon Press bid – a situation which finally dragged on into 1970.

general offer when significant holdings of shares are acquired and also took the opportunity of revising the definition of persons acting in concert and the rules governing partial bids. The latest revision took place in April 1976. The main areas of change (see Appendix III for the full version) include another attempt to strengthen the definition of persons acting in concert, mandatory bids, the treatment of convertible loan stock holders in bid situations and the application of the take-over regulations to foreign companies listed in London.

Although the City Code was drafted with quoted public companies particularly in mind, the fact remains that unlisted public companies also make use of the stock market facilities and these too will be expected to conform to both the letter and spirit of the City Code. The general principles may also be relevant to transactions in the shares of private companies but the Take-over Panel does not claim to have any authority in such cases.

Finally, it must be made clear that neither the City Code nor the Panel is concerned with the evaluation of the commercial or financial advantages or disadvantages of a take-over bid or merger proposal which in the final analysis can only be decided by the company and its shareholders.

By the very nature of its work the code administered by the Panel possesses a degree of flexibility and speed in action which a statutory body would find difficult, if not impossible, to match.

Moreover, the reconstituted Panel representative of the City, together with its permanent secretariat, is surely capable of more useful advice both before and during the course of a bid than would be possible if a statutory body were charged with the task of enforcing rigid regulations which, in the last resort, would have to be left to the courts for clarification. In fact, the Panel has already seen fit to publish several practice notes setting out their current views on the application of certain points of principle and particular rules in merger transactions.

As the Panel's Chairman, Lord Shawcross, went on to say in the foreword to the 1969–70 report:

'... the Panel has to apply the rules of the code in a manner which is easily intelligible, is manifestly fair and is, as far as ever-changing circumstances permit, consistent. I am firmly of the opinion that we are moving towards this ideal and that in a few years' time self-regulation in the take-over bid field will be taken for granted even by those who today are its sternest critics.'

Dealing with minorities

As already mentioned, an offer expressed to be conditional on acceptance by a stated proportion of shareholders may produce a situation in which a small number of dissentient members are left as a minority in a company intended to be operated as a member of a group. As such, their position is likely to be unenviable, for the parent company will wish to operate the subsidiary for the benefit of the group as a whole and not necessarily for the benefit of that particular subsidiary.[1] Equally ,they are likely to prove a thorn in the side of the parent company. Thus, section 209, Companies Act 1948, lays down a procedure whereby this position may be rectified in the case of registered companies. This it accomplishes by giving the acquiring company (which need not be a registered company itself) powers of compulsory acquisition and the minority a right to have second thoughts and compel the acquiring company to buy them out after all. If under any scheme or contract an offer to acquire the whole or any class of shares has been accepted within four months by nine-tenths in value of the shares affected, the transferee company can, within a further two months, give notice to any dissenting shareholder that it wishes to acquire his shares. The transferee company is then entitled and bound to acquire his shares on the same terms unless the Court, on application made by a dissentient within one month, thinks fit to order otherwise. Provision is made for executing transfers on behalf of recalcitrant members.

If, however, the transferee company does not avail itself of this power of expropriation but leaves the dissenting minority out on a limb, as it were, the latter are given a further opportunity of extricating themselves. Notice must be given to them that nine-tenths of the shares have been acquired, and they or any of them can within three months serve a counter-notice requiring the transferee company to acquire their shares. These shares must then be bought on the same terms or on such other terms as may be agreed or as the Court thinks fit to order.

Problems of minority shareholders
The position of shareholders who reject an offer (subject to a stated percentage acceptance) depends on the percentage of shares in respect of which holders accept. As already explained, if it *is* 90 per cent, a compulsory acquisition of the remaining shares can, subject to certain safeguards, take place. On the other hand, if it is less than 90 per cent of the shares not already held by the company making the bid, that company cannot compulsorily acquire the shares of the minority.

The attitude of the Courts to applicants under section 209 is indicated by the comment in *re Sussex Brick Co Ltd* ([1960] 1 All E.R. 772) that the shareholder who stands out against terms found acceptable by the assenting majority has a heavy onus to discharge. He has

[1] Oppressed minorities can seek relief under section 210. See also *Scottish Co-operative Society Ltd v. Meyer and another*. Times Law Report, July 24th, 1958.

to show the Court that he, being the only man in the regiment out of step as it were, is the only man whose views ought to prevail. The criterion of 'fairness' is important here. In *re Press Caps Ltd* ([1948] 2 All E.R. 638) the Court of Appeal approved the dictum of Maugham, J., in *re Hoare & Co Ltd* ([1933] All E.R. Rep., 105) that it was not for the Court to take action unless the scheme was unfair.

In this connection the validity of Stock Exchange prices as a measure of value has been judicially approved, the use of middle market quotations being preferred to 'marks' recorded in the *Official List*. Moreover in the take-over of Grierson, Oldham & Adams Ltd by John Holt & Co (Liverpool) Ltd (*The Financial Times*, November 5th, 1966) the fact that individual shareholders might be unfavourably placed from a capital gains tax standpoint was not accepted as a material factor in evaluating the fairness of the scheme as a whole.

Furthermore, the complainant must come to Court armed with his evidence. Roxburgh, J., declined to order discovery of documents, commenting on the serious consequences which might follow if the holder of 1 per cent of the shares of a company should in any large number of cases become entitled simply by making an application under section 209 to obtain an extensive investigation of the company's affairs.

On the other hand, the Courts are equally on the alert to prevent injustice through abuse of the machinery of the Companies Act in particular where the consenting majority is not genuinely independent of the bidder. In *re Bugle Press Ltd* ([1960] 3 All E.R. 791) the Court of Appeal denounced the transferee company as 'nothing but a little hut' built round the two co-shareholders of the complainant who had only to voice his grievance in order to bring his opponents' 'Jericho' to the ground.

The inference to be drawn from these cases is that while the Court pays close attention to the immediate pre-bid price in deciding whether a dissenting shareholder shall be compelled to transfer his shares under section 209, shareholders are expected to look to the recent average price in making their own judgement.[1]

If the minority shareholder retains his holding, because the company making the offer either does not want to acquire the whole of the share capital, or is unable to do so, he may find himself in an unhappy position. The market may become so narrow that he cannot later on dispose of his shares with ease, and the dividend paid on them, being at the mercy of the majority holder's policy (or whims), may dwindle.

The classic case of Crown Cork – a sub-subsidiary of Crown Cork

---

[1] See 'A fair price for the compulsory acquisition of shares', by R. R. Pennington, LL.D. – *Accountancy*, April 1967.

and Seal of America – is possibly an extreme example of the minority shareholders' weak position. The company paid no ordinary dividends between 1963 and 1970 (when the American parent made a fresh cash offer of £1·67½ a share which was accepted), although earnings were more than adequate to do so, because the company required additional funds to finance expansion plans. The bone of contention was that the initial decision to pay no ordinary dividend in May 1964, followed only three months after an even more curious decision to buy out preference shareholders for £500,000 in cash. Despite protests from shareholders the American parent was adamant in its view that funds must be conserved for a programme of capital expenditure.

Then came a change of policy and a new chairman was appointed. In March 1966 he promised that dividends would start again. Unfortunately, he had to break his pledge because the Treasury refused to allow it (under the then Prices and Incomes freeze).

As many outside shareholders are primarily interested in income they cannot be expected to welcome a policy – whatever long-term promise it may hold out – that condemns them to several dividend-less years.

Even with a foreign bid, the minority shareholders seem to be fighting a losing battle.

When the American company, Litton Industries, made a bid of 62½p a share for Imperial Typewriter they quickly acquired more than 90 per cent of the share capital.

Those left – the dissentients – went so far as to present their case to the Board of Trade, stressing the national interest in retaining a stake in the typewriter industry, but all to no avail.

As *The Economist* pointed out at the time: '. . . it is difficult to see how a holding of less than one-tenth can make much of an impression on the situation'.[1] Furthermore, an appeal by 368 shareholders in Marston Valley Brick Co to stop the compulsory sale of their shares to London Brick Co was dismissed by the Court of Appeal in November 1970.

Just over 90 per cent of Marston's shareholders accepted the £3·3 million take-over by London Brick, and the High Court had ruled that the dissenting shareholders must sell.

Led by chartered accountant, Miss Beryl Marsh, of Hove, Sussex, the dissenting holders claimed that the offer was unfair and inadequate.

In the Appeal Court Lord Justice Russell said the evidence did not justify overriding the rights of the Companies Act compelling sale by minorities. 'The fair and proper price for the stock units must be a question of opinion', he added. On the other hand, there are

[1] February 14th, 1967.

many cases on record where the minority holder has benefited considerably from refusing to part with his shares at the time the take-over bid was made.

Apart, however, from the genuinely 'stranded' minority share-holder who finds himself in an awkward predicament simply as a result of a merger or reconstruction, there are cases where a minority interest is considered preferable to an outright merger or take-over bid. Some years ago, Whitbread & Co Ltd, the brewers, started buying minority interests (seldom less than 10 per cent) in other brewery companies willing to accept association without amalgamation; it then used the associates to sell its bottled beers, and in return it strengthened management and provided know-how. Sometimes Whitbread takes a management fee; sometimes it sup-plies staff; and sometimes it trains the staff of the new associate. These preliminary moves were quickly followed up by an open invitation to breweries at large to shelter under the same umbrella. This technique, which stops a long way short of a complete take-over, seems to raise certain issues of principle. Firstly, Whitbread & Co Ltd uses its surplus cash resources to buy blocks of shares through the normal market channels. To get them it often has to pay a few shillings over the market price and when the buying ceases it is not unusual for the shares to fall back again. Secondly, Whitbread never act without the full knowledge and consent of the management of the company in which it proposes to invest (and it is interesting to note that it has far more proposals from would-be associates than it cares to accept). There are obvious advantages in this from the associates' point of view. Companies where management needs strengthening, especially if management is not itself a big share-holder, are natural targets for a bidder who is only too anxious to have the chance of employing the assets more effectively. Thus, a 10 per cent holding by Whitbread & Co Ltd added to the manage-ment's existing voting power goes a long way towards blocking the bidder's path. Consequently, the prospect of a safe and stable future opens up for directors and staff alike.

Certainly the group is just as much within its rights in buying a minority interest in another company as it would be if it were to make a bid for all the shares. And if it can secure its aim through a minority holding coupled with friendly association instead of a majority holding and domination it can hardly be condemned. The main differences, however, are that Whitbread spreads its available cash over a wider field; that outside shareholders of the other company do not necessarily have the chance of being bought out at Whitbread's price; and that the directors of the other company become associates, not the servants, of the Whitbread parent. As *The Economist* remarked: 'For an ageing industry like brewing, faced with the need for technological changes, the policy may have advantages, but it is not the up and coming founders of growing businesses that are likely to seek the shelter of the Whitbread umbrella. It is rather old family businesses where death duties have whittled down the controlling shareholdings. In essence, the umbrella is a blocking move.'[1]

The 'umbrella' was partially furled in 1961 when Whitbread successfully took over Tennant Brothers, Norman & Pring, and Flowers Breweries and later on added Duttons Blackburn Brewery and James Thompson.

Finally, in April 1967, Whitbread took another important step towards the concentration of the brewing industry by making a £24 million offer for Threlfalls Chesters, the Liverpool-based brewers.

Whitbreads revealed their 'umbrella' holdings for the first time in 1970.

Apart from their Boddingtons' Breweries interest, Whitbread Investment Co held 30 per cent of Brickwoods, 25 per cent of J. A. Devenish, 33 per cent of Marston Thompson, 36 per cent of Morland, 31 per cent of G. Ruddle and 11 per cent of Truman.

The reverse bid

In simple terms, this is a situation where the smaller company bids for the larger company, i.e., Small Ltd (at the instance of the controlling shareholders of Big Ltd) makes a share-for-share bid for the equity capital of Big Ltd. If the bid is accepted by the holders of at least 90 per cent in value of the equity capital of Bid Ltd and compulsory acquisition of any minority holdings is proceeded with, the result is that the former shareholders of Big Ltd will end up as the majority holders in the enlarged share capital of Small Ltd while the pre-existing shareholders of Small Ltd will be left with only a minority in the enlarged share capital.

But why should anyone want to traverse this unusual route? First, Small Ltd may be a quoted company and Big Ltd an unquoted one, and in order to maintain the quotation it is wiser for Small Ltd to finish up as the holding company (still quoted).

Secondly, where it is intended that Small Ltd shall act as the administrative focal point of the group, leaving Big Ltd as the effective operating and trading company. Thirdly, where Small Ltd happens to have very large undistributed profits which would be frozen in the hands of Big Ltd – if the latter was used as a vehicle for the take-over – as pre-acquisition profits and reserves. Fourthly, the gearing of the capital structures of the two companies may suggest that it is better for Small Ltd to take the bid initiative with the consent of Big Ltd. Fifth, where the larger of the two companies has

[1] July 13th, 1957.

preference shares or debenture capital in issue which might require the consent of the holders of such capital to a bid (or the immediate repayment of the capital as the case may be), then Small Ltd might be persuaded to bid from its own vantage point of having an all-equity share capital.

Example 1

Investment Registry Ltd – J. Sears & Co (True-Form Boot Co)

A take-over bid that caused some dispute at the time brought Mr Clore into the picture (through Investment Registry). His company made a bid for J. Sears & Co (True-Form Boot Co) in January 1953. And in notifying the shareholders of the offer, the board of directors of J. Sears advised them not to accept. On the face of it the offer was attractive. Investment Registry undertook to purchase the 25p ordinary shares in the first place at £1·62½ each. They then proposed to convert each 25p ordinary share into four ordinary shares of 5p nominal which they would retain, and one 'A' ordinary share of 5p nominal without voting rights but otherwise ranking *pari passu* in all respects with the ordinary shares. They then proposed to transfer free of charge to existing shareholders one 'A' ordinary 5p share for every 25p ordinary share sold to Investment Registry. The latter were willing to purchase these 'A' ordinary shares at 37½p each at any time in May and June 1954. Thus if the shareholders elected to dispose of their entire holding the offer was equivalent to £2 a share; alternatively, they could receive £1·62½ a share and still retain the equivalent of 20 per cent of their existing holdings. These prices were much above anything that had ruled in the market for years before the first approach to the directors of J. Sears. The directors of J. Sears were still full of fight, however, and in a circular to the shareholders reiterated their original advice to refuse the offer. Even so, they had to do something quickly to try and push up the market price of the sharesi n view of the ominous gap of 30p between the bid price (£2) and the current market price (£1·70). Their remedy was to recommend a final dividend of 47½ per cent, making a total of 62½ per cent for 1952, and making it clear that, in the absence of any serious deterioration in trading conditions, the board expected to be able to maintain that rate. Even so, it was noticeable that group earnings only gave a slender cover to the new rate of dividend. The board explained that annual dividends had been restricted previously to 'the conservative rate' of 22½ per cent, partly as a result of the Government's policy of dividend limitation, and partly because of the group's profits, which before taxation averaged some £1,200,000 a year for the five years ended December 31st, 1951, and were earned 'in the abnormal conditions of inflation and a "seller's market"'.

Furthermore, the board applied for Treasury consent to a free issue of three new ordinary shares for every two existing shares. In their circular, the directors remarked that even if this were to be satisfied wholly out of revenue reserves, these reserves would still remain in excess of £1 million. Finally, they touched on the matter which the would-be purchasers obviously had very much in mind – a valuation of the freehold and principal leasehold properties. This, it was said, was already in process and the indications were that the total amount of finance which could in case of need, be raised by means of these assets was at least £6 million, though the declared intention of the board was not to draw further upon the property resources since, in their view, the group already had ample working capital and liquid funds.

Nevertheless, allowing for the under-valuation of properties, the board intimated that the value of the tangible assets attributable to the existing ordinary capital exceeded £2 a share without any allowance for goodwill.

Investment Registry's rejoinder dealt with all these points. They emphasized the slender margin of earnings over the increased dividend and dismissed the scrip issue for what it was – a mere re-adjustment of issued capital so as to bring it more into line with the capital actually employed in the business. Next, they were anxious to draw the shareholders' attention to the full implications of the 1952 trading profits, suggesting that it represented an average profit per shop (the Sears group had over 900) of less than £1,300. 'For several years', the circular stated, 'the average profits per shop have compared unfavourably with those of similar undertakings.' And it proposed a reorganization of the company 'involving a vigorous policy of modernization'.

Soon afterwards, the requisite majority of shareholders accepted the offer and Mr Charles Clore and his associates in Investment registry gained control of J. Sears. In due course the valuable properties were sold but taken on lease, while the substantial liquid funds realized by this transaction were subsequently re-invested in more remunerative channels.

Today, Sears Holdings Ltd includes not only the British Shoe Corporation (comprising the multiple retail footwear businesses of Freeman, Hardy & Willis, Saxone Lilley & Skinner, True-Form, Dolcis, Manfield, Phillips Brothers, Character Shoes and Curtess Shoes and the Lewis's department stores, the group that includes Selfridges, but, through subsequent acquisition, the Bentley Engineering Group, the Furness Shipbuilding Co, Scottish Motor Traction, Shaw & Kilburn, Mappin & Webb, Garrards and Robinson & Cleaver.

Example 2

Tube Investments – British Aluminium

The long drawn out battle for control of British Aluminium started peacefully enough with a bland announcement by the British Aluminium board towards the end of November 1958 that discussions were taking place 'with other parties in the industry the outcome of which is as yet uncertain'. It subsequently transpired that talks had been going on between British Aluminium and the Aluminium Company of America (Alcoa) since June 1958, for the express purpose of getting finance for the former's development plans (which were particularly concerned with developing bauxite deposits in Australia and with the building of a new smelter in Canada). These negotiations finally led to a contract which was signed on November 14th whereby Alcoa agreed to purchase $4\frac{1}{2}$ million unissued ordinary shares in British Aluminium for £$13\frac{1}{2}$ million (£3 per £1 share) subject to Treasury consent. This would have given Alcoa a one-third stake in British Aluminium's ordinary capital.

Meanwhile, Reynolds Metals (another leading American aluminium company) which had been buying British Aluminium shares on some scale in the open market in association with Tube Investments Ltd, got wind of the negotiations which were afoot and early in November told the British Aluminium board of their intention to make a bid on terms favourable to the stockholders. On November 24th, Tube Investments made their offer known to the British Aluminium board on the basis of one Tube Investments share and £3·90 cash for every two of British Aluminium's nine million £1 ordinary shares. These shares would be vested in a company owned as to 51 per cent by Tube Investments and as to 49 per cent by Reynolds Metals. Events then followed in quick succession. Reynolds and Tube Investments publicly announced the terms of their offer, whereupon British Aluminium disclosed the existence of the Alcoa agreement, though without specifying its terms. These were not in fact published until December 5th, after Reynolds and Tube Investments had announced that they would make a direct offer to British Aluminium stockholders.

Official quarters were rather guarded in their reactions to these rival bids, but it was clear that Treasury consent (which was vital to both bids) would not be given until shareholders had had an opportunity of expressing their views on the subject.

On December 5th, a letter was sent to British Aluminium shareholders under the signature of Lord Portal, the then chairman, indicating the price to be paid for the new shares due to be taken up by Alcoa, and urging the shareholders to reject the Reynolds Metals-Tube Investments bid on the grounds that it was an attempt 'to acquire a powerful empire for the price of a small kingdom'. The British Aluminium directors pointed to the company's long-term growth prospects and emphasized how much better off the shareholders would be if they retained their stake in the company.

The formal offer by Tume Investments was sent direct to the shareholders of British Aluminium on December 15th, when it was revealed that Tube Investments and Reynolds already owned 1,157,173 ordinary shares, or just under 13 per cent of British Aluminium ordinary capital. The offer was to remain open until January 9th, 1959, an might be kept open for a further month at the directors' discretion. The terms of the offer were unchanged, namely, one Tube Investment share and £3·90 cash for every two British Aluminium shares – at the time equivalent to about £3·90 for each British Aluminium share

The British Aluminium board retaliated on December 20th by declaring their intention to raise the ordinary dividend from 12 per cent to $17\frac{1}{2}$ per cent for 1958 (thus bringing the British Aluminium dividend up to the same level as that currently paid by Tube Investments) and in the absence of unforeseen circumstances, to continue paying that same dividend for 1959 and 1960. At the same time, it was agreed that the dividend on the new shares to be taken up by Alcoa would be kept at the old rate of 12 per cent until 1961.

Although, at this stage, British Aluminium were committed to pay the same rate of dividend as Tube Investments, their margin of earnings was much lower. In 1957 British Aluminium earned 24 per cent, while 1958 was another poor year from the trading point of view. Thus earnings were now being distributed up to the hilt in sharp contrast with the high earnings margin shown on the Tube Investments side (where the dividend was covered four times). After a brief lull, the struggle for control of British Aluminium took a fresh turn on December 31st, 1958. A group of twelve City institutions, including five of the leading merchant banks, associated themselves with the British Aluminium company's two bankers in advising the rejection of the Tube Investments bid – an unprecedented move in take-over tactics. The group supported the British Aluminium board in the belief that: 'The maintenance of British Aluminium as a separate British company in partnership with Alcoa is in the national interest, and affords the best and indeed the only opportunity for investors to hold a direct interest in a British company engaged in the production, fabrication and sale of aluminium on an international scale.' This was an important point, because the alternative bid from Tube Investments merely secured an interest in a large engineering group, part of whose profits would flow from British Aluminium. In other words, it offered only a very indirect interest in the future prosperity of British Aluminium as such.

However, the group's view was backed up by something more solid than mere argument. It was based upon a partial cash offer amounting to £7 million in all. To be exact, existing shareholders in British Aluminium (other than Tube Investments group) were offered £4·10 for half their shares, on the understanding that they would keep the other half until the end of March 1959. The Reynolds –Tube Investments reply to this partial and conditional offer was immediate and defiant. Reynolds Metals came into the stock-market ready to buy (for cash) any British Aluminium stock that was on offer. There were two reasons for this. First, it increased the group's already sizeable holding of British Aluminium stock. Institutional holders and private investors alike sold heavily and in a matter of days the Reynolds–Tube Investments interest in British Aluminium was raised from 13 per cent to 45 per cent by the pur-chase of three million shares costing £12½ million or so. The second reason is that by open buying Reynolds kept the market value of British Aluminium shares above the figure of £4·10 offered by the group of fourteen City institutions. It was stated that any shares bought by Reynolds would ultimately be vested in the joint company in which Tube Investments was to hold a permanent 51 per cent control.

Then, on January 4th, Tube Investments came up with an amended offer in support of their partner in the form of an extra 25p cash for every British Aluminium share (costing another £2¼ million in all). This meant that Tube Investments was now bidding one share and £4·40 cash for every two British Aluminium shares. The circular letter made it clear that Tube Investments would not require 90 per cent acceptances to declare its offer unconditional. This latest Tube Investments offer was due to close January 9th, 1959. The battle was rapidly approaching its closing stages. At last, on the afternoon of January 9th, Tube Investments was in a position to announce that with acceptances still coming in, they owned about 80 per cent of British Aluminium share capital. A few days before this official announcement the fourteen City institutions released British Alu-minium shareholders from the previous undertaking not to dispose of their stock since it was clear that control of British Aluminium had then passed to Tube Investments. No doubt this move helped to swell last-minute acceptances.

Not for a long time had there been an industrial battle for contol on the scale and with such massive forces in conflict as that over British Aluminium. Once the dust had settled on the affair three important issues remained for discussion. First, when directors obtain approval for a substantial margin of authorized but unissued share capital, they should give an undertaking that an important issue will not be made without shareholders' approval (even though there is no legal obligation to do so). Secondly, when companies which already have unissued capital at their disposal issue shares, they should consult shareholders if the control or the nature of the business is affected to any important extent. The British Aluminium board failed on both counts. They had asked for and obtained the shareholders' approval to an increase in the authorized capital as far back as 1957, then treated their shareholders in a very cavalier fashion when the contract with Alcoa was concluded. The proprietors of a company are entitled to be consulted on major transactions; they cannot be expected to rubber-stamp board decisions (even where these are genuinely thought to be in the interests of the shareholders). The Association of Investment Trusts with the support of the British Insurance Association Investment Protection Committee published their views on the subject and in a key passage concluded that 'it is wrong for directors to allow any change in control of the nature of the business without reference to shareholders'.[1] In fact, several major companies have since given assurances of this kind when seeking extra authorized share capital. Lord Chandos, the chairman of Associated Electrical Industries, in speaking at an extraordinary meeting of that company, called to approve an increase in the authorized share capital, also came out in favour of full consultation on any deals which involved either an important proportion of the equity of where the nature of the business appeared to have altered – even at the risk of publicizing the situation. Nevertheless, he thought that directors might act with rather greater latitude when shares are offered to another body of shareholders, rather than to a single company or single portfolio.[2]

The third issue turned on the question of foreign control of a British firm. There was little to choose between the two contestants on this score since both the rival plans for British Aluminium involved large American interests. On the one side, a one-third American interest with no other single holding bid enough to offset it; on the other a 49 per cent American interest outweighed by a 51 per cent British holding.

[1] *The Times*, February 11th, 1959.
[2] *The Times*, January 24th, 1959.

CHAPTER IX

THE OFFER DOCUMENT

The first announcement of a take-over bid usually takes the form of a press notice revealing the bidder's name and his intentions. This preliminary information is put out as soon as possible in order to counter rumours and speculation in the shares of the offeree company. Rules 5–8 of the City Code outline the procedure in the early stages.

After an offer has been announced the offer document and a letter setting out the views of the Board of the offeree company should be circulated as soon as practicable (Rule 13).

Any document or advertisement addressed to shareholders must be treated with the same standards of care with regard to the statements made therein as if it were a prospectus within the meaning of the Companies Act 1948 (Rule 14). In one respect, the requirements are more rigorous for an offer document than for a prospectus, namely, in relation to profit forecasts. The intention is to provide shareholders with as much up-to-date information as possible so that they can make their mind up in full knowledge of the very latest position and outlook for their own company.

Distribution

A circular containing a take-over offer is necessarily one containing an invitation to dispose of securities, and as such its distribution is subject to the provisions of S.14 Prevention of Fraud (Investments) Act, 1958. Under this section, a take-over circular must be distributed either through an authorized channel (a member of a recognized stock exchange, a member of a recognized association of dealers in securities, a licensed dealer in securities, or an exempted dealer) or with the permission of the Department of Trade and Industry. If a take-over circular is distributed through a licensed dealer, the information given must comply with the Licensed Dealers (Conduct of Business) Rules 1960, which is concerned with the terms of the offer, the conditions attached to it and the interests in the offer of the directors of the two companies. A take-over circular which is distributed on the specific authority of the D.T.I. will also contain this information. Since the licensed dealers rules are narrower in their scope than the City Code, the D.T.I. make a point of drawing the applicant's attention to the City Code.

Statistics published in the annual reports of the Panel on Take-overs and Mergers suggest that the majority of merger documents submitted to the Panel executive were distributed through exempted dealers who are for the most part, merchant bankers:

Distribution of Formal Offers

	1972/73	*1971/72*	*1970/71*	*1969/70*
1. Circulated by Exempted Dealers	248	292	219	277
2. Circulated by Licensed Dealers..	26	20	9	21
3. Circulated by others exempted under Prevention of Fraud (Investments) Act, 1958 ..	42	31	36	37
4. Circulated on basis of specific authority of D.T.I.	25	26	30	27
5. Other (Schemes of Arrangements, etc.)	15	15	2	1
	356	384	296	363

The majority of offer documents then are distributed by one or other of the leading merchant bankers as the following random sample illustrates:

Offer	*Date*	*Distributed by*
Cerebos/Hugon & Co	1963	Morgan Grenfell & Co
Reed Paper/Field, Sons & Co	1964	J. Henry Schroder Wagg & Co and S. G. Warburg & Co
Cementation/Cleveland Bridge & Engineering	1967	Kleinwort, Benson
Hickson & Welch/Wm. Blythe & Co ..	1968	Hill, Samuel & Co
Burton Group/Ryman Conran	1971	Kleinwort, Benson
B.A. Tobacco/International Stores ..	1972	Lazard Bros & Co
Cadbury Schweppes/Jeyes Group ..	1972	Kleinwort, Benson
Reeves & Sons/Dryad	1973	Drayton Corpn

Contents

If the terms of the offer have been agreed by the Board of the offeree company, the formal offer will normally be circulated within about 21 days of the preliminary press announcement. In this case, the offer document will contain an explanatory letter from the chairman of the offeree company extolling the benefits and virtues of the proposed merger and recommending – in conjunction with their financial advisers – the offer to the shareholders at large, indicating at the same time, that the directors intend to accept the offer in respect of their own shareholdings. In the case of contested bids, the chairman's letter will not usually form part of the offer document. Instead, a separate circular will be distributed setting out the case – again prepared in conjunction with their own financial advisers – for rejection of the offer.

The information set out in the offer document itself normally falls into some nine sections:

(*a*) Terms of the offer, i.e., consideration or basis of exchange;
(*b*) Conditions;

(c) Financial advantages of Acceptance;

(d) Benefits of the merger;

(e) Information about the two companies concerned in the offer;

(f) Intentions regarding management, staff and employees;

(g) Capital Gains Tax implications;

(h) Procedure for Acceptance;

(i) Appendices – General Information (directors shareholdings, directors emoluments and service agreements, rights attaching to any new share or loan stock issues, market quotations, material contracts, documents available for inspection, financial information regarding the two companies including profit forecasts (if any).

The key points will now be examined in some detail.

Terms and conditions and financial advantages

The terms or basis of exchange takes many forms. Obviously an outright cash bid is the simplest form of consideration. It is a bid made in absolute terms and does not depend upon a comparison of values as is the case with share exchanges or bids made partly in shares and loan stock or even partly in cash and shares (or loan stock).

(a) *All-cash bids*

Thus the offer by Babcock & Wilcox Ltd for each ordinary share of 25p in General Electrical & Mechanical Systems Ltd not already owned by Babcock announced in the press on 1st November, 1972 and formally contained in the offer document dated 20th November, was simply expressed as being 145p in cash. This absolute offer was duly compared with the middle market quotations of G.E.M.S. 25p ordinary shares during the previous six months including 31st October, 1972 (the last dealing day prior to the announcement of the offer) viz:

Date					Ordinary Shares of 25p each
May 31st, 1972	..	..	..	..	$97\frac{1}{2}$p
June 30th, 1972	..	..	..	..	$82\frac{1}{2}$p
July 31st, 1972	..	..	..	..	$92\frac{1}{2}$p
August 31st ,1972	..	..	..	..	$107\frac{1}{2}$p
September 29th, 1972	..	..	..	..	$87\frac{1}{2}$p xd
October 31st, 1972	..	..	..	..	105p xd
November 17th, 1972	..	..	..	..	140p

It will be observed that the middle market quotations listed above also includes one post-bid quotation on November 17th, 1972 (the latest practicable date before the despatch of the offer document). In other words the market price has already been marked up in response to the announcement of the bid even though the full terms and conditions were not published until later. The offer document points to the advantages of acceptance by comparing the offer price of 145p with the middle market price of 105p ex-dividend on October 31st, 1972 stating that this represents an increase in capital value of over 38 per cent. It so happened that this particular offer was designated 'unconditional' mainly because Babcock had already acquired privately a large block of G.E.M.S. shares prior to the announcement of the bid and indeed had subsequently made further purchases in the market for cash. The formal bid was, therefore, only in respect of the remaining 2,483,754 issued ordinary shares of 25p each (out of a total of 4,070,000 ordinary shares in issue) not already owned by Babcock.

It is, however, more usual for a cash offer to be expressed as conditional upon acceptances being received in respect of *not less than 90 per cent* of shares (or such lesser percentage as the bidder may determine). For example, in another cash bid made by Babcock in the following month of 1972 (for the Woodall-Duckham Group) the 'lesser percentage' part of the offer was expressed as conditional upon Babcock acquiring or agreeing to acquire *more than 50 per cent* of the Woodall-Duckham Group Ordinary Shares.

The significance of these two percentage requirements soon becomes apparent. The former (90 per cent or more) permits compulsory acquisition of the minority holding of 10 per cent or less under S.209, Companies Act, 1948 while the latter (more than 50 per cent) does ensure voting or legal control. But whether or not the bidder is content with the bare legal control instead of the complete or 100 per cent control he envisaged at the outset, can only be decided by the percentage of acceptances received by the final date for acceptance. If 50 per cent or below the bid will lapse; if between 50·1 per cent and 90 per cent, the bidder can either settle for legal control thus leaving a substantial minority interest in the hands of outside shareholders or decide to withdraw the bid due to insufficient acceptances, i.e., failure to reach the 90 per cent target; if 90 per cent or over, the bid succeeds and the offer goes unconditional. Of course, failure to reach the specified 90 per cent in the first instance and dissatisfaction with any lower level of acceptances may lead to an improved bid which may in the end just turn the scales in the bidder's favour. However, going unconditional with a mere 50·1 per cent of acceptances is not unknown. When legal control is finally lost hitherto dissident shareholders usually decide to throw in their lot with the accepting majority, especially so when the bid has been firmly opposed by the directors. Once legal control has been lost, however, the directors usually – but reluctantly – accept the *fait accompli* and recommend other opposing shareholders to do the same. As a result, acceptances can increase quite dramatically from

50·1 per cent to over 90 per cent when the offer is extended for a further period in order to mop up last minute acceptances.

One other vital point for consideration in the case of a cash bid is the question of possible liability to capital gains tax. For acceptance of a cash offer constitutes a disposal for the purposes of taxation of capital gains which may give rise to a liability to tax depending on the circumstances of individual shareholders. For example, on April 6th, 1965 the 'market value' for capital gains tax purposes of each G.E.M.S. ordinary share referred to earlier was given as 118·75p in the offer document. Before acceptance, therefore, each shareholder would have to calculate the benefit (if any) remaining to him (or her) *after* deducting any capital gains tax from the cash proceeds receivable on acceptance.

(b) *Share exchanges*

Share exchanges, or paper-for-paper bids as they are sometimes called, are more difficult to assess than straight cash bids because the question of financial advantage depends upon two factors, both of a volatile or unpredictable nature, viz:

(i) comparative capital values, and

(ii) comparative income.

Comparative market quotations are given on one day, whereas market quotations can and do fluctuate from day to day, week to week, month to month and year to year. As for comparative income, dividends can and do vary over time depending upon the availability of profits and the board's recommendations thereon, i.e., the choice between high retentions and low distributions or vice-versa. In both cases, therefore, the recipient of a bid is bound to exercise foresight, judgment or opinion in coming to a decision. Future prospects have to be weighed in the balance just as carefully as recorded past performance. Perhaps, that is why the 'paper' offered in exchange is often contemptuously referred to in the City as 'Chinese money' or 'funny money'.

The comparison of market values and income in a typical take-over bid is presented in the following manner (based on the bid by Reed Paper Group for Field, Sons and Co on June 19th, 1964).

The terms of the offer were as under:

(*a*) Nine Ordinary Shares of £1 each of Reed, credited as fully paid *for* every twenty Ordinary Shares of 25p each of Field

(*b*) One 5½ per cent Cum. Redeemable Preference Share of £1 of Reed credited as fully paid, plus 17½p in cash *for* each 6 per cent Cum. Preference Share of £1 of Field

(*a*) The position of an accepting holder of 100 ordinary shares of

25p each of Field who would receive 45 ordinary shares of £1 each of Reed, would be as follows:

	Capital Value £	Income £
45 Reed Ordinary Shares of £1 each, @ 276p[1]	124·20	
Gross income on basis of a current dividend of 16 per cent payable on above		7·20
Compared with present holding:		
100 Field Ordinary Shares of 25p each, @ 102½p[2] ..	102·50	
Gross income based on 1963 rate of dividend of 12½ per cent		3·13
An increase of	21·70	4·07
Or an increase of	21%	130%

and

(b) The position of an accepting holder of 100 6 per cent Cum. Preference Shares of Field who would receive 100 5½ per cent Cum. Red. Preference Shares of Reed and a cash payment of £17·50 would be as follows:

	Capital Value £	Income £
100 5½ per cent Cum. Red. Preference Shares of £1 of Reed, @ 77½p[1]	77·50	5·50
plus Cash payment above invested, @ 6 per cent p.a.	17·50	1·05
	95·00	6·55
Compared with the value of the present holdings of:		
100 6 per cent Cum. Preference Shares of £1 of Field, @ 90p[3]	90·00	6·00
An increase of	5·00	0·55
Or an increase of	5½%	9%

Although there was no capital gains tax liability in 1964 (the tax was introduced a year later in 1965), the same type of offer today would constitute a part disposal and acceptance could, therefore, involve some liability to capital gains tax.

The increase in both capital value and income upon acceptance is considerably higher on the offer for the ordinary shares than is the case with preference shares. The reasons for this are twofold. First, the value of a *fixed* dividend share (or for that matter a fixed interest stock) is determined mainly by the prevailing market rate of interest. Secondly, the holders of preference shares are seldom entitled to a

[1] Middle market quotation on June 17th, 1964 (the latest practical date before printing of offer document).
[2] Based on middle market quotation on 10th June, 1964, the day before the first press announcement of offer.
[3] Middle market quotation on June 17th, 1964.

vote (unless the dividend on their shares is in arrears), conse-quently the bidder would not gain any voting advantage by taking them over. If he does choose to make an offer for the preference as well as the ordinary shares, it can only be for the sake of convenience, i.e., acquiring complete control of the whole share capital as a neat and tidy operation or extending the offer to the preference share capital where (as in this case) it comprised a relatively small pro-portion of the total share capital in issue, viz:

Field, Sons & Co, Share Capital Issued and fully paid

	£
150,000 6 per cent Cum. Pref. Shares of £1 each	150,000
6,867,588 Ordinary Shares of 25p each	1,716,897
	1,866,897

Assuming full acceptance,[1] the offer by Reed entailed the issue by them of the following shares (allowing for sale of fractions of new ordinary shares):

	£
150,000 5½ per cent Cum. Red. Preference Shares of £1 each ..	150,000
3,090,415 Ordinary Shares of £1 each	3,090,415

One other feature is worth noting here. The holder of a Cumulative Preference Share in Field (presumably with no right of redemption) is being offered an exchange into Reed's Cum. *Redeemable* Preference Shares where the rights attaching to these shares include the right by Reed to redeem at par together with any arrears of dividend all or any part of the shares on three months' notice in writing on or after March 31st, 1976. Thus, the acceptors had a possible maximum of twelve years assured income whereas their previous holding gave an assured income without any time limit (assuming, of course, that sufficient profits would always be earned).

(c) Mixed offer with cash option
This type of offer usually includes some ordinary shares (thus retaining a limited equity stake) combined with a larger amount of dated unsecured loan stock (with or without conversion rights into ordinary shares at a specified later date) or, at the option of the shareholder, a cash alternative.

An example of such an offer occurred when Ever Ready Co (G.B.) Ltd announced in the press on June 16th, 1972, that they intended making an offer for control of Crabtree Electrical Industries Ltd, documents being issued in July and August, 1972. The first two offers were firmly rejected by Crabtree directors, but they ultimately

---

[1] Which was the eventual outcome with this offer.

capitulated when the third and final offer from Ever Ready was just good enough to gain legal control of Crabtree.

The initial and improved offers were as follows:

For each Crabtree Ordinary Share of 50p:

	No. of Ever Ready Ordinary Shares of 25p each	Plus Nominal Amount of 6 per cent Conv. Unsec. loan Stock, 1992/97	Cash Option
1. First offer (July 14th, 1972)	One	£1·70	325p
2. Second offer (August 4th, 1972)	One	£2·55	405p
3. Third, and final offer (August 25th, 1972)	One	£3·10	500p

Note: The final date for acceptances was September 11th, 1972.

Taking the value of the final offer as the basis for comparison, then the (*a*) market values and (*b*) the relative income pre-bid and post-bid can be evaluated as follows in respect of a holding of 100 ordinary shares of Crabtree:

	Capital Value £	Income £
100 Ordinary Shares of Ever Ready @ 170p[1] each ..	170·00	
On which a dividend of 4p per share was last paid ..		4·00
Plus £310 nominal of 6 per cent Conv. Unsec. Loan Stock @ £107 per cent[2]	331·70	18·60
	501·70	22·60
As compared with:		
100 Ordinary Shares of Crabtree @ 252½p each[3] ..	252·50	
On which a dividend of 16p per share is recommended		16·00
An increase of	249·20	6·60
Representing an increase of	98·7%	41·2%

In the event, 61·8 per cent of Crabtree's Ordinary Share Capital was acquired by Ever Ready for cash and the remaining 39·2 per cent, in exchange for 917,376 Ever Ready Ordinary Shares of 25p each fully paid plus £2,843,865 6 per cent Con. Uns. Loan Stock, 1992/97. It is interesting to observe that at the date of the first offer, neither Ever Ready nor any of its subsidiaries nor any of its directors held any ordinary shares in Crabtree but subsequently began buying heavily on the Stock Exchange for cash and by September 4th, 1972,

[1] Based on middle market quotation on September 4th, 1972 – the day before the last letter was sent to Crabtree shareholders by Ever Ready.
[2] Based on advice from the company's (Ever Ready) brokers that the current value of the Convertible Unsecured Loan Stock (yet to be issued) is, in their opinion, not less than £107 per cent.
[3] Based on middle market quotation on June 14th, 1972, the day before the original offer was communicated to the chairman of Crabtree.

had amassed a holding of 405,000 ordinary shares of Crabtree out of a total of 2,400,000 shares (about 17 per cent). Clearly, many Crabtree shareholders must have opted for cash when the final bid was declared unconditional on September 12th, 1972. Ever Ready then stated that while the share and loan stock offer would remain open until further notice the cash alternative would only be extended for a further 14 days, i.e., until September 26th, 1972.

The majority who accepted might be liable to capital gains tax (the 'market value' on April 6th, 1965 given in the offer document was 145p for each Crabtree Ordinary Share), whereas the minority who accepted the Ever Ready Ordinary Shares and Convertible Loan Stock were not so liable. Obviously, the extent of the liability for capital gains tax purposes would depend on the price paid at the original date of purchase or the 'market value' on April 6th, 1965 and would vary from one shareholder to another.

As for the minority who accepted the mixed share and loan stock offer, they were faced with an exchange from an all-equity holding into a part equity holding and a fixed interest security with a final repayment date in 1997 at par (though with conversion rights attached). If the holder decides to keep the smaller equity part (thus giving him a stake in any further growth in the now combined group composed of Ever Ready and Crabtree), he is still left with the choice of either retaining the larger fixed interest security part with a 6 per cent coupon for the next 25 years until repayment at par or switching out of the fixed interest security back into ordinary shares by exercising his conversion rights. So the choice must depend upon the exact terms available for conversion. Briefly the terms were specified as follows:

(i) The convertible stock may be converted in whole or part at the option of the holder, into

(ii) ordinary shares of 25p each of Ever Ready at a conversion price of 180p per share, during

(iii) the conversion period (the month of July) in each of the years 1975 to 1981 inclusive.

Under these terms, the holder can postpone his final decision whether or not to convert until July, 1981 at the very latest, meanwhile continuing to receive a fixed income from his holding. In July 1975, and in each subsequent July up to and including 1981 he can review the position by comparing the market price of Ever Ready Ordinary Shares with the fixed conversion price of 180p and compare his potential income (by applying the then current ordinary dividend rate to his converted holding) with his previous income from fixed interest securities which he would now have to forego.

The choice and timing of any conversion will probably rest either on comparative capital values alone or on comparative income alone.

As the very last moment for conversion arrives one is still not relieved from the difficult task of judging the economic outlook generally, the trend of prices and indices on the stock market, and the future trading prospects of this firm in particular.

BENEFITS OF THE MERGER

The stated arguments in favour of the proposed merger range from the faintly condescending to the overtly eulogistic as the following random sample of extracts from published statements suggests:

1. Cerebos/Hugon – November, 1963.

'Hugon and Cerebos have maintained friendly relations for many years and the Boards of the two companies recognize that Hugon's products, including "Atora" suet and the "Lin-can" range of canned fruits and vegetables are complementary to the food products of the Cerebos group.'

2. Reed Paper/Field, Sons & Co – June, 1964.

'The Directors of Reed and Field envisage that there will be great advantages from the merger as the activities of Field and the Reed carton manufacturing company, Reed Cartons Ltd, are at present largely complimentary to each other. The Directors believe that the joining together of the two businesses under the management of Field will enable the outstanding skill and experience of Field in design and precision manufacture to be allied with the large-scale operations of Reed Cartons Ltd and to be supplemented by the financial, technical and research resources of the Reed Group as a whole.'

3. Cementation/Cleveland Bridge & Engineering Co – September, 1967.

'The Board of Cementation wish to expand its activities in the United Kingdom and consider that the business of Cleveland will fit in well with Cementation's operations in which emphasis is placed upon the provision of a wide range of specialized services to the construction industry. . . . This integration is also consistent with the Government's wish for larger operating units in the civil engineering industry.'

4. Hickson & Welch (Holdings)/William Blythe & Co – November, 1968.

'By joining the Hickson & Welch Group, William Blythe will safeguard the Group's supply of arsenic peutoxide, a key raw material for their "Tanaleth" water soluble timber preservatives.'

5. Burton Group/Ryman Conran – March, 1971.

'The retailing of products for the office is a growth industry and Ryman is the industry leader. However, Ryman needs properties and funds for development and is not yet represented in important areas of the country. Because of its widespread property interests, low gearing and high asset value, Burton is well placed to provide the sites and funds which Ryman requires to realize its full growth potential.'

6. Burmah Oil/Quinton Hazell – August, 1972.

'A main object of Burmah's marketing policy is to supply the goods and services that enable the motorist to enjoy the full advantages of car ownership. Thus "motorists market" is growing throughout the world. The acquisition of Hazell by Burmah is a logical step in the process of expansion in this market which has brought Castrol Ltd, Halfords Ltd, and more recently Tabbert GmbH, a leading West German caravan manufacturer, into the Burmah Group.'

7. Cadbury Schweppes/Jeyes Group – November, 1972.

'In making its offer for Jeyes, Cadbury Schweppes is implementing a policy to extend its range of activities in fields relating to its existing business. Jeyes will form the nucleus of a new group within Cadbury Schweppes comprising health, household care and packaging services. This will provide the basis for an important new development for Cadbury Schweppes which will broaden the company's opportunities for growth.'

8. British-American Tobacco Co/International Stores – November, 1972.

'Within the BAT Group, International would be able, in the opinion of both Boards, to pursue more vigorously plans for its development and expansion by reason of access to BAT's substantial resources. Both companies are specialists in the marketing and merchandizing of consumer goods. A merger of the business of International with that of BAT would create an opportunity to develop one of the most important retail groups in the United Kingdom and such a development would be in the best interests of stockholders and consumers.'

9. Babcock & Wilcox/Woodall-Duckham Group – December, 1972.

'Babcock has interests in activities which are similar to many of those of W-D Group. The Board of Babcock believes that the financial strength and world-wide organization of the Babcock Group would provide W-D Group with greater opportunities in process plant contracting and plans to build upon W-D Group's contracting team at Crawley as the base for further expansion in this field. Babcock also plan to develop other aspects of W-D Group's business including areas of common interest such as pollution control, materials handling equipment and food processing machinery.'

Alas, not all these grandiose statements of intent have been borne out by subsequent results!

MANAGEMENT, STAFF AND EMPLOYEES

A statement under this heading is usually couched in the following terms:

'If the offer becomes unconditional, it is the intention of X Ltd that Y Ltd should continue to be run as a separate business, that its existing goodwill should be maintained in every possible way and that the interests of its staff (including existing pension arrangements) should be fully safeguarded.'

The statement usually stresses the point that the merger will benefit the employees of Y Ltd by offering greater scope for personal advancement in an expanding group.

Moreover, the bidder usually takes the opportunity of pouring oil on troubled waters by announcing (if appropriate) that the existing Directors of Y Ltd will continue in office and that one or more of their number will be invited to join the Board of X Ltd and the Directors of Y Ltd will reciprocate by inviting one or more nominees of the main board to join the Board of the new subsidiary.

Failing this kind of amicable arrangement, the document will name those directors who propose to resign and what compensation (if any) it is proposed to pay them for loss of office.

PROCEDURE FOR ACCEPTANCE

It is important to follow out the acceptance procedure to the letter, noting carefully the final date and time for acceptances. Coloured forms of acceptance and transfer must be completed and delivered to the licensed dealers or other agents as instructed by the final date accompanied by the relative share certificate. Upon the offer becoming unconditional, Renounceable Allotment Letters (for shares) or Renounceable Certificates (for any loan stock) and cheques in respect of fractional entitlements or cheques in respect of any cash consideration are usually sent by post at the request of the persons entitled thereto within 28 days.

In the event of the relevant offer lapsing through insufficient acceptances, forms of acceptance and transfer and documents of title will normally be returned by post within 14 days.

CHAPTER X

DEFENCES AGAINST A BID

Despite the fact that more than 90 per cent of all take-over bids go through unopposed, the usual grounds on which a board of directors may decide to contest a bid can be classified as follows:

(1) The terms of the offer are unacceptable.
(2) There does not seem to be any industrial logic in the proposed link-up.
(3) Opposition expressed by employees, either key technical staff or the general body of employees as expressed in a formal resolution to that effect at union or other meetings representative of the workers.
(4) Implacable opposition by the founding family (with or without voting control) relying heavily on 'shareholder loyalty'.
(5) The take-over may foreshadow a boardroom 'shake-up' with consequent loss of jobs for the existing directors and some managerial staff.

'One of the most important lessons in any take-over battle', insists Sir Anthony Burney in an interview,[1] 'is to try and keep the initiative. The moment the other side gets the initiative you're in trouble. They have to have it for a moment of time because of the fact that when they issue a document the press tends to comment on the contents as a matter of course.' Sir Anthony claims that it was his idea to publish the defence document as a paid advertisement in the newspapers on the *same day* the shareholders received news of the offer from the bidder. The two come out together and the defence kills or dampens the effect of the surprise offer. He suggested this course of action when acting jointly with Baring Brothers, for Courtaulds in their battle with I.C.I. in 1961/62, and adopted the same technique once again in 1972, when, as Chairman of Debenhams Ltd, he successfully mounted a spirited defence against an uninvited bid from the rival United Drapery Stores. The bid was handed in at about 3 o'clock one afternoon. Later that same afternoon, Debenhams issued a rejection as a paid advertisement and as a press announcement. The result was that the headlines the next morning read: 'Debenhams rejects U.D.S. offer'. instead of 'Surprise U.D.S. bid for Debenhams'. Another novelty brought into the defence was a gramophone record which was sent out to all 46,000 shareholders and was well received by the shareholders, the press

[1] *Accountancy Age*, May 12th, 1972.

and the customers in the stores – many of whom were also small shareholders.

Reliance upon restrictive clauses in the articles or moves to disfranchise shareholders seldom achieve their object. Such moves only postpone the eventual bid: they do not avoid it for good.

If a company really wishes to avoid the attentions of a bidder, there are certain dispositions it can make in its own defence beforehand.

First, freehold properties could be revalued and the revised valuation brought into the balance sheet so as to bring the current worth of the asset to the notice of shareholders in an unmistakable manner.

Possibly, surplus property could be sold or a sale/leaseback transaction effected, thereby forestalling the designs of a bid altogether.

Second, the issued capital could be brought into line with the capital employed in the business by issuing bonus shares.

Third, the dividend could be stepped up on the ordinary capital so increased in order to distribute a higher proportion of earnings than formerly.

This course of action was permissible even during the control of prices and incomes, if a company was threatened by a bid.

If substantial capital reserves exist, then the annual dividend might be augmented by a special distribution out of capital profits (provided the latter are available for distribution). Fourth, cash and realizable investments in excess of current and future needs might be repaid to shareholders by way of a partial return of capital or, of course, might be reinvested elsewhere so as to yield a higher return.

Lastly, instead of congratulating themselves on their sagacity in financing the whole of their capital expenditure out of retained profits year after year, the directors of public companies might consider having recourse to the capital market – whose function it is to provide fresh capital – thereby releasing profits for dividend purposes.

As for more energetic and enterprising management, there is no simple solution except to import new blood from outside the business. Indeed, some bids are made with the prime object of bringing in an able management team built up by a successful competitor, rather than the acquisition of additional tangible assets as such.

In fighting off a bid, however, everything depends on the attitude of those who own the share capital or that part of it that confers voting control. Who exactly are the shareholders of a company? They are composed of three types of persons:

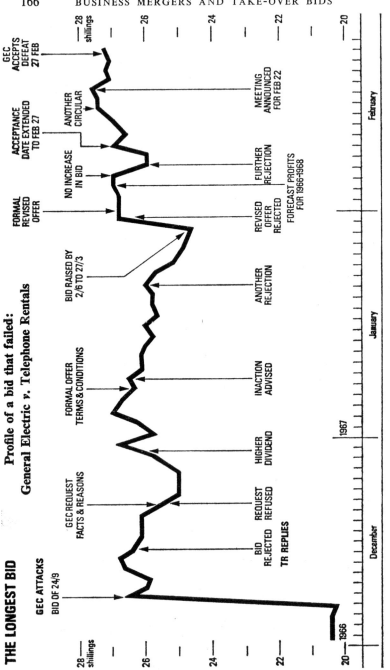

Profile of a bid that failed:
General Electric v. Telephone Rentals

THE LONGEST BID

GEC ATTACKS
BID OF 24/9

GEC REQUEST
FACTS & REASONS

FORMAL OFFER
TERMS & CONDITIONS

BID RAISED BY
2/6 TO 27/3

FORMAL
REVISED
OFFER

NO INCREASE
IN BID

ACCEPTANCE
DATE EXTENDED
TO FEB 27

ANOTHER
CIRCULAR

GEC
ACCEPTS
DEFEAT
27 FEB

BID
REJECTED

TR REPLIES

REQUEST
REFUSED

HIGHER
DIVIDEND

INACTION
ADVISED

ANOTHER
REJECTION

REVISED
OFFER REJECTED

FORECAST PROFITS
FOR 1966-1968

FURTHER
REJECTION

MEETING
ANNOUNCED
FOR FEB 22

December   1967   January   February

1966

Adapted from *The Economist*, February 25th, 1967.

(a) Small shareholders, i.e., the share capital is split ip into quite small holdings without any one holding dominating the rest.

(b) Directors and members of their families and close friends collectively owning a controlling interest or commanding a substantial block of shares.

(c) Institutional holdings which can outvote the aggregate holdings of a large number of small shareholders.

The interests of these three types may not always be identical, however, and shareholder loyalty (a tenuous link at the best of times) is often placed under severe strain. Have they been fairly treated in the past dividend-wise? Has the company shown a rising trend of profits? Is the return on capital employed satisfactory?

How does the bid price compare with recent pre-bid market quotations? How will they fare income-wise if the bid is accepted? Is the bid in cash, thus severing all connection with the company and bringing them face to face with the problem of reinvestment – or in the form of an exchange of shares (in this way they retain an indirect interest in the original investment)? What reliance can be placed upon the forecasts of future earnings disclosed by the bidder and the bid for company alike?

All these and many other questions have to be weighed in the balance. What lessons can be learned from contested bids?

In the first place, the 'sit tight and do nothing' approach is apt to leave the shareholder locked in as part of an outvoted minority.

Second, if the situation outlined above applies then it is often advisable to sell in the market for cash if the share price rises above the bid price in anticipation of a higher counter-bid.

Third, the book value of assets is certainly a factor but important though it is, it will not sustain share prices regardless of the past, present and prospective future earning power.

Fourth, it is wrong to suppose that share prices will never fall back to the pre-bid price if the bid is withdrawn or lapses through insufficient acceptances.

Many a shareholder in companies which have successfully rejected a bid (see Table XI) must rue the day that they – along with the directors – dismissed a genuine bid in such peremptory fashion.

Nevertheless, one of the most galling features of being on the receiving end of an uninvited take-over bid, is the cost of mounting a successful defence – a cost, moreover, which is not an allowable expense for tax purposes. Some idea of the expense incurred can be gleaned from the published annual reports of companies following the routing of the enemy:

Year	Successful Defenders	Cost £
1962	Courtaulds (v. I.C.I.)	163,000
1971	Reeves & Sons (v. Heenan Beddow)	12,500
1973	Ellis & Everard (v. Unilever)	72,500
1973	Fothergill & Harvey (v. James Stroud)	40,611
1973	British Steam Specialities (v. Bestobell and later U.D.T.) ..	34,000

Indeed, one or two chairmen have even gone so far as to suggest that there should be some recompense. 'It should not be difficult', suggested Mr J. A. Jordan, C.A., chairman of Fothergill & Harvey Ltd, 'for the Take-over Panel which regulates these matters, to introduce a system under which costs in such circumstances would be awarded against the bidder in the event of an unsuccessful bid'.[1] The same point was made particularly strongly by Mrs Helen Waudley, chairman of British Steam Specialities, the engineering group which successfully fought off two bids, both in the same year, first from Bestobill; then one from U.D.T.

Apart from the recorded expense, there were also additional costs which cannot be so easily quantified. 'In the same vein', remarked Mrs Waudley, 'I would like it to be known that in addition, the take-over situation lost us the opportunity of acquiring by mutual agreement, a public company of some standing with whom friendly negotiations were far advanced. Due to the sudden and unwanted interruption to our affairs and the period of uncertainty as to the final outcome, regrettably the company in question joined another group.'[2] She, too, felt strongly that the aggressors – when defeated – should pick up the bill. An understandable reaction, though not, one may surmise, a very practical one.

The price paid for acquisitions varied from 100 per cent to 199 per cent of the pre-acquisition price according to the results of a sample of 311 deals and bids made in 1967.[3] All but one acquisition were priced above the pre-bid price and the average consideration was a premium of one-third over the pre-acquisition price. Understandably, the premium tended to be small in the case of formal mergers (no more than 20 per cent higher) but relatively large with contested bids (about 60 per cent premium).

Payment for a company may be made either by an issue of shares (including preference shares) or loan capital of the acquiring company, or in cash (or a mixture of all three).

The analysis by the Department of Industry shows some remarkable variations in the composition of merger terms, over the period 1966–75. To begin with offers were financed mainly by the issue of equity or loan stock rather than cash, but from 1973 onwards the

[1] *The Accountant*, June 6th, 1974.
[2] *Accountants Weekly*, July 12th, 1974.
[3] *The 1967 Take-over Boom*, by Professor H. Rose and Mr G. D. Newbould, Moorgate and Wall Street, Autumn 1967. (Hill, Samuel & Co Ltd.)

TABLE XI
SOME BIDS THAT FAILED

Bidding company	Company bid for	Date of bid	Value of bid £	Reasons for failure
I.C.I.	Courtaulds (£1)	March 1962	2·50	Insufficient acceptances
London & Midland Industries	Bluemel Bros (£1)	November 1963	6·00	Insufficient acceptances
Horlicks	Burt Boulton & Haywood (£1)	June 1961	3·95	Insufficient acceptances
Thorn Electrical	Westinghouse Brake (£1)	December 1963	1·56	Offer lapsed due to lack of acceptances
Levy & Franks	Shorts (£1)	February 1965	2·00	Insufficient acceptances
Caravans International	Duple Motor Bodies (20p)	March 1965	0·50	Bidder withdrew
Vehicle & General Insurance	National Life & General Insurance (25p)	August	0·61½	Offer lapsed due to lack of acceptances
Pointvale	Stylo Shoes (25p)	December 1965	0·57½	Directors blocked bid
Viyella International	Jersey-Kapwood (25p)	March 1966	0·97½	Offer met with little success
Courtaulds	Bear Brand (25p)	April 1966	0·39	Offer not proceeded with due to 'lack of agreement on certain points'
Varian Associates	Edwards High Vacuum (20p)	September 1966	0·55	Talks terminated when bidders' conditions could not be met
A.V.P.	Barry Staines (40p)	October 1966	0·82½	Offer lapsed. Board produced more attractive capital reorganization scheme
Unilever	Smith & Nephew (10p)	June 1968	1·05	Offer lapsed due to insufficient acceptances
Allied Breweries	Boddingtons' Breweries (£1)	February 1970	4·56	Offer lapsed due to insufficient acceptances
Commercial Union Assurance (in conjunction with Trafalgar House Investments)	Metropolitan Estate & Property Corpn (25p)	December 1970	1·58½	Revised offer (conditional upon a new scheme of arrangement) withdrawn

Analysis of the consideration given by acquiring companies

			Total consideration £ million	Share and loan capital £ million	Cash £ million	Cash as % of total
1966	..	..	447	264	183	41
1967	..	..	781	521	260	33
1968	..	..	1,653	1,382	271	16
1969	..	..	1,069	773	296	28
1970	..	..	1,122	871	251	22
1971	..	..	911	626	285	31
1972	..	..	2,532	2,039	493	19
1973	..	..	1,304	613	691	53
1974	..	..	508	161	347	68
1975	..	..	291	118	173	59

Sources: *Board of Trade guide to mergers, 1969* and *Business Monitor 7.*

pattern has reverted to mainly cash bids following the sharp decline in share prices in 1973 and 1974 before the slow climb back in 1975. Indeed, there seems to be a close correlation between merger activity in general and the Financial Times Industrial Ordinary Share Index over this period.

Starting from a high point of 543 at the beginning of 1972, the index fell sharply throughout 1973 and 1974 reaching a 'low' of 146 in January, 1975. But the index recovered slowly in 1975 climbing back to around the 400 mark at the end of the year.

As the following analysis indicates, those mergers in 1968 involving consideration of more than £50 million were effected entirely with 'paper' (shares and loan stock), those where the consideration fell between £10 million and £50 million were also effected almost entirely with 'paper', but those where the consideration was under £10 million were effected as to 41 per cent in cash.

Since equity, or loan stock convertible into equity, has until recently been the main currency for acquisitions, the higher the value of a company's shares the better placed it is to buy up other companies. A high market value usually reflects the market's hopes of high and increasing earnings per share. Thus future expectations play a large part in the financing process where mergers are concerned.

Looking at the spectrum of individual bids, they range from all cash (all foreign bids have to be in this form anyway) through an issue of shares, with an added cash element (or an option to take cash instead of shares) to an all-share bid, or a mixture of shares and debt (sometimes with conversion rights into shares).

A cash offer is a matter of absolute value whereas a share offer is one of relative values. Nevertheless, it is important to remember that a share exchange represents money's worth, and can be converted into cash if the recipient so chooses. In fact, the market price of the shares of a company served with a bid in the form of an exchange of shares often falls as the result of advance selling by

Acquisition of U.K. companies	Acquired companies	Cash %	Consideration Shares/ Loan %
Consideration over £50 million			
British Leyland Motors	2	—	100
G.E.C./E.E.	1	—	100
Thorn/Radio Rentals	1	—	100
Allied/Showerings..	1	—	100
Land Securities/City Centre	1	—	100
Rank Hovis/Cerebos	1	—	100
Total over £50 million	7	—	100
Consideration over £10 million up to £50 million	28	4	96
Total over £10 million	35	1	99
Consideration up to £10 million	572	41	59
Total U.K. acquisitions	607	11	89
Acquisitions of overseas companies:			
Considerations up to £10 million ..	31	78	22
	638	12	88

(Source: *Board of Trade guide to mergers*, 1969)

Note. – The table above includes acquisitions of property companies and mergers involving the formation of new holding companies and the percentages therefore differ slightly from those given in the preceding table.

shareholders who either hold enough of the bidding company's scrip already or prefer to take cash through the market rather than throw in their lot with another company, whose shares they would not have chosen to buy in the normal course of events.

At the same time, selling out for cash constitutes a realization and may give rise to a liability to capital gains tax (which applied from 1965 onwards).

Scheme to frustrate threatened take-over

The case of *Bulmer and Others v. Commissioners of Inland Revenue* ([1966] T.R. 257) is of interest both because of the nature of the steps taken to frustrate a threatened take-over bid and because of the tax dispute that arose in consequence. It was in 1954 that the directors of Bulmer & Lumb (Holdings) Ltd became aware that shares in the company were being purchased on an unusually large scale. They ascertained that the purchaser was a rival company and took this to be an indication of a threatened take-over. In order to counter the threat a scheme was devised for making a take-over impossible, and for this purpose, the assistance of another public company (Sanderson) was obtained.

Sanderson formed a subsidiary finance company (Yorkshire) to whom it lent £250,000 at a commercial rate of interest. Yorkshire used this money to purchase Bulmer & Lumb shares on the open market. Yorkshire also purchased from certain Bulmer & Lumb shareholders who were party to the scheme a total of 552,262 of their shares at a price of 25p a share, which price was admittedly below the then market price. The amount due by Yorkshire to these shareholders was left outstanding. Yorkshire received dividends from time to time in the Bulmer & Lumb shares it owned, and it applied the dividends in servicing the £250,000 Sanderson loan. Eventually, after a period of years, the loan was extinguished and the shareholders purchased back the remainder of Yorkshire's holding in Bulmer & Lumb at the price of 25p a share.

The Revenue claimed that the scheme amounted to a revocable settlement by the Bulmer & Lumb shareholders who had been a party to it, and that dividends received by Yorkshire were liable to surtax as part of the income of those shareholders.

Mr Justice Pennycuick decided in favour of the taxpayers. He considered that the scheme was not a settlement since it was a commercial transaction without any element of gift or bounty. Accordingly there was, in his view, no justification for treating the dividend income of Yorkshire as part of the total income for surtax purposes of the individuals who had been parties to the scheme.

In the case of *Bamford v. Bamford* (*The Times*, February 1st, 1969) the question at issue was the ratification of allotment. Under a power conferred by the articles of association, the directors of B Ltd allotted 500,000 unissued shares of 20p each to X for cash at par.

Certain shareholders attacked this allotment as being made, not for the benefit of B Ltd, but to thwart a take-over bid. Later the company called an extraordinary general meeting at which this allotment was ratified and approved by ordinary resolution. The dissentients brought an action to determine the validity in law of the purported ratification.

The Court of Appeal unanimously found the ratification to be valid and the allotment good. Acts by directors which were initially defective (as for want of a quorum, irregularity of their appointment, or improper motives) could be validated, after full disclosure of the facts, by the general body of shareholders. In the present case, even had the directors not acted bona fide, the company had waived any such impropriety and the allotment must stand.

Imperial Chemical Industries v. Courtaulds
The hotly-contested I.C.I. bid for Courtaulds is, perhaps, the out-standing example of a bid that failed.

In sheer size alone the offer – worth close on £200 million – towered above every other take-over bid made in the United Kingdom at the time (1961). The original offer consisted of £3 ordinary stock of I.C.I. for every £4 ordinary stock of Courtaulds and offers were also made for the Courtaulds preference stocks. In rejecting the terms of the bid, the Courtaulds board stated that profits had been substantially better in the second half of that current year and forecast a final dividend of 6p a share – to maintain the same total dividend as for the previous year in spite of an ill-timed cut in the interim dividend. I.C.I.retaliated by raising the terms of the offer to £4 I.C.I. ordinary stock for every £5 Courtaulds ordinary stock.

The battle was now joined in earnest, with Courtaulds vigorously opposing the new offer on the grounds that it seriously undervalued their earning capacity in relation to that of I.C.I. Impressive forecasts of the future growth expected in profits were given and, at the same time, trade and other investments were shown to be worth £120 million (against a book value of only £70 million), equivalent to more than £1·50 per £1 ordinary stock in issue without taking in the manufacturing side at all. It is interesting to observe that Courtauld's £1 ordinary stock was quoted at £1·50 just before the bid.

I.C.I. came back with a statement expressing the view that the world demand for chemicals would double in the next ten years; that despite the sharp fall in group income last year, 1962 was expected to bring better trading and, looking beyond 1962, the trend of profits was confidently expected to continue upwards; at the same time the I.C.I. board wisely refrained from entering the realms of detailed forecasting by stating that:

'. . . these depend in part on factors outside its control and can be influenced by political events – both at home and abroad – by labour conditions and, above all, by the success or failure of plans to raise living standards throughout the world'.

Moreover, it was asserted that a complete merger between I.C.I. and Courtaulds would increase efficiency and reduce costs in a number of ways. For instance, a large integrated organization would be able to spread the cost of research and development over a large production volume and a wide field of fibres; common ownership of the plants for the manufacture of the polymers and the fibres would lead to substantial reductions in capital and operating costs; a common marketing organization would lead to lower selling costs as well as better advice and technical service to the user; and above all, the United Kingdom industry would be in a much stronger position in competing for overseas markets.

While confirming the terms of the share exchange offer, the board of I.C.I. decided to include an alternative offer of £25 6½ per cent convertible unsecured loan stock, 1972–77, for each £10 of Courtaulds ordinary stock. This exchange effectively offered increased income with the option of converting into I.C.I. ordinary stock over a period when the growth potential of I.C.I. and the benefits of the merger might have accrued.

By this time the value of the offer was equivalent to £2·50 for every £1 ordinary stock unit of Courtaulds (assuming the value of the convertible loan stock to be par).

The directors of Courtaulds made a dramatic ripost to this statement by proposing an increase in dividend, the payment of a tax-free capital distribution, the free issue to shareholders of £40 million of loan stock, and the creation of a new subsidiary to contain most of Courtaulds trade investments.

The I.C.I. rejoinder came on February 28th, 1962, when they informed Courtaulds that they had decided to declare their offer for the ordinary stock of Courtaulds unconditional *irrespective of the percentage of acceptances received by the closing date* – in this case March 8th, 1962.

After more than two months of bitter wrangling, the moment for decision had arrived. Acceptances received up to the closing date amounted to only 36·7 per cent of the Courtaulds ordinary stock, 44·6 per cent of the 5 per cent preference stock, and 59·8 per cent of the 6 per cent preference stock. As this was not enough to give control, the I.C.I. directors extended the offer for a further four days. On Monday, March 12th, 1962, I.C.I. conceded defeat. By mid-morning they had received acceptances for 37·4 per cent of Courtaulds ordinary stock, only fractionally more than the 36·7 per cent counted on the original closing date. The offers for the Courtaulds preference stocks also lapsed.

As *The Times* leader commented:

'. . . one of the major lessons of the I.C.I.–Courtaulds fight has been the ample demonstration that financial inducements are not in themselves enough. Both the handling of the battle by I.C.I. and the feeling that Courtaulds had acknowledged their recent failures and were willing to learn from their mistakes (quite apart from a certain ingrained loyalty among Courtaulds shareholders) played a greater part in the final result than the financial shrewdness of the I.C.I. offer.'

The very magnitude of the offer was by no means the only mark of distinction, however, for there were several other issues involved, any one of which would have been enough to incite public controversy and attention.

While the two contestants were locked in conflict, public attention centred upon the question of monopoly for, if the merger had gone through, the combined group would have controlled over 90 per cent of Britain's synthetic fibre production. This prospective concentration of resources had caused some public disquiet which had found expression through questions raised in Parliament, demands for a public inquiry, and a request that the matter be referred to the Monopolies Commission.

In those days, the Government had little or no power to intervene until a merger was complete and until the new combine was operating in a way which appeared to be against the public interest. The President of the Board of Trade explained that it had been the policy of successive Governments to judge monopolies by their actual effects in practice, and not to attempt to reach conclusions on the possible effects of any particular monopoly before it has come into existence and there had been experience of its working.

In point of fact, monopoly conditions already existed in the man-made fibres industry, because I.C.I. and Courtaulds jointly owned a third firm, British Nylon Spinners. A formal merger would therefore only have had a marginal effect upon the position. In any case, the new giant would, in all probability, have been in competition with the fully-integrated giants of Europe and the United States.

This take-over battle underlined the weakness of the Government's policy towards monopoly, and thereby prepared public opinion for the legislative changes incorporated in the Monopolies and Mergers Act 1965. However, the story of the bid that failed would be incomplete without the tailpiece. This came two years later, in 1964, when Courtaulds 50 per cent shareholding in British Nylon Spinners was exchanged for I.C.I.'s $37\frac{1}{2}$ per cent holding of Courtaulds ordinary stock.

CHAPTER XI

FOREIGN BIDS

The issues raised by a whole series of foreign bids in the past few years have caused disquiet in many quarters. The frequency of these deals has led to the feeling that American interests are poised to take over important sections of British industry.

Sometimes these bids have amounted to a complete take-over like the Texas Company's offer for the Trinidad Oil Company; the offer by Reynolds Metal (in conjunction with Tube Investments) for British Aluminium; the bid by the Swiss Nestle Co for Crosse & Blackwell, the bid by the Canadian company Massey-Ferguson for F. Perkins Ltd; or the offer by Philips, the Dutch giant, for Pye; the acquisition of Smith's Food Group (formerly Smith's Potato Crisps) by General Mills of the U.S.; at other times they have taken the form of a repatriation of the British-owned minority holdings in American controlled subsidiaries established in this country as with the bid for shares in British Timken, British United Shoe Machinery, Crown Cork, Ford, IBM United Kingdom, Monsanto and Technicolor by their respective parent companies in the United States.

In general the objections to these bids are misplaced. American investment in Britain makes a considerable contribution to the British balance of payments position on capital account. American management has often introduced new and novel methods of production, put labour to more productive use, and provided the benefits of research undertaken in the United States on a scale that British Industry alone can seldom match. Moreover, some British subsidiaries of American groups are well to the fore in Britain's export drive.

In theory, it is possible to imagine the process of foreign investment in Britain being carried to the point where *The Times* list of the 500 largest industrial companies consisted of wholly-owned American or other foreign subsidiaries. No one would want this to happen nor would they want American interests to become as dominant in the United Kingdom as they are, for example, in Canada. But the present threat is much more limited; it can be summed up as the emergence of too great a United States influence in particular industries.

Including components, groups with headquarters in the United States already control roughly half Britain's motor industry. That is why the Government insisted upon writing in certain conditions to the agreement before giving their consent to the Rootes-Chrysler deal. For the same reason were a foreign bid made for British Leyland

176

Motor Holdings it would probably be frowned upon in the light of recent events. Even so, one has to remember that this is an age when industries and companies are becoming international. Indeed, there is a strong case for arguing that Britain needs more giant firms to match the size and strength of other giants in international trade. Even today, fragmentation is rife in many sections of British industry in spite of all the mergers and take-overs in the post-war period.

Speaking on this theme to the National Liberal Forum in November 1965, Mr H. G. Lazell, Chairman of the Beecham Group, said: '(International companies) will inevitably capture a bigger and bigger share of world trade, and if Britain wants to stay in the international league it must put its international companies on an equal basis with their American competitors.'

One important principle must, however, be proclaimed at the outset – important, that is, for a country that prospers from the free flow of capital. Impediments ought not to be placed in the path of foreign investment in Britain through prejudice, envy or an outbreak of xenophobia. There has been a healthy movement of capital both ways across the Atlantic since the war and any discriminatory legislation imposed here might have invited retaliation against substantial British investment in the United States (including Beechams, Bowaters, Courtaulds, Shell Oil and Unilever). So far as the strength of sterling allows, a two-way flow of international investment should be encouraged.

The Multinational company

The operations of multinational companies – sometimes called international or transnational companies – seem likely to hold the centre of the stage in the 1970s.

For Britain, the growth in the output of multinational companies has two major implications. One is the result of direct foreign investment on the British foreign exchange reserves and the effect on the balance of payments. The other is the effect that multinational companies may have on prospective British sales that might result from entry into the Common Market.

A multinational company may be defined as an international firm with substantial operating assets in a number of countries, trading through branch offices, subsidiaries or affiliated companies owned wholly or in part. Such a company wields considerable power, not only financial but industrial and no one really knows how they exercise it since a multinational company pursues its own goals; it will not voluntarily accept a nation's priorities. Nevertheless, there is a two-way interest in all this, the firms themselves leaning over backwards in an attempt to show that they are sensitive to national interests, while governments, for their part, repeatedly proclaim that they can bring pressure to bear on them in order to protect the public interest. At the same time, it must be acknowledged that home countries retain basic authority derived from nationality, and the control derived from having the board of directors and headquarters within their countries. In addition, they also retain the vital right of taxing the earnings of the multinational company.

In the developed countries, the host countries probably do have the political power to control the activities of multinational firms within their borders but this may not be altogether true of under-developed host countries. Even so, the mere threat of nationalization can exert some control in these situations. For all countries the key question is: Does investment increase national income by an amount greater than the cost of servicing the investment (i.e., interest and dividends flowing out to other countries)?

The increase in the contribution of these concerns to world industrial output is one of the most impressive economic features of the last two decades. About three-quarters of this growth has originated from American and British owned and controlled enterprises, though the greatest percentage increases have been recorded by European and Japanese firms.

According to Professor J. H. Dunning[1] the estimated book value of total assets owned by these firms in 1968 outside the countries in which they were first incorporated was about $94 billion, and their total foreign sales (both exports and local output) were reckoned to exceed in value the gross national product of any country except the U.S.A. and the U.S.S.R. About 55 per cent of these international assets were owned by U.S. enterprises, 20 per cent by British firms and the rest largely by European and Japanese companies.

Some countries, like Britain, are two-way investors. While more than 30 per cent of the profits of British-owned enterprises stem from overseas operations, foreign multinational firms in the U.K. account for 25 per cent of manufacturing exports and, on present trends, seem likely to supply the same proportion of manufacturing output by 1980.

In Britain, companies like British Petroleum, Unilever, Philips, I.B.M., Rio Tinto-Zinc and the recent link-up between Dunlop and Pirelli late in 1970 seem to qualify as multinational concerns.

Suffice to say that the trans-frontier development is just beginning. The difficulties are real, even where the will and the opportunity exists. As well as company control and domicile, accounting conventions, national attitudes and susceptibilities, there are different company laws, fiscal systems, stock exchange regulations, exchange restrictions and anti-trust rules, which create a veritable barbed-wire entanglement and governments have taken very few steps to cut

[1] 'The Multinational Enterprise'. *Lloyds Bank Review*, July 1970.

paths through it. The pressure of events may well force their hand in the next few years.

It would, of course, be wrong to suggest that multinational companies are the direct result of mergers (indeed some are very much the product of internal growth over the years), but it is often cheaper and easier to buy out established firms abroad rather than have the problem of setting up your own plant from the outset and recruiting a local work force.

Treasury consent

The Government has certain means at its disposal whereby Treasury consent can be refused if the bid is not considered to be 'in the national interest'. Under the Exchange Control Act 1947, section 9, Treasury permission is required for the transfer of securities by United Kingdom residents to persons resident outside the sterling area and to any action whereby a company controlled by United Kingdom residents passes out of such control. So far, these powers have not been invoked against a foreign bid, but in a statement about the offer for Ford shares, the Chancellor of the Exchequer made it clear that:

> 'There may well be cases where proposals may seem attractive from a commercial point of view, but where nevertheless it may be necessary to refuse consent to transfer of control for reasons of national security or the significance of a particular firm or industry to our economic life.'

Furthermore, the Treasury stands by its ruling that cash bids only are acceptable from abroad.[1] In August 1959, National Dairy Products of America made a bid for the equity of the Typhoo Tea Co which, after being accepted in principle by the directors, foundered on the terms, i.e., 40 per cent in cash and the rest in National Dairy Products shares. In the case of another foreign bid, that made by the United States Timken Roller Bearing Co for British Timken Ltd, the directors stated that they would have preferred to exchange Timken Roller Bearing shares for British Timken shares, but Treasury permission was not forthcoming for such a transaction.

The Treasury's insistence on wholly cash bids relies on the argument that while the general ban on purchases by United Kingdom residents of foreign securities at the official rate of exchange remains in force, it would be somewhat anomalous to permit some people to gain possession of such securities at the official rates just because they happened to own certain shares in a British company which were coveted by a foreign bidder. The ruling means that the official exchange reserves receive the full benefit of the transfer; British shareholders being paid out in the sterling equivalent. Consequently,

[1] In exceptional circumstances, a share-for-share exchange could be approved, but even so it is thought that the Bank of England would require payment of the security dollar premium.

there is much to be said for a relaxation of this rigid ruling. Foreign bids might not appear so objectionable if British residents were allowed to hold American shares in private (and traceable) hands as a result of a share exchange offer, especially as the reverse situation is condoned, viz., the Royal Dutch-Shell Co's share offer for the Canadian Eagle Oil Co (a dollar concern) in April 1959.

Although the Government might be justified in withholding consent to a transaction because it considered the bid price to be inadequate, the precise terms of the offer are primarily a matter for the shareholders of the company concerned. It is for them to decide whether or not to accept the bid price, and sometimes this gives rise to differences of opinion. Thus the cash bid of £4·19 made by Timken Roller Bearing for the minority holding in British Timken Limited (compared with the then market price of £3·52½) was not considered attractive enough by some institutional investors. In their view, the offer was too low for really long-term holders. Timken Roller Bearing, however, quickly gained control of about 85 per cent of the British Timken equity and after extending the date for acceptances, announced that if enough assents were not secured they might force British Timken into liquidation – a course of action well within their power by virtue of their holding more than 75 per cent of the equity. Faced with this prospect, the institutional investors finally assented to the bid, stating that the existence of a small group of minority shareholders opposed to liquidation would not only create difficulties for the liquidator but would prove damaging to the best interests of the business and staff alike. So, even with a foreign bid the minority shareholders' lot can be most unrewarding.

At first glance, it seems difficult to understand why a foreign company is so ready to pay a high price for the minority interest in a British company which it already controls and in which it intends to preserve the existing British management and staff. As with the bid by the Ford Motor Co of the United States, and previous bids by Timken Roller Bearing and IBM World Trade Corporation of New York, the answer seems to be greater operational flexibility. Perhaps recent developments in the European trading area – the establishment of the Common Market and the European Free Trade Association – have shown that it is difficult to reconcile the just interests of minority shareholders with the necessity to integrate the businesses concerned with a world-wide organization. It is a hard choice to make, for most of these corporations are only too well aware (from experience in Canada, Australia and Germany) that local investors relish the opportunity of having a stake in the equity of prosperous foreign corporations.

Foreign investment in this country may be divided into three types:

(a) direct investment, which consists of the phyical establishments of plants in this country;

(b) the complete or partial acquisition of existing United Kingdom concerns;

(c) 'portfolio' investment in British securities.

According to United States Government estimates, the book value of direct private investment by United States companies in the United Kingdom amounted to £884 million at the end of 1959. Against that, unofficial estimates of United Kingdom direct investment in the United States suggest that the total is in the region of £700 million.

Some of the gaps in this surprisingly uncharted sea are now filled in by the regular inquiry initiated by the Board of Trade into Britain's private direct investment overseas and corresponding overseas investment in Britain. The first results were published in the *Board of Trade Journal* for October 7th, 1960. The inquiry covers investment in overseas branches, subsidiaries and associated companies; it does not cover public investment or portfolio investment – or direct investment by oil and insurance companies (which is being dealt with in a separate inquiry.

At the end of 1970, United Kingdom private investment overseas was listed under the following headings:

	£m
Direct investment (less oil, insurance, banking)	6,550
U.K. oil companies net (a)	1,900
U.K. insurance companies in U.S. (a)	500
Portfolio investment (b)	5,450
	£14,400

(a) Estimated book value of net assets.
(b) At estimated market value.

Whereas private overseas investment in United Kingdom only totalled £7,185 million, at the same date.

In addressing the Institute of Export in October 1959, Mr Anthony Barber, the Economic Secretary of the Treasury, asserted that 'if a full inventory could now be made of all United Kingdom assets and liabilities, I have no doubt that we should be seen to be a creditor nation'. In spite of recent foreign bids, the overall position is evidently much stronger than some gloomy prophets would have us believe.

The whole problem of foreign bids must be seen in perspective. The following points may help to redress the balance:

(1) Europe's population and aggregate national product exceed those of the United States.

(2) The American share in new investment in the major European countries is surprisingly small.[1]

[1] See estimates for 1966. *The Economist*, December 17th, 1966.

(3) The stock of European investment in the United States is in fact larger than that of the United States in Europe. The flow of American capital is exactly the same phenomenon – in reverse as it were – as the flow in earlier decades of European investment to the United States. In those days the American market was the chief area of growth and thus the magnet for capital; nowadays it is the growth prospects in Europe that provide the attraction.[1]

The real difference is in the form of the investment. The United States has gone in more for direct investment. Over 90 per cent of the net private United States capital outflow goes in this form – that is into companies controlled from America – whereas less than 20 per cent of Europe's investment in the United States was direct. European investors preferred to put their money into marketable American securities.

Moreover, the Americans have been far more selective than were their European counterparts. In the three biggest European markets, West Germany, Britain and France, 40 per cent of American direct investment is accounted for by the three firms – Esso, General Motors, and Ford. In all Western Europe, twenty firms account for two-thirds of American investment. Concentration upon the newer technologies means that in computers and carbon black, American companies often hold a dominating position in the major European countries.

Having regard to the level of merger activity in the U.S.A. in recent years it is perhaps rather surprising that foreign companies have been far less active in the British merger market than one might have expected. The U.K.-based foreign-owned companies seem generally to have concerned themselves with internal expansion; they are strongly represented in the motor vehicles and tyres, petroleum, electronic products (of which office equipment forms an important part), agricultural machinery and pharmaceutical industries as the following table shows.

Some of these companies could well be described as multinational.

Example 1

Rootes – Chrysler

In January 1967, the Chrysler Corporation undertook to inject further funds into Rootes Motors Ltd amounting to £20 million in all, thereby acquiring control of Rootes.[2]

Prior to this, Chrysler had first taken a share interest in Rootes in 1964 and acquired further shares later on when their Dodge truck interests in Great Britain were sold in exchange for shares. The

[1] *Transatlantic Investment*, by Christopher Layton, published by Atlantic Institute, May 1966.
[2] Since renamed Chrysler U.K. Ltd.

NET ASSETS OF SOME OF THE LARGEST U.K.-BASED, FOREIGN-OWNED
MANUFACTURING COMPANIES 1957 AND 1968

Company	Parent Country	Business	Net assets 1957 £m	1968 £m
Esso Petroleum	U.S.A.	Petroleum	116	257
Ford Motor Co	U.S.A.	Motor vehicles	82	240
Vauxhall Motor	U.S.A.	,, ,,	55	120
American Tobacco	U.S.A.	Cigarettes	41	114
Philips	Holland	Electrical	24	85
I.B.M. U.K. Holdings	U.S.A.	Office equipment	N/A	79
Standard Telephone	U.S.A.	Telecommunications	17	74
Chrysler	U.S.A.	Motor vehicles	21	60
Mobil Oil	U.S.A.	Petroleum	26	58
Massey-Ferguson	Canada	Agricultural machinery	5	56
Nestlé	Switzerland	Food	12	48
Alcan Industries	Canada	Aluminium	N/A	45
H. J. Heinz	U.S.A.	Food	14	41
Goodyear	U.S.A.	Tyres	15	38
National Cash Register Co	U.S.A.	Office equipment	N/A	31
Caterpillar Tractor	U.S.A.	Heavy duty tractors	N/A	29
I.B.A.[1]	Switzerland	Pharmaceuticals	N/A	28
Honeywell Controls	U.S.A.	Electronics	N/A	28
Geigy (U.K.)[1]	Switzerland	Pharmaceuticals	N/A	27
Burroughs Corporation	U.S.A.	Office equipment	5	25
Pirelli-General	Italy	Electrical cable	N/A	25

Source: *A Survey of Mergers*, 1958–68. H.M.S.O., 1970.

position then was that Rootes had £1·4 million in voting ordinary shares, the majority owned by the Rootes family and 45 per cent by Chrysler, and £6·66 million in non-voting 'A' ordinary shares – the latter two-thirds owned by Chrysler.

The new arrangement was put into effect by a rights issue at par of 50,407,597 new preferred ordinary shares of 20p each, carrying one vote per share, to holders of the ordinary and 'A' ordinary shares on the register at the close of business on January 24th, 1967, on the basis of five preferred ordinary shares for every four ordinary of 'A' ordinary shares held. The issue was underwritten without commission by Chrysler, who, on taking up their entitlement under the rights issue gained voting control of Rootes (the major part of the Rootes family interests did not take up their rights).

In addition to the above, Chrysler agreed to subscribe up to £10 million 8 per cent unsecured loan stock at par. At the same time, the Industrial Reorganization Corporation put up £3 million by acquiring 15 per cent of both the new rights and loan issue, I.R.C. having the right on January 1st, 1972, to call upon Chrysler to buy back these securities at par with dividends and interest accrued. In

[1] These two companies merged in 1970.

the meantime, I.R.C. has the right to nominate a director to the Rootes board. The necessary Treasury consent under the Exchange Control Act 1947 was given subject to certain undertakings by Chrysler, viz.:

(a) maintenance of a majority of British directors on the board of Rootes;

(b) exchange of directors with Chrysler International S.A. and Simca S.A.;

(c) confirmation of Rootes' expansion and development plans, particularly at Linwood in Scotland;

(d) expansion of exports to all practicable markets.

In the light of the heavy trading losses incurred by Rootes in recent years and the urgent need for fresh working capital, those terms were, perhaps, the best that could be expected in the circumstances.

Example 2
Texas Co – The Trinidad Oil Co
The offer made by the Texas Co to purchase the entire issued ordinary stock of the Trinidad Oil Co produced one of the biggest take-over bids in British financial history. The price offered was £4·01 for each 25p stock unit,[1] of which 15,738,740 were in issue, equivalent to a sum of £63·2 million for the entire holding. The offer was subject among other things to any necessary consents being obtained from Governments or other official agencies. The Texas Co also indicated that, if control of the Trinidad Oil Co was acquired, they would wish to transfer its domicile from the United Kingdom.

The Treasury was informed by representatives of the Trinidad Oil Co on June 5th, 1956, that the Texas Co had made a conditional offer to purchase the whole undertaking. The offer was made public on the following day.

Although Trinidad Oil Co had paid a tax-free dividend of 21⅔ per cent in respect of 1954–55, the dividend yield alone could not be said to justify a doubling of the market price of the shares. For the year ended June 30th, 1955, there was a group net profit of £2,312,682 after providing £1,849,448 for depreciation, £2,480,439 for taxation and £42,459 for contingencies; of the group net profit the parent company's share was £1,937,559; of this dividends absorbed £710,429 and £1 million was placed to reserve. Nor did the balance sheet enlighten the situation. The parent company's current assets stood at £10,793,735 and its interests in subsidiaries and investments at £8,841,437. Liabilities were £7,283,255 and reserves £12,561,270.

[1] Prior to the bid, the 25p stock units had stood in the market at approximately £2 per unit.

The reasons for the doubled valuation placed upon the company's stock by the American firm must, therefore, be sought in other directions.

But, first, one must delve a little deeper into the status and operations of the Trinidad Oil Co. This company directly controlled some 135,000 acres in Trinidad. From these and from its share of joint venture holdings, it produced about 1,150,000 tons of crude oil a year (in 1955, world crude oil production totalled about 707 million tons). In addition to being the largest oil producing and refining company in Trinidad, the company had a number of subsidiary and affiliated interests which mainly comprised:

(1) Regent Oil Co Ltd – marketing in the United Kingdom and Eire, owned jointly by the Trinidad Oil Co and California Texas Corporation (CALTEX). The latter comprises the Texas Co jointly with the Standard Oil Co of California.

(2) Regent Refining (Canada) Ltd – an 89 per cent subsidiary, with a substantial refining and marketing business and some unproven acreage.

(3) Trinidad Northern Areas Ltd – owned as to one-third each by Trinidad Oil, Shell and D'Arcy Exploration Co, then in course of developing the marine oil areas of Trinidad.

The company's operations were of great importance to the economy of Trinidad, being responsible for about a third of the island's crude oil production and about two-thirds of the $5\frac{1}{2}$ million tons treated in the refineries there. Furthermore, in 1955, the company provided by way of royalties, income tax, etc., about 19 per cent of the Trinidad Government's total revenue and about half of the Revenue provided by the oil industry s aa whole. The company had about 8,000 people on its payroll, again representing about half of the total number of persons employed in the oil industry as a whole and as much as 3·5 per cent of all persons employed in Trinidad. What, then, gave rise to a bid for a company of such proportions?

The 'blunt truth' according to the chairman, Mr Simon Vos, was that the company could no longer afford to stay in the hunt with the major oil companies owing to a shortage of capital. The oil business, with its rapidly changing character, needs tremendous capital resources to meet the ever-growing necessity to install new facilities to acquire a volume of outlet for the vast quantities of crude oil available in the world, particularly in the Middle East.

So far as Trinidad Oil was concerned, the fundamental weakness was that it had no cheap source of crude Middle East oil to support its business, although its main market (the United Kingdom) was almost wholly based on Middle East crude. Trinidad Oil, therefore, found itself at a considerable disadvantage, not only with its competitors, but also in maintaining its position with its partner, Caltex.

Another factor was that Trinidad Oil's crude oil production in Trinidad represented less than one-third of its refinery capacity, which refinery must be of sufficient minimum size to compete with those elsewhere in the Caribbean area. While the company had managed to secure the best possible terms for buying the balance of its crude requirements, it nevertheless remained highly vulnerable. Moreover, it was known that Middle East production was being obtained at a cost of around 35 United States cents a barrel – just less than one-third of the cost of Trinidad Oil's own production in Trinidad.

Then the advent of refineries here in recent years placed the Regent Oil Co Ltd at a serious disadvantage as compared with its competitors. So much so that Caltex had decided to erect a large refinery in the United Kingdom at the earliest possible moment. Quite apart from the lack of crude resources, the very magnitude of the investment (of the order of £25 million) precluded Trinidad Oil from participating in the project with its partner, Caltex, and so weakened its standing in the partnership.

At the same time, competition in world markets in general, and in the United Kingdom in particular, had reduced Trinidad Oil's revenue to a margin insufficient to allow it to finance any material portion of its requirements from revenue. Furthermore, the large sums required for putting down facilities in connection with the distribution of fuel oil and entry into the civil aviation business as well as the oil resources to back them, ran into figures far beyond the reach of a company like Trinidad Oil. Investment on such a massive scale was thought to be unjustified since the margin of profit on marketing oil did not permit an adequate return on the capital involved.

In the light of all these drawbacks, it was finally decided to seek a solution through an arrangement with the partners, the Texas Co. And the result was the bid already mentioned.

On June 14th, 1956, the Chancellor of the Exchequer made a statement in the House of Commons in which he said that Her Majesty's Government had decided that they were in principle willing to give permission for this transaction, subject to the ordinary law, both in the United Kingdom and in Trinidad, being complied with, but more particularly subject to two specific conditions and six undertakings. At the same time, a White Paper[1] was laid before Parliament setting out the factual basis on which the Government's decision had been reached.

[1] Cmd 9790.

Two essential legal formalities remained to be settled. First, under the Exchange Control Act 1947, sections 9 and 30, Treasury permission is required for the transfer of any securities by United Kingdom residents to persons resident outside the Sterling Area and to any action whereby a company controlled by United Kingdom residents passes out of such control.

Secondly, without Treasury consent, it is unlawful for a body corporate resident in the United Kingdom to cease to be so resident, or for the trade or business of a body corporate so resident to be transferred to a person not so resident (Income Tax Act 1952, section 468). In considering applications for transfer of residence, the practice is to weigh the prospective loss of revenue together with the other factors in the case. As already stated, the Texas Co fully intended to transfer the residence of the Trinidad Oil Co from the United Kingdom, if the bid was accepted. And in due course this was done.

An interesting postscript to this take-over bid came nearly ten months later, when *The Times* reported the hearing of a case brought by a shareholder,[1] challenging the Texas bid for Trinidad Oil. The case is reported as follows:

Chancery Division

In re TRINIDAD OIL CO LTD

Before Mr Justice Wynn-Parry

His lordship dismissed this summons by Colonel William Henry Gardiner, holder of twenty 5s shares in Trinidad Oil Co Ltd, asking for an order under section 209 (1) of the Companies Act 1948, declaring that the Texas Company of East 42nd Street, New York, United States, was neither entitled nor bound to acquire the ordinary stock units held by him in the Trinidad Oil Co Ltd, on the terms of an offer made on June 18th, 1956, notwithstanding that such an offer had been approved by holders of not less than nine-tenths in value of such stock units.

Mr Justice Wynn-Parry, giving judgment, said that the evidence disclosed that either within the time limited by the offer or after its expiry stockholders holding approximately 99·5 per cent of the issued ordinary stock had voluntarily accepted the offer, and the remainder had had their stock acquired under the section without making any objection. It had been pointed out by this Court again and again that, in the case of schemes of arrangement or schemes under section 209, prima facie the best judges of the scheme were the shareholders themselves. Stockholders who saw fit to accept the scheme included a number of well-known insurance companies, and that fact must have some influence with the Court on such an application, because while great care had to be taken to see that justice was done to the applicant, it was also very necessary that attention should be paid to views of the majority of the shareholders. To leave outstanding such a small number of shares would be most inconvenient from the point of view of the Texas Company.

[1] April 13th, 1957.

That was not of itself a decisive ground, although it was a circumstance which the Court ought, and indeed had, to take into consideration.

But matters went much further, and the basis on which the scheme put forward by the Texas Company had been accepted was to be found in a passage of the speech of Mr Macmillan, when he was Chancellor of the Exchequer, in a debate in the House of Commons on June 20th, 1956, when he said: 'Seriously . . . what is it proposed to do if we refuse permission for this transaction? The Trinidad Oil Co could not, I think, raise the money on the market. It has not the resources, and could not command the resources it needs. . . .' That passage was redolent of common sense having regard to the position in which the Trinidad Oil Co found itself. When the circumstance was considered, and the high price offered by the Texas Company, and the fact that (as was necessary in the circumstance) the making and carrying through of the transaction had been authorized by Her Majesty's Government in the interests both of the country and the stockholders, and the fact that it had been accepted voluntarily by an overwhelming majority of the shareholders, it appeared to him (his lordship) that this summons could not succeed. He took the positive view and thought that he should say so, that this offer was eminently a fair one.

CHAPTER XII

RECONSTRUCTIONS

The tangled undergrowth of financial jargon so seldom has any exact legal meaning that one must set about closely defining the conventional phrases used right at the beginning so as to avoid any misunderstanding. The expression 'reconstruction' is employed here to denote those types of exceptional change which are often the prelude to a merger. In general the expression 'reorganization' or 'scheme of arrangement' is frequently employed when only one company is involved and the rights of its members, and, sometimes of its general creditors, too, are varied – the latter expression being more commonly used when creditors' rights are affected. At this point it must be made clear that changes commonly known as 'capital reorganization schemes' or 'rearrangement of capital schemes', which are usually far more limited in scope than formal reconstructions, are treated separately in Chapter XIII.

Capital reduction schemes also fall outside the ambit of reconstructions as defined above. We are left, therefore, with two distinct types of reconstruction which can be resorted to when the circumstances demand radical treatment. Such schemes can be initiated under two headings:

(*a*) schemes of arrangement (under sections 206–208, Companies Act 1948); or

(*b*) reconstructions (under section 287, Companies Act 1948).

It is probably true to say that more reconstruction schemes are borne out of adversity than otherwise. The primary cause is usually a maladjustment of capital related to earnings and assets. Either some of the capital has been absorbed by trading losses or the original capital structure has proved to be inflated to such an extent that normal earnings fail to yield a reasonable return on the amount issued. The reconstructions inevitably involve an ascertainment of the capital lost, or not represented by available assets, followed by a scheme which attempts to spread the loss fairly on the owners of the capital. A new issue is not necessarily involved, although a company in need of a 'capital spring-cleaning' may also be in need of new capital in order to make a fresh start, and the reconstruction may be delayed until the decline in assets and earning power has levelled off and the business has established itself on a firm footing again, thereby enabling lost capital to be determined with some degree of accuracy. Once this situation has been resolved, the time is ripe for fresh investment. The terms for the issue of new capital may be arranged conditionally on the reconstruction being approved by the present holders and by the Court. Alternatively, the method most appropriate may require liquidation and refloatation, the present holders being offered a reduced stake in the new company.

Attention must now be turned to the detailed procedure associated with the two main methods mentioned above and the comparative advantages displayed by each.

(a) SECTIONS 206–208

These sections apply to any company liable to be wound up under the Companies Act 1948, and to any compromise or arrangement between a company and its members or any class of them. It has been established that the 'compromises and arrangements' dealt with by these sections are exceptionally wide in content, ranging from a simple composition or moratorium to a merger of companies, with a complete reorganization of their share and loan capital. The rights of debenture-holders and other creditors may be modified, as may those of shareholders even though embodied in the memorandum and therein expressly referred to an unalterable and their liability may be increased as well.

On the other hand, the scheme cannot authorize something contrary to general law (which has been held to include the conversion of issued shares into redeemable preference shares since section 58 merely authorizes new issues of shares)[1] or wholly *ultra vires* the company, and that if capital has to be reduced the formalities of sections 66–71 must, perforce, be complied with.

It is not even necessary for the company to go into liquidation in order to avail itself of sections 206–208. If, however, it is already in liquidation it has the choice of proceeding under these sections or relying on certain additional powers of compromising claims, viz. under sections 245, 303 and 315. Furthermore, a company which is about to be or is in the course of winding-up may enter into arrangements with its creditors which will be similarly binding on the company, but only if sanctioned by an extraordinary resolution, and on the creditors side if acceded to by three-fourths in number and value. Since it is necessary to obtain the consent of three-fourths in value of *all* creditors, and not merely of those present and voting *at* a meeting, the latter provision is difficult to comply with, so procedure under sections 206–208 is almost invariably followed instead.

If, as is often the case, the scheme under section 206 involves the transfer of the company's undertaking to another company, the Court is empowered to make orders under section 208 for transfer of all the company's assets and liabilities and for its dissolution.

[1] *Re St James's Court Estates* ([1944] Ch. 6).

This opens up a convenient path by which solvent firms can be merged in addition to the reconstruction of companies in desperate financial straits. Thus, the scheme may provide for the formation of a new company to take over the undertaking of the old (the acquiring company might, however, just as easily be an existing company) or on a merger to acquire the undertakings of a number of companies, the members and creditors of which accept shares or debentures in the new company in substitution for their former claims.[1] All consequential orders for completing the transaction can then be made by the Court, subject to two restrictions. First, section 208 applies only when *all* the companies concerned are registered companies, and, secondly, it does not permit contracts of a personal nature to be transferred, which infers that arrangement will have to be made to secure a voluntary novation of contracts of service and such-like. If the reconstruction merely applies to members, meetings of creditors will not be needed, even so the Court will not make orders under section 208 without making sure that the creditors are protected.

Another problem is the difficulty of securing the same unanimity of view among trade and other unsecured creditors as prevails between shareholders and debenture-holders. Indeed, the problem is made no easier through the need to hold separate meetings of the various classes of creditors, and it may not always be easy to determine whether all unsecured creditors can be treated as a single class, or whether their rights are so diverse as to make it essential to divide them into separate class compartments. For these reasons it is quite usual for the scheme to include provision for payment in full of unsecured creditors, thus dispensing altogether with the need for their consent, in spite of the fact that there may have been a variation of the debenture-holders' rights. As Professor Gower pertinently observes on this point: 'This, of course, is an extreme illustration of the extent to which debenture-holders are equated with share holders in economic reality notwithstanding their legal position as secured creditors.'[2]

The usual procedure under section 206 is for application to be made to the Court by the company although it can be done by the liquidator, a creditor, or member. The Court then directs meetings to be convened of the classes concerned and, under section 207, the notice convening the meetings must be accompanied by a circular explaining the scheme, and disclosing any material interests of the directors and of the trustees for debenture-holders. If at a meeting of each class a majority in number representing three-fourths in

---

[1] Dissentient shareholders may be dealt with under the procedure outlined in Chapter VIII.

[2] *Modern Company Law*, second edition, page 556.

value of those present and voting in person or by proxy approve the scheme, then, if subsequently sanctioned by the Court, it becomes binding on all once an office copy of the Court order has been delivered to the Registrar.

(b) RECONSTRUCTIONS UNDER SECTION 287

In general, this section is narrower in its application than the previous method examined. Against that, the fact that application to the Court is avoided may make it cheaper and more convenient, especially in straightforward mergers when a new company can be formed to take over the undertakings of the various companies to be merged. But it is still subject to the serious drawback that dissenting shareholders can insist upon being paid out.

The procedure here is for the company to resolve upon a voluntary winding-up, and by special resolution, to authorize the liquidator to sell to another company (not necessarily one newly formed, though normally that is the case) receiving in payment shares or debentures of that company for distribution *in specie* among the members of the company now in process of liquidation. Such an arrangement is binding on the members of the transferor company, but any of them not voting in favour of the special resolution may within seven days express his dissent in writing to the liquidator and require him either to refrain from carrying the resolution into effect or to purchase his interest at a price to be determined by agreement or arbitration.

At the same time it is questionable whether the protection afforded of dissentients under section 287 is of much value. Certainly, the section provides that their interests shall be purchased at a price to be determined by arbitration in default of agreement. The intention is clear enough. The shareholder is meant to receive what he would have been entitled to had liquidation proceeded in the usual manner by way of actual realization of assets. But in practice it is extremely difficult *to prove* just what he is entitled to, because so many obstacles are put in his way. It has been held, for instance, that he is not entitled to examine the books or the directors in order to obtain evidence for his purpose. Apart from nuisance value – which obviously depends upon active support from his co-dissentients – he is in an unenviable position. On the other hand, of course, a host of dissentients can be a real source of embarrassment to the liquidator particularly if there is not a ready market for the new shares.

Another pitfall can occur by reason of those members, who, without formally dissenting, fail positively to agree to take up their shares in the new company, for they cannot be compelled to do so and the new company is not entitled to place them on the register as members without their agreement. Where new shares are partly paid it is a wise precaution to have them underwritten, otherwise those shareholders who have not signified their wishes, one way or the other, could defeat the scheme just as effectively as the more vocal dissentients. Consequently, the liquidator may have to cope with three groups of shareholders:

(1) Those who accept the new shares unreservedly. These cause no difficulty at all and the shares will normally be allotted to them direct.

(2) Those who actively dissent. These will have to be bought out for cash (unless the scheme is withdrawn completely), and the liquidator must keep sufficient assets in hand to enable them to be paid off.

(3) Those who 'sit on the fence'. It is normally provided that shares to which they are entitled shall be sold by the liquidator and the proceeds divided among them. The scheme may, however, provide that they shall forfeit all rights unless they accept the new shares within a fixed period of time.

The great danger looming up in all these cases, however, is that relief from stamp duty[1] may be lost simply through sheer dilatoriness on the part of the shareholders.

In comparing the above procedure with that outlined under sections 206–208, the following differences of approach may be noted:

(a) Only *registered* companies can take advantage of section 287, since it is expressly confined to cases of voluntary liquidation (and an unregistered company can only be wound up compulsorily). Against that, it is expressly provided that the company to whom the undertaking is to be transferred need not be a company within the meaning of the Act.

(b) There can be no variation of creditors' rights. Creditors are still entitled to prove in the liquidation of the old company and the liquidator must ensure that claims are met to the extent of the company's assets and cannot rely upon any indemnity given by the acquiring company. The sale of the undertaking will, however, be binding on the creditors who will have to look to the securities obtained in substitution for the former assets. Since this could affect them adversely, especially if the securities happened to consist of unquoted shares, it is provided that if an order is made within a year for the winding-up of the old company, compulsorily or under supervision as the case may be, the special resolution shall not be valid unless sanctioned by the Court.

(c) The extent to which there can be a variation of the rights of

[1] See Chapter IV.

members is also limited. The shares in the new company must be distributed among the members of the old company strictly in accordance with their class rights on a winding-up. Yet the shares in the new company could be very different from those in the old (partly paid, for example, so as to leave the way open for raising new capital). The section is, therefore, very difficult to apply unless all the shares in the old company happen to have equal rights on a winding-up or unless all those with special rights expressly agree or failing that, dissent and elect to be paid out.

(d) The transferor company must be put into liquidation, and normal liquidation procedure is followed with the exception that assenting members are paid out in the shares of the acquiring company instead of in cash.

Unlike section 208, there is no procedure for dispensing with formal assignments of property or of winding up.

(e) Shareholders cannot be forced to²accept new shares. Instead, they have the option of either dissenting as a body thus forcing the liquidator to abandon the whole scheme, or of being paid out with due regard to their previous rights.

(f) On the other hand, the scheme can be implemented without the need for application to the Court for confirmation. It is, therefore, the only method of reconstruction which avoids application to the Court and, furthermore, does not afford dissentients a special statutory right to apply to the Court.

The accountant's task

The first practical question claiming the accountant's attention is the timing of the reconstruction. If there is a series of past losses, it is pointless to attempt a reconstruction until the tide has turned. On the other hand, if there has been a record of profits, though on too small a scale to cover dividends and reasonable transfers to reserve, the reconstruction can be put in hand at once. In very general terms, the reconstruction may take place whenever earnings are high enough to warrant the resumption of dividends though based on a more realistic capital structure.

In preparing the ground, the accountant will be asked to assemble the data, viz. statements of maintainable revenue, and of assets and liabilities valued in relation to the estimated profits.

The maintainable revenue computations may be extracted on the assumption that recent trading conditions are fully representative of future trading prospects. The profits computation will include revised provision for depreciation on the basis of revalued assets even where these are materially less than the sums allowed for taxation. While the reconstruction may justify an abnormally low depreciation provision, it would be no more than prudent to transfer additional sums to a fixed assets replacement reserve before arriving at the profits freely available for distribution, otherwise the shareholders' sights may be set too high. This point is of some importance as the directors in commending the scheme to the proprietors may give some indication of the dividend on the equity capital which, based on current trading experience, they hope to pay for a period following reconstruction.

In framing the assets and liabilities valuation, it is imperative for the accountant to have the professional support of qualified valuers. Where a writing-down of fixed assets to the recommended levels still leaves a net asset position which is inadequately covered by maintainable revenue, further drastic reduction may be accepted on the advice of the accountant. A writing-down should be regarded as a 'once-for-all' occurrence in every respect.

This question, however, cannot be isolated altogether from the peculiarities of the capital structure. If the existing structure contains preference and ordinary capital, both calling for some measure of reduction, the total amount to be written off the fixed assets may be influenced, within limits, by the equitable rights, present and future of the two classes of shareholders. If there is only one class of capital, the precise amount of the writing-down is of less importance since an under- or over-valuation of assets will affect all shareholders equally.

The final step in preparing the reconstruction scheme is the manner of spreading the total reduction. Here the accountant may be called upon to tabulate appropriations of profits at various levels for several possible schemes of reconstruction. These tables can be most rewarding in demonstrating the comparative result of the different proposals at varying levels of prosperity.

Where preference capital suffers some reduction, either in the annual rate of interest or in the nominal value of the capital, some recompense by way of a share in the equity is now a well-established principle, so as to give them a small stake in future profits, should events turn out unexpectedly favourable. In general, reconstruction schemes are far less in evidence these days than they were about the time of the economic depression in the early 1930s. Then, the word 'reconstruction' was used in a much wider context, based initially on a capital reduction scheme and often followed up by some kind of merger designed to eliminate redundant capacity. Nowadays a 'reconstruction' seldom goes much further than an internal re-arrangement of capital for one reason or another.

CHAPTER XIII

THE CAPITAL STRUCTURE

Looking back over the hundred years or so during which limited liability companies have been in existence, it is possible to trace periods in which definite changes occured in the type or style of the capital raised. In fact, three main phases can be identified.

In the very early stages of limited company life, the members were still imbued with partnership ideas and hence it was common to find shares with a large nominal value, partly paid, and all of one class. This, however, was found to be attractive only to the investor who was ready to take an active interest in the day-to-day affairs of the company. Once it became known that one of the great advantages of the limited liability company was that it enabled fresh capital to be obtained from those who were unconnected with the business beyond holding a financial stake therein, the way was clear for companies to adapt their capital structure accordingly. The capital was so arranged as to provide an appeal to this type of investor. From about 1880, therefore, it became fashionable to reduce the amount of the unpaid liability as well as the size of the nominal value. Furthermore, the advantages of a low-priced share which was easily marketable soon became apparent when it was realized that the small investor's pocket must also be tapped. This development quickly gave rise to an increase in the classes of security on offer. In particular, an effort was made to cater for those investors who were anxious to secure a steady return plus a greater measure of security than that conferred by ordinary shares. The obvious solution was to make use of the method, hitherto popularized by railway and other statutory companies, of issuing preference shares offering a fixed preferential dividend, with or without a corresponding right to preferential treatment as regards capital on a winding-up. Another leaf was also taken out of the statutory companies' book by issuing mortgage debentures, thus appealing to the more safety-inclined investors who, until now, had been content with Government securities. Among the latter type of investor were to be found many who welcomed the opportunity of getting a higher return of their savings without losing much by way of security. The popularity of debentures was given a fillip when the legality of the floating charge was finally established in 1870.

All this time the number of share classes was also being increased. In the first place, the rise of the professional company promoter led to the practice of creating a special class of founders' or deferred shares which the promoters usually retained partly by way of remuneration for their services and partly as an act of good faith – a gesture of continued confidence in their own flotations. These shares were of low nominal value in most instances but conferred substantial participating rights in profits after the other shareholders had received a stated return. Again, the need to raise further capital led, just as it had done in the case of statutory companies, to the issue of pre-preference shares on terms which were even more attractive than those obtainable on the existing shares. Another factor, too, which goes a long way to explain the proliferation of classes, is the case with which a small minority – often the original proprietors of a business – could retain voting control of the company despite the fact that their financial interests were far less than those of the public. The second phase is, therefore, exemplified by highly complicated capital structures comprising both shares and debentures of many different types and classes.

The third phase which dates from about 1920, and is still in progress, has seen a distinct trend towards simplification. Deferred and founders' shares are on their way out while the same may be said of partly-paid shares. Lately, even the joint-stock banks and finance houses have taken steps to reorganize their out-of-date capital structures by eliminating the uncalled liability. Moreover, companies with several classes of preference and pre-preference shares in issue have proved unpopular with investors and managements alike. The former, particularly, suffer from loss of purchasing power, value during an inflationary period, if they are tied to a fixed interest stock. Nowadays, therefore, it is rather unusual to find a public company with more than one, and at the most two, of each of the primary classifications of debentures, preference shares and ordinary shares. In general, the same applies in even greater degree to private companies which often make do with a single class of capital. The other main tendency which was observed in the second phase – smaller nominal values – continues to operate, perhaps, with greater emphasis. Consequently, shares today seldom go above a £1 denomination and frequently fall as low as 5p.

During this last phase, however, two special factors have been instrumental in shaping the modern capital structure. First, the incidence of taxation. Post-war taxation policy veered towards the imposition of a heavy tax on distributed profits while undistributed profits were let off comparatively lightly (that is so far as profits tax is concerned). Companies can scarcely withhold payment of their preference dividends if they have earned sufficient distributable profits during the year. If they do pay the preference dividend, increased liability to profits tax arose and the burden of it fell paradoxically enough upon the ordinary shareholders. For this reason alone, new issues of preference shares have been unpopular with companies and their ordinary shareholders. Hence, the increased popularity of debentures, for the simple reason that debenture interest is an allowable expense for profits tax purposes (except under certain circumstances in a director-controlled company).

At long last, however, Mr Heathcoat-Amory, in introducing the Budget of 1958, bowed to the weight of opinion by removing the tax distinction between distributed and undistributed profits. As from April 1st, 1958, the two rates were replaced by a single rate of 10 per cent levied on the whole of a company's profits (though the existing provisions for exemptions and abatements to companies with small incomes continue). The general effect was that companies that had distributed their earnings cautiously in the past and so leaned more towards a policy of placing a very high proportion of profits to reserves paid more profits tax; those that have pursued an open-handed dividend policy, distributing a high proportion of their earnings, paid less. On the face of it, a result which, perhaps, runs counter to all the past exhortations for thrift. Yet the Royal Commission on Taxation forewarned us of this reaction in stating:

'It is always possible to label as discriminatory a process which merely aims at restoring uniformity through the removal of a discrimination imposed at some earlier date.'[1]

As we have seen, there were a number of specific defects in the old differential system. In the first place it made it more difficult to raise new capital. It gave an artificial advantage to the firm which could plough back, as against the expanding firm which needed new money, because new money cannot be raised without paying or promising to pay a fair return on the money. It inhibited the transfer of capital back to shareholders and through them to new uses. It tempted firms to build up cash balances they did not need and even to embark upon physical investments which were wasteful in character.

The old tax was also most unfair as between different companies. It was a far heavier burden on companies with preference than with loan capital. Two companies with the same total capital, the same ordinary dividend and the same profits could pay very different amounts. It encouraged too great a reliance on loan financing, and the removal of the differential has effectively cut by two-thirds the incentive to make loan rather than share issues. The old tax also inhibited joint ventures, as the dividends of a jointly owned subsidiary were liable to distributed profits tax even though the money never reached the general public at all. The implementation of the Royal Commission's recommendation, therefore, can only improve the efficiency of industrial financing. Once the defects in the old and

[1] Cmd 9474, pages 164–165.

unwieldy differential system were exposed, the case for its replacement by a single rate became overwhelming.

The form of new issues will continue to be partly determined by a company's capital structure and partly by what sort of stock investors are willing to buy at the time.

The type of investor has changed since pre-war days, and with this change have come different requirements. The wealthy personal investor of pre-war days who was prepared to take risks has largely given way to the institutional investor – assurance and insurance companies, finance companies, investment trusts, pension funds, unit trusts, etc. – all of whom act as collecting centres for the fragmentary savings of a multitude of people. Not surprisingly, these institutional investors cannot indulge in risk-taking to anything like the same degree as the former personal investors whose place they have now taken. The security of the funds entrusted to them is paramount. Consequently, companies seeking fresh capital pay great attention to their needs, which, more often than not, are centred upon debentures (though not exclusively, for institutions are prepared to invest in the ordinary shares of a well-established public company with a first-class record).

The manner in which capital is raised by a limited company is, therefore, largely determined by the advice tendered by the market. In general, however, the issue will take the form of one or more of the following types of permanent capital:

(*a*) preference shares;

(*b*) ordinary shares;

(*c*) debenture or loans.

In addition, the effective use of capital may also be obtained by bank overdraft, a loan from the Finance Corporation for Industry Ltd or the Industrial and Commercial Finance Corporation Ltd, and by credit extended by trade creditors, hire-purchase finance houses, etc. These methods are essentially short-term in character, however, and cannot be considered as part and parcel of the permanent capital structure. Needless to say, the method of capitalization to be adopted in any particular case can only be determined after full consideration of the special requirements and circumstances of the case. There is no such thing as a formula for determining the capital structure. Thus, it may sometimes be intended that the whole of the capital shall be held only by members of a family or a small group of friends or business associates, and the rights attaching thereto may be simply a matter of mutual agreement.

In other cases, it may be possible to obtain the use of additional capital by inviting the public to subscribe thereto. In these circumstances, careful consideration will be devoted to:

(i) the past record of the business, and its future prospects as exhibited by the state of the order books;

(ii) the state of the capital market, the prevailing yield on similar classes of investment, and the current demand for and supply of capital;

(iii) having regard to (i) and (ii), the type of offer which is most likely to meet with a successful response from the public.

Preference shares

By issuing preference shares in addition to ordinary shares, capital is raised at a fixed rate of interest, thus allowing all surplus profit to go to the ordinary shareholder. In other words, use of additional money is obtained without the necessity of extending to the subscribers the right to participate in the future prosperity of the company.

An additional advantage may be obtained, if desired, by issuing to the vendors both ordinary and preference shares in satisfaction of the purchase price of the business acquired. By so doing the vendors are placed in possession of shares (the preference shares) which they can, if they so desire, realize for cash, without disturbing their control of the company. The same result would, however, be attained by paying part of the purchase consideration in cash, leaving the vendors to subscribe in cash for some of the preference shares should they so desire.

In some cases, in order to make the shares more attractive to the public, participating preference shares are issued which carry, in addition to a fixed rate of dividend, the right to some further participation in profits, after a specified rate of dividend has been paid upon the ordinary shares. The right to participate in surplus profits may be limited to a certain percentage, or it may be unlimited.

Where, owing to increasing prosperity, a company accumulates surplus funds, considerable advantage would be conferred upon the ordinary shareholders by the repayment to the preference shareholders of the capital subscribed by them. This could not normally be done, however, except by way of a proper reduction of capital duly sanctioned by the Court. If, however, under powers in the articles, redeemable preference shares are issued, the company obtains the right to repay the preference share capital on, before, or after an agreed date, or at the option of the company, according to the terms of the issue. The temporary nature of such shares may, therefore, be of considerable value.

In accordance with the provisions of section 58, Companies Act 1948, redeemable preference shares can be redeemed either out of profits, or out of the proceeds of a fresh issue and, in the former case, require the establishment of a capital redemption reserve fund which is treated as it it were paid-up capital. On a redemption, therefore, there is no reduction of the capital yardstick. If the shares are redeemed out of the proceeds of a fresh issue, the capital raised on that issue will, of course, replace the capital redeemed. Alternatively, if they are redeemed out of profits, then, as already explained, an amount equivalent to the nominal amount of the shares so redeemed must be transferred to the capital redemption reserve fund which is then treated as equivalent to paid-up capital. The result is that although the shares disappear on redemption, the capital which they represent must be retained from an accounting point of view.

In passing, it may be mentioned that the precise rights attaching to preference shares must be defined in the memorandum or articles of the company, or in the prospectus of the issue.

In particular, it should be remembered that in the absence of express provisions in the articles, preference shares are:

(a) cumulative as to fixed dividend;

(b) not preferential as to repayment of capital in the event of winding-up of the company;

(c) not entitled to participate in any surplus assets, because, prima facie, the memorandum or articles contain their full rights (*Scottish Insurance Corporation Ltd v. Wilsons & Clyde Coal Co Ltd*). The onus of proof, that the rights specifically given to them are not exhaustive, is upon the preference shareholders (*The Isle of Thanet Electric Supply Co Ltd*).

Voting power

Some take-overs, notably the bids for Harrods, focused attention on the voting rights of preference shares and show that in certain cases preference shares can command a price far in excess of their intrinsic value. As a general rule preference holders have a vote only when their dividend is in arrear or when a resolution is submitted directly affecting their rights. But some shares carry the same votes as the equity capital and it is these shares that suddenly acquire an added value when a bid is made for the control of their company.

How substantial that extra value can be was illustrated by the bid for Harrods: House of Fraser's original proposal for Harrods' $7\frac{1}{2}$ per cent preference was £2 a share, whereas the market price prior to the announcement was only about £1·40.

Harrods was in a somewhat special position in that the total preference vote was equal to the total equity vote. Thus, in a take-over offer the preference ownership could be decisive. But Harrods is by no means unique. Indeed, with some companies the preference vote actually exceeds the equity vote. In normal times the price will continue to be determined largely by the course of other fixed interest or dividend securities. But in a bid situation their value will be just whatever a bidder is prepared to pay for their votes.

Ordinary shares

As the name implies, ordinary shares or 'equities' as they are sometimes called constitute the residuary class in which everything is vested after the special rights of other classes, if any, have been satisfied. They are the ultimate proprietors of the business and so bear the main weight of the business risks. Since they are bound to feel the effect of falling profits in lower dividends or the passing of the dividend altogether for a year or more. they may find recompense in the prospect of taking the lion's share of the profits in good years after the directors and managers have been remunerated. Moreover, in many cases, the control of the company is vested in the holders of the ordinary shares by means of the voting power attached to them, since preference shares invariably carry no votes unless their dividends are in arrear.

Even so, there are several subsidiary classifications or ordinary shares which are designated as 'preferred ordinary' (it is really just a matter of nomenclature whether they are called preference shares instead for the right of participation in income or capital, or for that matter in both, is identical whichever name applies), deferred, management, founders' and, in a rather restricted sense, employees' shares.[1]

The name only serves as a distinguishing mark or, perhaps, as a reminder of the origin.[2] Provided that the company's regulations are complied with, the company has complete freedom as to the creation of classes and as to the names it gives them, while the nature of the rights attaching to each class is a matter of construction of the terms of issue.

Other distinctions may be drawn between ordinary shares so named, ranking equally as regards participation in profits, by dividing them into separate classes with quite different voting rights. In this case a distinguishing label or prefix such as 'A', 'B' or 'C' will be attached to the ordinary shares. Indeed, in the past there have been very many issues of non-voting 'A' ordinary shares consideration in take-over bids. By this device control may be vested in a relatively small proportion of the equity, thereby calling attention to the divorce of ownership from control.

The voteless equity

The expression 'non-voting shares' is generally applied to a class of ordinary shares which carries the same risks and – with one

[1] For a full treatment of this special subject, see: *The Challenge of Employee Shareholding*, by Dr G. Copeman, Business Publications, 1958.
[2] Though the *voting* rights may vary.

exception – enjoys the same rights as the rest of the equity holders in any particular company. The exception being that the holders do not have the same right to vote, even in the circumstances which normally entitles a preference shareholder to vote, viz. when no dividend is paid. The number of these non-voting shares has grown steadily since the Second World War, partly through new introductions to the Stock Exchange, but mainly through free scrip issues of non-voting equity stock. In both cases the prime motive has generally been the retention of control by families or other small groups.[1] Although the subject has been discussed in a desultory and abstract way for some time, it is only in the last year or two that opinion in the City began to harden against the voteless equity. Institutional investors, who until things go wrong are generally the least vocal of all investors, led the way. Many spokesmen in the investment trust movement publicly expressed their disapproval of the voteless equity and some of the institutions, especially those in the insurance world, became so chary of equities of this kind as to refuse to buy them. This was reflected in a widening of prices between the voting and non-voting shares in many public companies.

There are two main objections to non-voting ordinary shares. In the first place they are equal in all other respects to voting shares but embody no advantage to offset their lack of votes. Secondly, it is generally accepted that those shareholders who carry the residual risk of profit and loss in a business should have the right to vote in matters affecting the conduct of the business. At the present time, over 100 public companies appear to have non-voting shares in their capital structure and some of the leading examples are given in the following table.

Company	Share unit £p	Non-voting capital £	Voting capital £	Proportion of non-voting to total ordinary capital %
British Electric Traction	25	6,680,016	790,752	89
Great Universal Stores..	25	38,315,219	1,360,513	97
Ropner Holdings ..	1·00	2,639,409	1,759,606	60
Sears Holdings	25	15,732,559	2,225,000	88

At length the Stock Exchange Council came out into the open with their considered views. In a formal statement issued to the Press on August 23rd, 1957, they made it clear that they did not 'look with favour' on the voteless equity share. They did not propose, however, to use the 'high-powered sanction' of refusing a quotation

[1] There is no guarantee, however, that such a family or group will continue to provide the necessary directorial skills and there is a risk that control may eventually pass to an irresponsible minority.

to non-voting shares, which would have had the effect of taking away from companies powers which they legally possess.

The Council went on to say that they had 'watched with attention the growth of the practice of issuing non-voting equity share capital', but they had taken such steps as they could to ensure that the public was not misled as to what they were buying or were being offered.

Even if the Council considered it possible to take some action, the statement added, there would be formidable difficulties. If the Stock Exchange required that in future applications all ordinary shares should have equal voting rights, it would necessarily result in the refusal of quotation in all cases of non-compliance. It would follow that where new issues were to be identical with, and indistinguishable from, existing ones, the quotation for the latter would have to be cancelled.

'This would inevitably result in denying the facilities of a free market to companies who have exercised their legal rights in creating non-voting shares and also to those shareholders who have preferred to buy non-voting shares because they are cheaper.

'The proper remedy against the issue of non-voting shares is an amendment of the Companies Act; but in the meantime no person or company is compelled to hold or buy or to subscribe for or underwrite non-voting shares, and if such attitude were consistently adopted the issue of non-voting shares would cease to be a practical proposition.'

Pressure of this kind has already begun to produce its result: a number of leading public companies have seen fit to enfranchise 'A' ordinary shareholders (House of Fraser, J. Lyons & Co, Marks & Spencer, Rank Organization among the major converts) but the procedure is not without its domestic complications where a price differential exists.

For instance, British Home Stores called meetings to effect their plans for consolidating the non-voting equity shares and ordinary stock into one class of capital.

'The directors consider that the existence of the non-voting "A" stock might be prejudicial to any raising of fresh capital for the development of the company's business. Accordingly, they are convinced that the interest of the company and of stockholders generally would be best served by the elimination of the "A" stock altogether. There has been since the issue of the "A" ordinary shares in 1955 a price difference on market quotation in favour of the ordinary units. The directors consider that it would be equitable for the ordinary stockholders to receive six new units for every 100 units held at the close of business on October 11th, in consideration of the extension of voting powers" to the "A" ordinary stock.'[1]

Even so, the widely held assumption that non-voting and voting shares would rate the same price in a take-over was rudely shattered

[1] *The Times*, October 12th, 1957.

in the terms of an offer by Ranks Ltd for shares of Energen Foods Ltd, reported in *The Financial Times*.[1] The terms were nine Ranks' 50p ordinary shares for every twenty Energen 10p voting – or non-voting 'A' ordinary. But holders of voting shares were given a 50p cash premium. This was equal to 36p for the voting ordinary against a market quotation of 30p. For the non-voting 'A' shares the terms equalled $33\frac{1}{2}$p against a quotation of 24p. So Ranks were offering only $2\frac{1}{2}$p more for the voting ordinary than for the 'A' ordinary, whereas the difference in the market between the prices of the two types of shares was 6p.

The precarious position in which non-voting shareholders can sometimes find themselves was demonstrated in the take-over bid made for Carreras by The Rembrandt Tobacco Co Ltd, a wholly owned subsidiary of Rembrandt Tobacco Corpn (South Africa).[2] The bid of £5·50 in cash for each Carreras share was confined to the 240,000 voting ordinary shares of £1 each (well over half of which was owned by the Baron family). The remainder of the ordinary capital – no less than £7,200,600, consisting of 57,604,800 'B' ordinary shares of $12\frac{1}{2}$p each – was voteless and its owners therefore had no say in the running of the company and received no bid. Thus control changed hands and Carreras was merged with another business without consulting the interests of the 'B' shareholders – who, as it happened, held the majority of the ordinary share capital.[3] As with other family businesses, the capital structure seems to have been adopted originally as a protective device against the possibility of absorption by some other group. No doubt all is plain sailing while the family control is enterprising and both earnings and dividends are on the increase, but the voteless shareholders are powerless to change the management when the business is on the decline. Moreover, the existence of voteless shares seldom prevents a bid being made; they merely expose the value placed upon the right to vote by a potential bidder. It may be argued that an investor who buys non-voting shares is fully aware of the risk he assumes. One wonders, however, whether the average investor is always conscious of the difference between voting and non-voting shares, especially when they are simply distinguished by the addition of an 'A' or 'B' to the class title. The disparity in price between voting and non-voting shares quoted on the Stock Exchange does suggest that while some investors prize the right to vote at all times, others are quite indifferent so long as their company prospers.

While nobody is compelled to *buy* non-voting shares in the

---

[1] March 12th, 1958.
[2] *The Economist*, November 8th, 1958.
[3] Since then, the 'B' ordinary shares have been given 1 vote per $12\frac{1}{2}$p share, the other $12\frac{1}{2}$p ordinaries are entitled to 4 votes per share.

market, those shareholders who are given non-voting ordinary shares as a result of a capitalization of reserves (bonus issue) have no option but to accept them. All too often, that it the channel by which many non-voting shares reach the market in the first place. Clearly the remedy rests with the corporate body venturesome enough to make an issue in this form.

Nevertheless, it seems probable that the issue of the non-voting equity will solve itself in time, simply because the institutions are nowadays called upon to provide the bulk of the new money needed by industry. Failure to meet the wishes of the institutions could have very serious implications for companies with non-voting shares that require fresh capital. Others disappear from the list of quoted 'A' shares through take-overs like F. W. Hampshire & Co (taken over by Reckitt Colman Holdings) and Yardleys (taken over by British-American Tobacco). Yet one is bound to recognize the fact that non-voting shares may have a special significance; in particular, companies where the main aim is to prevent foreign interests from obtaining control of the company.

The New York Stock Exchange has also been confronted with the same problem, and has taken active steps against the listing of shares which limit a stockholders right to vote. The board of governors recently ruled that the Exchange would refuse to list voting stock of a company if the right to vote was restricted by a voting trust, irrevocable proxy, or any similar arrangement to which the company or any of its officers was a party, either directly or indirectly.[1]

Shares of no par value

Almost all expert opinion supports the report of the Gedge Committee which was favourably inclined towards no par value shares when it reported in 1954. Shares of a fixed nominal value, the only kind permitted at present, are really an outdated legal fiction which not only confuses the small investor and the ordinary layman but occasionally causes the better informed to put the wrong construction on such things as bonus issues etc.

Given the necessary safeguards, there is every reason for allowing companies the freedom to resort to this form of capitalization. Incidentally, the existence of no par value shares would permit companies to raise risk capital at times of poor trading when their ordinary shares (under existing conditions) would stand way below par in the market.

The only real opposition to the introduction of no par value shares is likely to come from the trade unions on the grounds that this type of capital might be used to conceal the payment of high dividends. However, critics can always look at the total amount of

[1] *The Times*, October 23rd, 1957.

cash distributed in dividends instead of the amt
that objection is of little consequence.

However, no early moves in this direction are ex
Government, because the introduction of no par valt
involve many clauses and consequential amendments t
financial Acts.

Speaking on the second reading of the new Companie
House of Lords (Novmeber 1966), Lord Brown, Ministt
at the Board of Trade, explained that 'there is in the Gov\. _ient's
mind nothing in principle against this matter, but it has been delayed
for the purpose of simplicity'. And there, for the moment, the
matter rests.

Debentures
The relative advantages and disadvantages of an issue of debentures
may be summarized as follows:

Advantages
  (i) an issue of debentures is attractive to the public by reason of
      the security afforded;
 (ii) income from the debentures is payable to the holders even
      though no profits are made by the company;
(iii) from the viewpoint of the company the debentures represent
      temporary capital, and can be repaid when the company's
      financial position will allow, subject to the terms of issue;
 (iv) no voting rights are held by the debenture-holders, and there-
      fore, so long as their interest is duly paid and their security
      is not in jeopardy, they cannot in any way interfere with the
      management of the business. In law the debenture-holder is a
      creditor and entitled to all the remedies of a creditor to obtain
      payment of the sums due to him whether they be principal or
      interest;
  (v) a lower rate of interest will normally be expected by debenture-
      holders than by preference shareholders owing to the security
      given to the former;
 (vi) subject to any provisions to the contrary contained in the
      terms of issue, a company may, when it has surplus funds,
      purchase its own debentures in the open market and either
      hold them or cancel them. Such a procedure is not possible
      with shares;
(vii) debenture interest is an allowable expense for the purposes of
      corporation tax (and previously for profits tax), whereas the
      gross amount of preference and ordinary dividends has to be
      provided for.

.sadvantages which may arise from an issue of debentures

(i) interest thereon must be paid even though insufficient profits are earned;

(ii) in order to make the issue attractive the company should possess fixed assets of sufficient value which can be charged specifically in favour of the debenture-holders;

(iii) when debentures are redeemable, some provision for their redemption must be made. This provision would, normally, take the form of annual appropriations of profit, thus reducing the possible dividend to the ordinary shareholders for some years;

(iv) in the event of default in the payment of the debenture interest, or for any other cause provided for by the terms of issue, the debenture-holders will have power to appoint a receiver, and thus take away from the shareholders the control of the company;

(v) the existence of debentures may restrict the company's ability to borrow in the future, and perhaps restrict also its trade credit.

Debentures may be redeemable or irredeemable. When the need for the money is of a temporary character a redeemable issue should be made. When, however, the capital to be raised in this manner will be utilized in the acquisition of fixed assets, it must be remembered that redemption can only be effected by providing the funds therefore by appropriation of profit or by a new issue of capital.

The provision of the necessary funds by appropriations of profit will impose a temporary burden upon the ordinary shareholders, whose dividends must be restricted, but the subsequent elimination of the charge for debenture interest will confer considerable benefit in the future. In the case of an expanding business, however, it may be necessary to retain in the business a proportion of the profits made each year to provide the capital necessary to meet the requirements of expansion, and therefore too large a burden may be imposed upon profits if annual appropriations must also be made, to meet a redemption of debentures. In this event it will be necessary to raise further capital to repay the debentures, and if interest rates have advanced since the original issue was made, an increased burden will be imposed upon profits. When, therefore, debentures are issued at a time when interest rates are exceptionally low and the capital raised is required for permanent purposes, irredeemable debentures may offer considerable advantages.

A few years ago many large and well-established public companies made use of a new type of security for short-term industrial financing.

Issues of short-dated unsecured loan stocks or unsecured notes were made sometimes without the benefit of a Stock Exchange quotation. The loan stock or notes are issued under the seal of the company, but they give no specific charge on the company's assets. They are usually repayable at the end of a short term of years (ten years is usual), or redeemed by means of annual instalments. The attraction of this method of financing is based largely on the support given to this type of security by institutional investors who are now the only major group of investors with funds accruing regularly for investment in the market. Private placings of this type of security offer material advantages to large borrowers and institutional lenders; they avoid all the costs and complications of a public issue, and the institutions acquire large blocks of high-grade stock in first-class companies on favourable terms.

From the debenture-holder's point of view, a debenture can be very inadequate security during a period of inflation. In the first place, the fixed interest payments settled at the time of issue may become worth less and less as time goes on as the purchasing power value of money continues to fall steadily. Secondly, the eventual return of the nominal value of the money originally advanced is also tantamount to repayment at a severe discount if purchasing power value is taken into account. In inflationary conditions, of course, *all* prior charges[1] are vulnerable. On the other hand, with a stable price-level or, going to the other extreme, during a period of deflation prior charges are sound holdings.

A neat way of getting round the drawback is the convertible debenture or convertible unsecured loan stock. It confers on the holder a right to convert into ordinary shares during a set period and at a specified price, thus giivng him the security appropriate to a debenture-holder while market conditions pull in that direction, but with the option to take up ordinary shares instead when conditions seem favourable for switching. Just how popular convertible prior charges are can be gauged from the fact that during the period 1961–75 over £1,000 million was raised in this form (representing about one quarter of all debt issues during the period).

The table shows continuing reliance upon issues of debt until the end of 1972. The total amount raised by all types of securities fell sharply in 1973 and again in 1974. In fact the 1974 total was the lowest amount recorded – even in money terms – for ever 20 years and nearly 40 per cent of that was accounted for by one issue (Commercial Union Assurance £62 million rights issue). However,

---

[1] The customary Stock Exchange meaning is attached to this phrase, viz. all securities conferring a fixed maximum return, whether charged by law in favour of a creditor (debentures) or merely extending a preferential right to dividends in favour of a member (preference shares).

TYPES OF SECURITIES ISSUED BY COMPANIES[1]
(excluding railway, gas and water undertakings before 1961)

Year	Debt		Capital				Total £ million
			Preference		Ordinary		
	£ million	% of Total	£ million	% of Total	£ million	% of Total	
1946	20·1	15·7	30·5	23·7	77·8	60·6	128·4
1950	71·5	55·6	10·9	8·5	46·2	35·9	128·6
1960	121·8	25·5	10·4	2·2	345·5	72·3	477·7
1966	479·5	75·1	16·4	2·6	142·5	22·3	638·4
1967	343·5	81·5	5·8	1·4	72·6	17·2	421·9
1968	309·5	45·8	3·1	0·5	363·7	53·8	676·4
1969	397·4	67·1	—	—	195·0	32·9	592·4
1970	312·9	82·0	17·2	4·5	51·9	13·6	382·0
1971	340·3	51·3	12·8	1·9	310·4	46·8	663·6
1972	295·6	30·9	10·9	1·1	649·9	68·0	956·4
1973	42·9	20·4	14·0	6·7	153·6	73·0	210·5
1974	42·8	26·4	—	—	119·3	73·6	162·1
1975	212·8	13·5	44·9	2·8	1,320·7	83·7	1,578·4

1975 saw a dramatic reversal of the trend, and total issues rose steeply to over £1,500 million for the year, and of this figure, no less than £1,400 million was raised by 168 rights issues (accounting for 89 per cent of all company issues). No wonder 1975 has been described as 'The Year of the Rights Issue'. For the second successive year, though, no *new* companies raising capital were floated on the Stock Exchange,

Loan capital is a much cheaper form of financing than issues of preference or ordinary shares because the interest payable on borrowed money is allowed as an expense for corporation tax purposes; whereas dividends together with the income tax deducted therefrom have to be paid out of income that has borne corporation tax.

The series of capital switches introduced during 1965 and 1966 with the simple aim of reducing the liability to corporation tax had given rise to fears that the Chancellor of the Exchequer might legislate for a change in the system. In the event, he decided to leave well alone and merely contented himself by bringing the stamp duty on borrowed money into line with that charged on ordinary capital. On loan capital this has been $12\frac{1}{2}$p per cent whereas on ordinary capital it has been 50p per cent; as from April 6th, 1967, both will be 50p per cent.[2] Local authority stocks and bonds are exempt from the duty on issue or transfers.

[1] *Midland Bank Review*, February 1976.
[2] Capital duty increased to £1 per cent under Finance Act, 1973 and doubled in 1974. £2 per cent duty was, however, abolished on transfers of debentures and other fixed interest stock in 1976.

On Wall Street, however, convertible stocks extend from railroads and public utilities to steel and other industries. Yet in Britain, convertible issues were confined largely to mining and plantation companies where risks were high and where commodity prices were subject to violent fluctuations; they also remained the favourite device of mining finance houses while unquoted preference shares and loan stocks with conversion options have been used by the Finance Corporation for Industry and the Industrial and Commercial Finance Corporation for the companies they nurse. In this way, the lenders hope for the best of both worlds: a prior claim on earnings and assets if results fail to come up to their expectations and a finger in the 'equity' pie if things go right.

In recent years, however, British industrial companies of the highest standing have been borrowing on the strength of convertible issues. To attract money they have had to offer the double option of a fixed prior charge acceptable in itself even if it runs right through to its final redemption date, plus rights to exchange meanwhile into ordinary shares if the earning of the business and the market price of its shares makes the switch an attractive and profitable proposition.

Thus, a convertible stock appeals to the institutional investor who is continually confronted with the task of finding suitable investment outlets, whatever the state of the market may be. Moreover, some of them are also keen to hold more equities and proportionately less gilt-edged stocks. In the amounts that are usually dealt in, such switches can seldom be executed save on a falling market, which means that some capital depreciation is almost unavoidable. Consequently, the attraction of the convertible stock issue is that it opens up the prospect of an ultimate stake in the equity on terms that offer a satisfactory yield in the meantime and a valuable hedge against the risk of fluctuating prices. In a sense, it is a type of security that is tailored to fit the current needs of the pension funds and life assurance offices.

If the borrower, rather than the lender, called the tune, British industry might have devised some other form of issue. But as it is, the convertible issue is useful when a known sum of money is required to finance a definite capital project, especially one where the constructional process is lengthy and the profit-earning stage is delayed. For one thing, the costs are fixed until the new capital is fully remunerative, while the borrower pays no distributed profits tax in respect of the loan interest as he would otherwise have done in respect of ordinary and preference dividends (though loan stock interest coming into the hands of the instutitional investor suffers from the fact that it is not classified as franked investment income unlike dividends). When the new capital has reached the profit-

REPRESENTATIVE TERMS OF CONVERTIBLE LOAN STOCK ISSUES

Company and Stock		Issue date	Issue price	Amount issued £000s	First conversion date	First conversion price
Mercantile Credit	$7\frac{1}{4}\%$ Convertible Unsecured Loan Stock, 1987–92	January 1967	100	10,000	1970	0·96
Cerebos	7% Convertible Unsecured Loan Stock, 1985–90	September 1965	100	3,500	1968	$0·67\frac{1}{2}$
Arndale Property Trust	$7\frac{3}{4}\%$ Convertible Unsecured Loan Stock, 1994–99	February 1967	100	3,000	1970	0·79
Dunlop	$7\frac{3}{4}\%$ Convertible Unsecured Loan Stock, 1989–94	August 1966	100	21,000	1969	1·53

earning stage, the conversion options can be exercised – given the right market conditions – and the risk capital is thus increased forthwith (and, of course, the loan stock simultaneously decreased).

Nevertheless, the conversion option is not without its effects upon the owners of the existing equity. Clearly, they suffer partly through having to accept a dilution of the ordinary capital as and when the conversion rights are exercised and the possible cost to them depends on the extent of the dilution. Holders of the ordinary stock may also have to pay in another way since their directors have less freedom of action in raising further capital at some future date.

No doubt some companies will willingly accept them, confident that their shares will continue to rise and the conversion rights will be fully exercised. The true position cannot be clarified, however, until all the conversion dates have passed by. The possibility must always remain that some (or even most) of the loan stock will not be converted and will have to be paid off on maturity. To that extent the company's capital sturcture is at the mercy of the market and not under the complete control of the directors. A convertible loan stock issue will make its maximum appeal to an industrial borrower when the amount raised will not unduly disturb the capital structure (whether conversion rights are exercised or not), where the need for more new money is unlikely during the lifetime of the options, and where, above all, an upward trend of earnings is foreseen on a sufficient scale to ensure that the dilution of the existing equity does not rebound to their disadvantage in the long run.

Where prior charges already loom large in the capital structure, a convertible loan stock is out of the question. For instance, when the Steel Co of Wales Ltd was sold back by public offer in March 1957, the Iron and Steel Holding and Realization Agency must have been sorely tempted to make an issue of convertible loan stock instead of the ordinary shares which eventually came on offer. Though a convertible issue would have found a ready response from the institutions, the Steel Co of Wales Ltd was already burdened by heavy prior charges and could not, therefore, be expected to shoulder any more prior capital. To do so would have created an exceptionally highgeared capital structure.

Perhaps the last word on this thorny matter may be left to Sir Frank Morgan, chairman of the Prudential Assurance Co. Investors and issuing houses alike would do well to heed what he has to say about convertible debenture and loan stocks.

'This is a type of security which has become increasingly popular in recent years, but it should be borne in mind that the incorporation of options could prove to be disadvantageous to the borrowing companies and their shareholders. We, as institutional investors, would generally prefer capital to be raised directly in fixed interest securities or ordinary shares rather than in a convertible form, but we do recognize that there can be special circumstances which make an issue in this form appropriate in a particular case.'[1]

Loans or mortgages
Except in the case of private companies, loans can rarely be raised without adequate security. In the case of private companies, the directors, who are possibly the sole shareholders, may be willing to meet the company's cash requirements with temporary loans without security.

Where a public company is concerned, long-term *secured* loans have little advantage over debentures. The cost of raising loans privately may be less than a public issue of debentures, but greater difficulty may be experienced in finding persons willing to advance large sums for long periods. When, however, short-term borrowing is necessary, the most economical method is undoubtedly by means of loans.

Where mortgages are granted on the company's property a long-term loan is necessary to warrant the expenses entailed. Money raised in this manner will usually be obtained through private sources, and the expenses necessary to a public issue are thus avoided, although a negotiation fee may have to be paid to the persons who arrange the loan.

Capital planning
When a company is contemplating its future financial structure a few simple rules must be kept in mind:

(1) in general, the whole of the intangible assets, such as goodwill, patents, trade-marks and copyrights, etc., should be represented by ordinary or deferred capital;
(2) so far as revenue is concerned, a company should not allow the fixed annual obligations including preference dividends to absorb more than about 40 per cent of the net profit and the preference dividend *alone* should be covered at least *three times* by the average earnings available for dividend;
(3) so far as capital is concerned, it is wise to leave some major asset uncharged which can be used as security in an emergency. In particular any preference capital should be covered at least twice by net tangible assets.

Once a company has settled the method(s) by which it will raise capital, i.e., the choice between temporary and permanent capital

[1] 1957 Annual Report and Chairman's Statement.

and the different ways and means available and so on, the next question before it is:

What particular pattern or financial structure should it seek to build? As we shall see, certain broad generalizations emerge.

Where a company is formed to acquire a successful business, the vendors of the business or promoters of the company usually wish to retain for themselves the largest interest in the profits and the control of the company, and at the same time obtain for the company the use of capital subscribed by the public. These objects may be achieved by the issue of ordinary shares to the vendors in part or full payment of the purchase consideration, and the offer of preference shares or debentures for subscription by the public. If the business is one which commands the confidence of the public, the preference shares or debentures will form an attractive investment by reason of the priorities attaching to them.

Assume that the capital required by a company is £100,000, of which amount £80,000 must be raised by a public issue, and that an average profit of £10,000 per annum is anticipated. If the whole of the capital (including that allotted to the public) were issued in the form of ordinary shares, the promoters would enjoy no greater benefit per share than other members, whilst such other members, or a group of them, might by virtue of their weight of voting power be in a position to wrest the control of the company from the promoters. If, however, ordinary shares for £20,000 were allotted to the promoters, and the £80,000 required from the public were issued in the form of preference shares, carrying a fixed cumulative dividend of, say, 5 per cent, although this would probably be sufficiently attractive to ensure a satisfactory response from the public, only £4,000 per annum would be required to pay the preference dividend, leaving £6,000 available for the promoters, representing 30 per cent on their capital. At the same time the full control of the company's affairs would remain in their hands if the preference shares carried no voting power except when their dividends were in arrear. If, instead of preference shares, debentures were issued, even a lower rate of interest might be offered with every prospect of success, but the debentures would probably have to be secured by some charge on the assets of the company, and this might, to some extent, restrict its activities.

The articles of the company may further provide that any surplus of assets, after repayment of the share capital in full, shall, on a winding-up, belong wholly to the ordinary shareholders, whose shares may thus have a very considerable actual and potential value.

It should be pointed out that where an issue of preference shares is made on terms analogous to those described above, whereby the preference shareholders enjoy no interest in the super-profits beyond their fixed dividend, the goodwill of the business is automatically vested in the ordinary or deferred shareholders, who are entitled to the whole of the super-profits after the payment of the preference dividend. Where, therefore, on the acquisition of an existing business by a company in consideration partly of cash and partly of shares, the whole, or practically the whole, of the ordinary shares are allotted to the vendors of the business, only preference share being offered for subscription to the public, the purchase consideration should include nothing for goodwill, as this asset is vitually retained by the vendors in the ordinary shares allotted to them, and they should not be paid, out of cash contributed by the public, for something which they are not selling. If, however, ordinary shares are offered for subscription to the public, there would usually be nothing inequitable in the inclusion in the purchase consideration of a reasonable sum for the goodwill which the vendors are selling. Of course, nearly every business possesses certain individual characteristics or features and in recommending a sutiable capital structure full account should be taken of these.

Gearing of capital
The use of the word 'gearing' means the relationship between the various classes of loan and share capital to each other, i.e., the expression is applied to the proportions in which the capital is divided between fixed interest or dividend-bearing securities (such as debentures and preference shares on the one hand) and 'equity' or risk capital (in the form of ordinary or deferred shares on the other hand). When the amount of the former is unduly high, in proportion to the latter, the capital is said to be 'highly-geared'; when the proportion is low, it is described as 'low-geared'.

This question of gearing is the most vital point to consider when deciding on the future capital structure of any business. It will be appreciated that it is entirely possible at a stroke of the pen to convert a normal business into a speculative one by high gearing (from the investors' point of view, of course). This is because even a relatively stable business experiencing a mild recession in profits may be forced to default if it is saddled with unduly heavy commitments for the annual service of prior charges or prior claims as they are sometimes called.

In short, a company may be forced to withhold payment of debenture interest (which may lead to the appointment of a receiver and, perhaps, eventual liquidation of the company) or it may be obliged to pass the cumulative preference dividend (and start piling up arrears which may lead eventually to a capital reduction scheme), while the preference-holders are normally entitled to a vote in such circumstances.

It is true that the evils of high gearing are now widely recognized and that the lengths to which this was carried in the 1920s and 1930s are unlikely to be repeated. But so long as the desire to speculate or to retain voting control by the possession of a comparatively small percentage of the total capital obtains, so long will high gearing be resorted to.

Effects of high gearing
The effect of a highly-geared capital structure is that an unduly large amount of the company's earnings may be required to satisfy the interest and/or dividend on the priority capital, with the result that any fall in earnings may cause a wholly disproportionate reduction in the rate of dividend payable on the equity (or ordinary) capital. Consequently, the market price of the ordinary shares may be subject to extremely wide fluctuations. Moreover, the margin of security given to the debenture-holders and preference shareholders is reduced (not only in terms of *earnings* but also in terms of actual *assets*), and a correspondingly high yield will be demanded by investors.

Professor Sargant Florence set out to test the validity of some 'Stock Exchange folk-lore', among which he investigated the common assumption that high gearing increases the chance of capital appreciation in a time of prosperity – an assumption that was vindicated in the main. He showed that the shares of the more highly-geared companies (that is, those with a high proportion of prior charges, debentures and preference shares) tend to gain more in capital value than others. This, it has always been assumed, is because any increase in earnings has a marked effect on this type of company's relatively small amount of ordinary shares. The investigations certainly established a close relation between highly-geared companies and those whose shares gained most during the fifteen years covered. But it was not quite so close as expected, because several highly-geared companies suffered losses during this period. Thus, while the largest capital gains may be found among companies with this sort of capital structure, most of the risks are run by shareholders in these companies, too.[1]

In a study of company finance,[2] Dr R. F. Henderson commented that the effect of the inflation of the past twenty years has been greatly to reduce gearing in general. He thought that after such an inflationary period, there is great scope for the issue of loan capital without the gearing ratio being raised to pre-war levels (when it was one of the more important obstacles to progress in modernization and technical improvement). Provided that the inflation had not

[1] *The Three Banks Review*, March 1958.
[2] 'Comments on company finance', *Lloyds Bank Review*, January 1959.

been severe enough to discourage purchasers of loan stock and preference shares, he thought that sound companies with few prior charges have something like a hidden reserve of borrowing power.

Indeed there are many examples of companies with once highly-geared structures which have built up substantial reserves over many years, thereby improving their financial structure, and now exhibit a fairly low-geared capital.

Example 1

Question: A company with a capital of £200,000 in ordinary shares and £100,000 in 6 per cent preference shares and making an annual profit of £30,000 wishes to purchase for £200,000 a similar business earning £16,000 per annum. How would you recommend the additional £200,000 capital required should be raised, assuming market conditions are equally good for the issue of 5 per cent debentures, 6 per cent preference shares and ordinary shares with a yield of 10 per cent? Give reasons for your recommendation. *Ignore tax.*

Answer: In the case in point, the proportion of the ordinary shares to the preference shares is 2 : 1, and the amount of the fixed prior dividend is covered five times. After payment of the preference dividend, the earnings on the ordinary capital are equivalent to 12 per cent and, assuming a dividend of 10 per cent to have been paid, profits of £4,000 have been retained in the business. The gearing of the capital may thus be regarded as satisfactory.

The earnings of the business which it is proposed to purchase are not sufficient to pay a dividend of 10 per cent in the proposed purchase price of £200,000, so that it would be impossible to issue ordinary shares for the whole of that amount. On the other hand, if the whole of the capital were raised in the form of 6 per cent preference shares or 5 per cent debentures, or partly in one and partly in another, the capital of the company would become too highly geared, and an unhealthy situation might arise if difficulty were experienced in earning the increased amount of the fixed prior charge on the profits.

It is suggested that the new capital be raised in the form of £150,000 in 6 per cent preference shares and £50,000 in ordinary shares. The additional profits of £16,000 would thus be sufficient to leave £2,000 to carry forward after providing for the dividend of £9,000 on the new preference shares and a dividend of 10 per cent on the new ordinary shares.

The capital of the company would now be represented by £250,000 in 6 per cent preference shares and £250,000 in ordinary shares, and the earnings of £46,000 would be applied as follows:

					£
Preference dividend – 6 per cent on £250,000	..	..	..	..	15,000
Ordinary dividend – 10 per cent on £250,000	..	..	..	..	25,000
Carry forward	..	..	..	..	6,000
					£46,000

The issue of 5 per cent debentures is not recommended because:

(1) the debentures would carry a first charge on the assets of the company for principal and interest;

(2) the interest would be a first charge on earnings, and would be payable whether or not profits were available to meet it;

(3) the margin of profit appears to be insufficient for the creation of a sinking fund for the redemption of debentures, after providing for dividends, and maintaining the reserves necessary for the company's normal requirements and development.

Example 2

In times of rising profits a highly-geared capital structure will give greatly accelerated earnings on the ordinary shares, but when profits are falling earnings will fall even faster. Consequently, figures purporting to show the earnings or cover for the ordinary dividend can be misleading without an appreciation of 'gearing'.

In the following example, for instance, if the amount available for distribution were doubled from £123,000 to £246,000, the earnings yield on the ordinary capital would climb from 25 per cent to 66 per cent, but if the amount available were halved to £60,000 the dividend would not be fully earned.

Example 3

One special feature of the financial affairs of investment trusts which deserves attention is this vexed question of the 'gearing' of capital.

Gearing can best be illustrated by considering a new trust having total funds of £1 million divided into £300,000 preference shares, £200,000 ordinary shares, and as much as £500,000 of debentures – by no means an uncommon ratio. Assuming that something like £800,000 (or 80 per cent of the total funds) out of the investment portfolio were invested in equity stocks there would be a gearing ratio of 4 : 1 on the trust's own ordinary capital and it would, therefore, be providing for investment purposes four times as much risk capital as it had originally issued. Unquestionably, the special place of investment trusts in the capital market depends upon thier ability to provide a flow of risk capital for industrial ventures, while at the same time offering a wide measure of security to investors seeking a remunerative outlet for their savings. Nevertheless, owing to the prevalence of 'highly-geared' capital, the ordinary shares of investment trusts are apt to carry rather greater risks of capital fluctuation than many industrial equities, simply because of the existence of prior charges which have to be serviced before the equity shareholders come into their own.

Throughout the war years and right up to the middle of 1953, investment trusts had languished under the ban on the raising of new capital (then in excess of £50,000), though the gearing ratio was noticeably reduced during this period owing to the accumulation of reserves. Consequently, when the ban on new issues was lifted investment trusts no longer suffered quite so much from the handicap of 'high gearing', and henceforth were in an altogether much stronger financial position from which to expand their activities.

STOCK EXCHANGE METHOD
OF SHOWING DIVIDEND COVER

A HIGH GEARED CO LTD – PROFIT AND LOSS ACCOUNT

		£
Profit after all charges except interest		200,000
Deduct Debenture interest, net		23,000
		177,000
Deduct Corporation tax		77,000
	£	100,000
Deduct Preference dividend, gross	20,000	
Ordinary dividend (10 per cent, gross) ..	30,000	
Transfer to debenture sinking fund ..	5,000	
		55,000
		£45,000

TABLE SHOWING COVER FOR INTEREST AND DIVIDENDS

	Net interest or dividend payable £	Times covered	Amount available £
Debenture interest	23,000 ⎫	4·4	123,000
Debenture sinking fund	5,000 ⎭		
Preference dividend	20,000	4·7	95,000
Ordinary dividend (10 per cent)	30,000	2·5[1]	75,000
Surplus	45,000		45,000
	£123,000		

[1] Percentage earned calculated as follows:

$$\frac{75,000}{30,000} \times 10 \text{ per cent} = 25 \text{ per cent}$$

If amount available for distribution is increased to £198, then earnings are

$$\frac{198,000}{30,000} \times 10 \text{ per cent} = 66 \text{ per cent.}$$

Price/earnings ratio (P/E ratio)

Complications such as those inherent in the dividend-cover yardstick are avoided by the price-earnings ratio. This method of evaluating shares is general practice in many countries, notably the United States. The ratio is the share price expressed as a number of years net earnings. The P/E ratio is calculated by dividing the latest year's net earnings per share (expressed in £p terms) into the current market price of the shares. For instance, if company A has its capital in £1 ordinary shares offiically quoted on a Stock Exchange at £4, and it last earned 50 per cent on the equity capital after corporation tax, i.e., 50p per £1 share, it has a P/E ratio of 8.

The object of the P/E ratio is to provide a means of assessing various shares on a common footing and it is particularly useful when judging the relative merits of companies engaged in the same industry.

Thus, if the P/E ratio of company B – in, say, the chemical industry – comes out at 9·2 when the average for the chemical industry as a whole is 11·3, the shares of company B would seem relatively cheap. The P/E ratio is, however, only *one* of the factors to be taken into consideration when assessing the merits of a share. Needless to say, the treatment of capital allowances, franked investment income and investment grants can also affect the base figure for earnings in the P/E calculation.

Capital Issues Committee

At one time, all new issues required Treasury approval which was operated through the Capital Issues Committee. This committee, known as the C.I.C., was dissolved in November 1967.

The committee was originally set up under the Defence Regulations of 1939, to consider and advise on applications made to the Treasury for the issue of capital to the public, the offer of securities for sale or the renewal or postponement of the maturity of securities. In 1946 its responsibilities were further extended to take in all applications for the issue of capital, but since 1959 its activities have been limited, mainly to issues made by local authorities and overseas residents. The work of the committee was further curtailed early in 1967, when it no longer became necessary for an overseas resident to obtain Treasury permission to borrow in the United Kingdom by way of an issue of securities denominated in a currency other than sterling.

From now on, the Bank of England will handle those few issues which still require Treasury consent and will also continue to regulate the 'queue' for public sector issues.

CHAPTER XIV

CAPITAL REORGANIZATION SCHEMES[1]

Where the memorandum and articles create merely one class of share, the company will nevertheless be entitled to take power to issue, say, preference shares notwithstanding that this clearly dilutes, as it were, former rights of the existing shares.

Once a distinction has been drawn in any way between various shares then any rights must be regarded as special class rights if either, (a) they are expressly described in the memorandum, articles, or terms of issue, as rights attaching to one or other class; or (b) they relate in some way to dividends, return of capital, or voting.

Variation of rights

In the vast majority of cases, it is customary for the rights attaching to shares to be set out in the articles only, and not in the memorandum, and for the articles to provide that, where shares are divided into separate classes, rights can be varied or abrogated with the consent of a prescribed majority of the class (usually referred to as the 'majority clause'). This right, is, however, subject to the possibility that a dissenting minority of the class may apply to the Court under section 72, Companies Act 1948.

On the other hand, if the rather unusual circumstance arises where the rights of shareholders are expressed in the memorandum, they are deemed to be unalterable unless the memorandum itself prescribes a method of alteration, or unless the consent of the Court is obtained to a 'scheme of arrangement' dealt with under section 206, Companies Act 1948.

It should be noted that the power to alter the memorandum conferred by section 23, Companies Act 1948, does not extend to any variation or abrogation of the special rights of any class of members.

The procedure for variation of class rights described above applies only to registered companies and does not permit the liability of the shareholders to be increased. Moreover, shareholders cannot be compelled to take up more shares in the company. Consequently, a scheme of this kind is applicable only in a limited range of cases and should not be confused with the more formal schemes of arrangement which are recognized under section 206, Companies Act 1948. The latter type of scheme is apt to be rather more ambitious in scope, since it also enables the rights of debenture-holders or creditors to be brought within its terms.

[1] This chapter is based on an article of mine in *The Accountant*, April 13th, 1957.

Capital reorganization

In general terms, then, the entrenched rights of the members of a company are subject to a considerable measure of protection. However, even entrenched rights are liable to be modified or abrogated where exceptional procedure is adopted. Such exceptional changes are variously described as capital reconstructions, reorganizations or rearrangements; but it will be observed that none of these expressions is a term of art with a clearly defined and distinguishable legal meaning. Instead, they are just phrases well established in company and Stock Exchange jargon.

It is customary, therefore, to employ the expressions 'capital reorganization' or 'rearrangement of capital' to schemes which concern only one company where the rights of its members (or some of them) are varied. So the reorganization of the share capital of an existing company, however drastic, in no way constitutes a reconstruction of the legal entity itself (dealt with under section 287, Companies Act 1948).

It will be evident that the difficulties met with in capital reorganization schemes arise, not so much from any complexity of law, as from the infinite variety of schemes which may be formulated so as to cover all possible kinds of internal reorganizations and rearrangements of the capital structure. Indeed, the vast majority of schemes come into effect without involving reference to the Court at all, because the companies concerned take good care to obtain expert financial advice in the first place, and often enter into consultations with large shareholders so as to obtain their support beforehand.

Purposes

Although the alteration of the capital structure of a company clearly presents many facets, it is still possible to identify certain main purposes from some of the schemes announced during the past few years. These may be listed as follows:

(*a*) The simplification of the existing complicated capital structure of a business, i.e., converting or consolidating several classes of shares into one or two main classes. Quite often this need has arisen through a process of 'tidying-up' the capital structure, as it has survived from an earlier capital reduction or company reorganization scheme, where, for instance, the share capital is divided into rather unusual denominations, like preference shares of a nominal value of 75p each, or ordinary shares of $33\frac{1}{2}$p each.

(*b*) The capital structure is rearranged so as to remove high gearing.

(*c*) The existence of prior capital carrying an unusually high fixed, or participating rate of dividend, sometimes gives a misleading impression of the financial standing of the company, especially where it is accompanied by complicated or unusual voting or other rights. Whereas in the great majority of cases ordinary shareholders have voting control, there are a few companies where the preference shareholders are in command. Invariably the valuable voting rights of these preference shares are over-looked and the market price continues to be judged by the unusal considerations of yield, cover and prospects. There have been several instances recently where belated recognition of such voting rights have resulted in offers from outsiders attempting to gain control. Any company where the preference shareholders are in control is exposed to such a possibility, and in order to forestall a 'take-over' bid, may seek to put its internal capital structure on a more orthodox basis.

(d) In order to pave the way for a further issue of shares, since the existence of unusual nominal capital units or complicated rights attaching to shares might otherwise hamper a company's plans for expansion when it contemplates approaching the public for additional permanent capital.

(e) Substitution of an equivalent amount of fixed interest loan stock for existing preference share capital in order to reduce the burden of taxation on profits – thus applied both to the inadequate post-was period when a two-tier profits tax was in operation and to the corporation tax era which began in 1965.

Examples

A few samples taken from actual schemes may suffice to illustrate the main principles that have a decided bearing upon the type and style of capital reorganization scheme which is finally submitted to the members for approval.

(1) Scheme for simplifying the capital structure combined with capitalization of reserves in order to bring the issued capital into closer relationship with the funds employed in the business.

Structure before scheme £	SHARE CAPITAL					*Reclassified after scheme* £
1,143,023	6 per cent preference stock	..	..	..	..	1,380,209
1,897,485	Ordinary stock	..	..	..	..	5,883,744
919,387	Deferred ordinary stock	..	..	..	..	—
200,000	Co-partnership stock ..	..	..	..	..	—
£4,159,895						£7,213,953

The above scheme included the capitalization of reserves amounting to £3,054,058 applied as follows:

	£
One new 6 per cent cumulative preference share of £1 for every £8 of existing ordinary stock	237,186
One new ordinary share of £1 for every £1 of existing ordinary stock (£1,897,485) and deferred ordinary stock (£919,387) ..	2,816,872
	£3,054,058

At the same time, the existing deferred ordinary stock and co-partnership stock was converted into ordinary stock. The voting rights of the ordinary stock, as reorganized, were then reduced to one vote for every complete £2 of stock, so as to preserve, approximately, the original ratio between the voting rights of the preference stockholders and those of the other stockholders.

(2) A capital structure which exhibits some degree of high gearing is improved by capitalization of reserves, while preference shares (carrying an unusual rate of interest) surrender voting control to the ordinary shareholders.

Before scheme
SHARE CAPITAL

£
500,000   5½ per cent (tax free) cumulative preference stock
400,000   Ordinary shares

£900,000

Each £1 unit of either class was entitled to one vote.

After scheme

£
500,000   5½ per cent (gross) cumulative preference stock
1,450,000   Ordinary shares

£1,950,000

The preference shareholders receive 250,000 ordinary shares on a one-for-two basis as compensation for having their various rights altered – the 5½ per cent dividend is now subject to tax, instead of being tax free, and the voting powers are restricted. On the other hand, they have improved rights in a winding-up. The ordinary shareholders receive 800,000 shares on a two-for-one basis, again out of the capitalization of reserves. On the basis of an expected ordinary dividend of 10 per cent, the preference shareholders slightly improve their net income position on £100 stock from £5·50 to £6·04 (made up of £3·16 net from the new preference shares and £2·87½ net from the block of fully-paid ordinary shares allotted). As far as the old ordinary shareholders are concerned, they, too, increase their income, since the previous dividend under the old capital was 27½ per cent, equivalent to just over 9 per cent on their new holdings.

(3) The 12½p ordinary shares of the one-class £37,500 issued capital of Brown Bayley's Steel Works represented one of the extreme examples of 'heaviness' in a share price, being quoted around £10·50 each some time prior to the reorganization scheme. The board had such a scheme in mind for the purpose of:

(a) reducing the 'top heavy' quotation per share;

(b) bringing the capital of the company more into line with its net asset position;

(c) rendering the dividend expressed as a percentage of the issued share capital more realistic. Just how necessary this was is illustrated by the 250 per cent tax-free dividend then currently paid.

Whilst (a) above could easily have been met by subdividing the existing shares into shares of, say, 2½p each, this would not meet points (b) and (c). Furthermore, a ruling was required from the Inland Revenue regarding the safeguarding of relief from profits tax in respect of retained profits amounting to approximately £160,000. Considering the company's unusual capital structure, a reorganization was certainly long overdue. Behind the parent company's single-class issued capital of only £37,500 in 12½p units, the balance sheet as at July 31st, 1956, disclosed net assets of £1,045,277 – no less than twenty-eight times the nominal capital. The real position, however, was even more complicated, for those net assets included investments with a market value of some £3 million, against the book value of just over £1 million. These investments consisted of a 60 per cent holding in Hoffmann Manufacturing, the bearing makers, and a more than 50 per cent holding in Brown Bayley Steels. The former interest was valued at only £419,909, yet the market value was £2,190,000. Hoffmann's balance sheet as at December 31st, 1955, revealed net tangible assets of £3,938,000 attributable to the equity, so that the portion attributable to Brown Bayley's was around £2·36 million. Likewise, the interest in Brown Bayley's Steels (not to be confused with Brown Bayley's Steel Works Ltd – the parent company) was given a book value of only £601,950 while the market value at July 31st, 1956, was £811,350. Yet this company's net tangible assets attributable to the equity came to £2,968,000 on the balance sheet to October 1st, 1955, so that the portion attributable to the controlling group's holding must have been close on £1½ million.

The result of this statistical exercise is that a more realistic figure is brought to light for the asset value of Brown Bayley's Steel Works Ltd 12½p shares, which, based on the £3·88 million asset value of underlying shares in the subsidiaries, may be estimated at 103 times their nominal value, or £12⅞.

To some extent, the true earnings picture is also concealed, since the £169,819 received in dividends from the subsidiaries represented only around one-quarter of the available earnings. When the two major subsidiaries were consolidated, the 250 per cent tax-free dividend then being paid revealed over threefold cover, allowing for the full profits tax. The 12½p shares yielded 7⅛ per cent at the then current market price of £7¾ each.[1] Six months later, when the capital reorganization scheme was formulated, the shares stood at £10·50 each.

Following a satisfactory ruling from the Inland Revenue in regard to the incidence of profits tax, a new holding company was formed to take over the undertaking and assets of the parent company, which was then placed in liquidation. Shareholders received eight £1 ordinary shares in the new company for every one 12½p share then held – giving a capital of £2·4 million. At the same time, the directors added that they had carefully considered a proposal that the substantial holdings in the trading companies, Hoffmann Manufacturing and Brown Bayley Steels, should be distributed *in specie* among the shareholders of the parent company. But both they and the directors of the trading companies were unanimous in their opinion that, apart from the substantial cost by way of tax which such a distribution would involve, the maintenance of the group through a common holding company was in the best interests of each of the trading companies on account of the close liaison in relation to supply and demand both as to quality and quantity which had contributed to the satisfactory results achieved in past years. If suitable opportunities arose, the new holding company fully intended to extend the scope of its interests by acquiring further businesses complementary to the activities of either of the existing trading companies.

Group treatment

Large groups with interlocking subsidiaries often find it advantageous to tidy up their capital structures, particularly when savings in profits tax are apparent through the replacement of preference shares (dividends on which count as a distribution) with loan stock (interest on which is allowed as an expense). Within the last decade the Beecham Group and Bowater Paper have done so and during the same period Distillers issued details of its scheme to convert the preference shares of its subsidiaries into an undated 5½ per cent consolidated unsecured loan stock of the parent company.[2] On a maximum

[1] December 1956.
[2] *The Economist*, May 6th, 1957, page 76. There is, however, no saving in stamp duty for in addition to capital stamp duty on the new loan stock, stamp duty is also payable on the transfers of the preference shares to the parent company in exchange for the stock.

conversion £9,910,870 of the new stock would be issued. This new loan stock is redeemable by purchase up to a price of £110. Although no minimum proportion of acceptances was laid down, the directors recommended shareholders to accept.

The terms were fixed by reference to the market prices of the shares and to the rights of the different classes of holders. The upshot was that shareholders gained in income, and cash payments were duly made when required so as to cover accrued dividends on the existing preference shares.

The choice of an unsecured loan stock of the parent company is particularly apt because the method of exchange ensures that there is no dilution of the security attaching to the preference shares, now superseded. Indeed, so far as security was concerned the unsecured loan stock was covered about six times by assets and about twenty-two times by earnings.

Moreover, the method should relieve the Distillers group of some profits tax liability, though that was not the primary object of the scheme. In fact the main purpose was to smooth the way for transfers of assets and shares between subsidiaries within the group (and in so doing make possible some saving in stamp duty).

Another company, Boots Pure Drug Co Ltd, has also applied to the Court for directions to proceed with a scheme for the replacement of the retail subsidiaries' preference shares by a 6 per cent unsecured loan stock of the parent company.[1]

The grounds for this plan were announced as simplification of the internal administration and improvement in the marketability of part of the fixed interest capital; reasons that look convincing enough because no less than fifteen different classes of preference shares were in issue, with amounts ranging from £50,000 to £300,000 outstanding. Assuming maximum conversion, something like £2,065,867 of unsecured loans stock would be issued.

The new stock was expected to have a twenty-five years' life and to be redeemable at the company's option after twenty years. The scheme envisaged that holders of the two 7 per cent issues would receive £1·16½ of new stock for every £1 preference share; holders of the eleven 6 per cent issues, £1·01; and holders of the two 5 per cent issues 91½p – terms which were pitched above the market prices then ruling while in all cases income rights were preserved or improved.

In 1959 Great Universal Stores, aided and advised by Helbert Wagg & Co, brought out its long-awaited plan for the rationalization of the group's untidy preference capital structure. The plan,

[1] *The Investors' Chronicle*, December 20th, 1957. Stamp duty was avoided here by adopting a scheme under section 206, Companies Act 1948, whereby the preference shares were *cancelled* so that no transfers took place at all.

which dealt with the parent's own two straight preference issues and with twenty-four out of the forty separate preference stock of the many subsidiaries, is relatively simple and straightforward. It consists of conversion offers into two new preference issues of the parent, one bearing a $4\frac{1}{2}$ per cent coupon, and the other one of 7 per cent, both ranking *pari passu*. The capital structure after reorganization is as follows:

Authorized £	CLASS OF CAPITAL			Issued £
1,250,000	$4\frac{1}{2}$ per cent Redeemable Pre-Preference		..	1,250,000(a)
6,000,000	$4\frac{1}{2}$ per cent Cumulative Preference	..	..	3,808,619(b)
7,000,000	7 per cent Cumulative Preference..	..	..	5,169,132(b)
2,000,000	Ordinary 25p shares	..	..	1,360,513
21,000,000	'A' Ordinary 25p shares	..	..	21,731,828(c)
£37,250,000				£33,320,092

(a) Existing issue.   (b) Ranking *pari passu*.   (c) After one-for-ten scrip issue.

The sixteen omissions mentioned above have been made for a variety of reasons, but they comprise, apart from overseas subsidiaries, those of the United Kingdom subsidiaries 'whose trade is largely overseas, whose ordinary capital is not wholly owned, private companies and so on'.

No doubt may others will see fit to follow the lead given by the groups mentioned above.

Conclusions

In examining these and other schemes of the same type, one may detect a few underlying principles:

(1) when converting several classes of shares into one or more main classes, it is necessary to guard against altering relative voting strength;

(2) the income position of a particular class should, at least, be maintained after the scheme, though it is usual to award slightly more income in order to gain the consent of the affected shareholders;

(3) where *participating* preference rights are yielded, an interest in the equity seems a suitable form of compensation as a means of removing the considerable equity element previously embodied in those shares;

(4) in view of the capitalization of reserves which invariably takes place simultaneously with capital reorganization schemes, it would seem that such schemes occur more often in times of prosperity than in times of financial stress and depression.

APPENDIX I

FINANCE ACT 1927, SECTION 55

Relief from Capital and Transfer Stamp Duty under section 55 (as amended by section 31, Finance Act 1928, and section 41, Finance Act 1930).

(1) If in connection with a scheme for the reconstruction of any company or companies or the amalgamation of any companies it is shown to the satisfaction of the Commissioners of Inland Revenue that there exist the following conditions, that is to say:

(*a*) that a company with limited liability is to be registered, or that since the commencement of this Act a company has been incorporated by letters patent or Act of Parliament, or the nominal share capital of a company has been increased;

(*b*) that the company (in this section referred to as 'the transferee company') is to be registered or has been incorporated or has increased its capital with a view to the acquisition either of the undertaking of, or of not less than 90 per cent of the issued capital of any particular existing company;

(*c*) that the consideration for the acquisition (except such part thereof as consists in the transfer to or discharge by the transferee company of liabilities of the existing company) consists as to not less than 90 per cent thereof:

(i) where an undertaking is to be acquired, in the issue of shares in the transferee company to the existing company or to holders of shares in the existing company; or

(ii) where shares are to be acquired, in the issue of shares in the transferee company to the holders of shares in the existing company in exchange for the shares held by them in the existing company; then, subject to the provisions of this section:

(A) the nominal share capital of the transferee company, or the amount by which the capital of the transferee company has been increased, as the case may be, shall, for the purpose of computing the stamp duty chargeable in respect of that capital, be treated as being reduced by either:

(i) an amount equal to the amount of the share capital of the existing company . . .[1] or, in the case of the acquisition of a part of an undertaking, equal to such proportion of the said share capital as the value of that part of the undertaking bears to the whole value of the undertaking; or

(ii) [the amount to be credited as paid up on the shares to be issued as such consideration as aforesaid and on the shares, if any, to be issued to creditors of the existing company in consideration of the release of debts (whether secured or unsecured) due to accruing due to them from the existing company or of the assignment of such debts to the transferee company][2] whichever amount is the less; and

[1] The words 'in respect of which stamp duty has been paid' were struck out at this point (as from August 1st, 1930) by the Finance Act 1930, section 41, which also made special provision for cases arising before that date.
[2] As amended by section 31, Finance Act 1928.

(B) Stamp duty under the heading 'Conveyance or Transfer on Sale' in the First Schedule to the Stamp Act 1891 shall not be chargeable on any instrument made for the purposes of or in connection with the transfer of the undertaking or shares, [or on any instrument made for the purposes of or in connection with the assignment to the transferee company of any debts, secured or unsecured, of the existing company][1] nor shall any such duty be chargeable under section 12 of the Finance Act 1895 on a copy of any Act of Parliament, or on any instrument vesting, or relating to the vesting of, the undertaking or shares in the transferee company:

Provided that:

(a) no such instrument shall be deemed to be duly stamped unless either it is stamped with the duty to which it would but for this section be liable or it has in accordance with the provisions of section 12 of the Stamp Act 1891 been stamped with a particular stamp denoting either that it is not chargeable with any duty or that it is duly stamped; and

(b) in the case of an instrument made for the purposes of or in connection with a transfer to a company within the meaning of the Companies (Consolidated) Act 1908,[2] the provisions of paragraph (B) of this subsection shall not apply unless the instrument is either:

(i) executed within a period of twelve months from the date of the registration of the transferee company or the date of the resolution for the increase of the nominal share capital of the transferee company, as the case may be; or

(ii) made for the purpose of effecting a conveyance or transfer in pursuance of an agreement which has been filed, or particulars of which have been filed, with the registrar of companies within the said period of twelve months; and

[(c) the foregoing provision with respect to the release and assignment of debts of the existing company shall not, except in the case of debts due to banks or to trade creditors, apply to debts which were incurred less than two years before the proper time for making a claim for exemption under this section].[3]

(2) For the purposes of a claim for exemption under paragraph (B) of subsection (1) of this section, a company which has, in connection with a scheme of reconstruction or amalgamation, issued any unissued share capital shall be treated as if it had increased its nominal share capital.

(3) A company shall not be deemed to be a particular existing company within the meaning of this section unless it is provided by the memorandum of association of, or the letters patent or Act incorporating the transferee company that one of the objects for which the company is established is the acquisition of the undertaking of, or shares in, the existing company, or unless it appears from the resolution, Act or other authority for the increase of the capital of the transferee company that the increase is authorized for the purpose of acquiring the undertaking of, or shares in, the existing company.

[1] As amended by section 31, Finance Act 1928.
[2] Now the Companies Act 1948.
[3] As amended by section 31, Finance Act 1928.

(4) In a case where the undertakings of or shares in two or more companies are to be acquired, the amount of the reduction to be allowed under this section in respect of the stamp duty chargeable in respect of the nominal share capital or the increase of the capital of a company shall be computed separately to each of those companies.

(5) Where a claim is made for exemption under this section, the Commissioners of Inland Revenue may require the delivery to them of a statutory declaration in such form as they may direct, made in England by a solicitor of the Supreme Court, or in Scotland by an enrolled law agent, and of such further evidence, if any, as the Commissioners may reasonably require.

(6) If:

(*a*) where any claim for exemption from duty under this section has been allowed, it is subsequently found that any declaration or other evidence furnished in support of the claim was untrue in any material particular, or that the conditions specified in subsection (1) of this section are not fulfilled in the reconstruction or amalgamation as actually carried out; or

(*b*) where shares in the transferee company have been issued to the existing company in consideration of the acquisition, the existing company within a period of two years from the date, as the case may be, of the registration or incorporation, or of the authority for the increase of the capital, of the transferee company ceases, otherwise than in consequence of reconstruction, amalgamation or liquidation, to be the beneficial owner of the shares so issued to it; or

(*c*) where any such exemption has been allowed in connection with the acquisition by the transferee company of shares in another company, the transferee company within a period of two years from the date of its registration or incorporation or of the authority for the increase of its capital, as the case may be, ceases otherwise than in consequence or reconstruction, amalgamation or liquidation, to be the beneficial owner of the shares so acquired;

the exemption shall be deemed not to have been allowed, and an amount equal to the duty remitted shall become payable forthwith, and shall be recoverable from the transferee company as a debt due to His Majesty, together with interest thereon at the rate of 5 per cent per annum in the case of duty remitted under paragraph (A) of subsection (1) of this section from the date of the registration or incorporation of the transferee company or the increase of its capital, as the case may be, and in the case of duty remitted under paragraph (B) of the said subsection from the date on which it would have become chargeable if this Act had not been passed.

(7) If in the case of any scheme of reconstruction or amalgamation the Commissioners of Inland Revenue are satisfied that at the proper time for making a claim for exemption from duty under subsection (1) of this section there were in existence all the necessary conditions for exemption other than the condition that not less than 90 per cent of the issued share capital of the existing company would be acquired by the transferee company, the Commissioners may, if it is proved to their satisfaction that not less than 90 per cent of the issued capital of the existing company has under the scheme been acquired within a period of six months from the earlier of the two following dates, that is to say:

(a) the last day of the period of one month after the first allotment of shares made for the purpose of the acquisition; or

(b) the date on which an invitation was issued to the shareholders of the existing company to accept shares in the transferee company;

and on production of the instruments on which the duty paid has been impressed, direct repayment to be made of such an amount of duty as would have been remitted if the said condition had been originally fulfilled.

(8) In this section, unless the context otherwise requires:

References to the undertaking of an existing company include references to a part of the undertaking of an existing company.

The expression 'shares' includes stock.

APPENDIX II

FINANCE ACT 1930, SECTION 42

(1) Stamp duty under the heading 'Conveyance or Transfer on Sale' in the First Schedule to the Stamp Act 1891, shall not be chargeable on an instrument to which this section applies.

Provided that no such instrument shall be deemed to be duly stamped unless either it is stamped with the duty to which it would but for this section be liable, or it has in accordance with the provision of section 12 of the said Act been stamped with a particular stamp denoting either that it is not chargeable with any duty or that it is duly stamped.

(2) This section applies to any instrument as respects which it is shown to the satisfaction of the Commissioners of Inland Revenue:

(a) that the effect thereof is to convey or transfer a beneficial interest in property from one company with limited liability to another such company; and

(b) that either:

(i) one of the companies is beneficial owner of not less than 90 per cent of the issued capital of the other company; or

(ii) not less than 90 per cent of the share capital of each of the companies is in the beneficial ownership of a third company with limited liability.

See also Finance Act 1938, section 50, and section 27 (2) (3) of the Finance Act 1967.

APPENDIX III

THE CITY CODE ON TAKE-OVERS AND MERGERS (REVISED APRIL 29th, 1976)

The City Code on Take-overs and Mergers first appeared in its present form in March 1968. It was prepared and issued by the City Working Party, a body originally set up in 1959 and reconvened by the Governor of the Bank of England in 1967 for that purpose. The new Code, now in its fourth edition, incorporates a limited number of revisions and additions made by the City Working Party in the light of experience gained in its operation since that date. Certain of these modifications are the result of suggestions made by the Panel on Take-overs and Mergers established in September 1969 on the proposal of the Governor to supervise the operation of the code.

The provisions of the code fall into two categories. On the one hand, the code enunciates general principles of conduct to be observed in bid situations. On the other it lays down certain rules, some of which are precise, and others are no more than examples of the application of principles.

Definitions

The Panel. The Panel means the Panel on Take-overs and Mergers set up at the request of the Bank of England.

Acting in Concert. Persons acting in concert comprise persons who, pursuant to an agreement or understanding (whether formal or informal), actively co-operate, through the acquisition by any of them of shares in a company, to obtain or consolidate control (as defined below) of that company.

Without prejudice to the general application of this definition the following persons will be presumed to be persons acting in concert with other persons in the same category unless the contrary is established:

(1) a company, its parent, subsidiaries and fellow subsidiaries, and their associated companies, and companies of which such companies are associated companies, all with each other. For this purpose ownership or control of 20% or more of the equity share capital of a company will be regarded as the test of associated company status;

(2) a company with any of its directors (together with their close relatives and related trusts);

(3) a company with any of its pension funds;

(4) a person with any investment company, unit trust or other fund accustomed to act on such person's instructions;

(5) a financial adviser with its client in respect of the shareholdings of—

  (a) the financial adviser; and

  (b) all the funds which the financial adviser manages on a discretionary basis, where the shareholdings of the financial adviser and any of those funds in the client total 10% or more of the client's equity share capital.

Associate. (This definition has relevance only to disclosure of dealings under Rule 31.)

It is not thought practicable to define associate in precise terms which would cover all the different relationships which may exist in a take-over or merger transaction. The term associate is intended to cover all persons (whether or not acting in concert) who directly or indirectly own or deal in the shares of the offeror or offeree company in a take-over or merger transaction and who have (in addition to their normal interests as shareholders) an interest or potential interest, whether commercial, financial or personal, in the outcome of the offer.

Without prejudice to the generality of the foregoing, the term associate will normally include the following:

(1) the offeror or offeree company's parent, subsidiaries and fellow subsidiaries, and their associated companies, and companies of which such companies are associated companies. For this purpose owner-

ship or control of 20% or more of the equity share capital of a company will be regarded as the test of associated company status;

(2) bankers,[1] stockbrokers, financial and other professional advisers to the offeror, the offeree company or any company mentioned in (1);

(3) the directors (together with their close relatives and related trusts) of the offeror, the offeree company or any company mentioned in (1);

(4) the pension funds of the offeror, the offeree company or any company mentioned in (1);

(5) any investment company, unit trust or other fund accustomed to act on the instructions of another associate.

(6) a holder of 10% or more of the equity share capital of the offeror or offeree company. Where two or more persons act as a syndicate or other group, pursuant to an agreement or understanding (whether formal or informal) to acquire or hold such capital, they shall be deemed to be a single holder for this purpose;

(7) a company having a material trading arrangement with the offeror or offeree company.

Cash purchases. References to purchases for cash and cash prices paid for shares shall be deemed to include contracts or arrangements for the acquisition of shares where the consideration consists of a debt instrument maturing for payment in less than 3 years.

Control. Control shall be deemed to mean a holding, or aggregate holdings, of shares carrying 30% or more of the voting rights (as defined below) of a company, irrespective of whether that holding or holdings gives *de facto* control.

Directors. References to directors shall be deemed to include persons in accordance with whose instructions the directors or a director are accustomed to act.

Offer. Offer includes, wherever appropriate, take-over and merger transactions howsoever effected, including reverse take-overs, partial offers and also offers by a parent company for shares in its subsidiary, but offers for non-voting non-equity capital do not come within the Code.

Offeror. Offeror includes companies wherever incorporated and individuals wherever resident.

Offer period. Offer period means the period from the date when an announcement is made of a proposed or possible offer (with or without terms) until the first closing date or (if this is later) the date when such offer is declared to have become unconditional as to acceptances or to have lapsed.

Voting rights. Voting rights shall mean all the voting rights attributable to the share capital of a company other than rights exercisable only in restricted circumstances. However, the Panel should be consulted where rights exercisable only in restricted circumstances have in fact been exercisable for a long time, as it may consider the relevant shares to have voting rights for the purposes of the Code.

[1] Note: The definition associate does not apply to a banker whose sole relationship with a party to a take-over or merger transaction is the provision of normal commercial banking services or such activities in connection with the offer as confirming that cash is available or handling acceptances and other registration work.

GENERAL PRINCIPLES

1. It is impracticable to devise rules in such detail as to cover all the various circumstances which arise in take-over or merger transactions. **Accordingly, persons engaged in such transactions should be aware that the spirit as well as the precise wording of these General Principles and of the ensuing Rules must be observed.** Moreover, it must be accepted that the General Principles and the spirit of the Code will apply in areas or circumstances not explicitly covered by any Rule.

2. While the boards of an offeror and of an offeree company and their respective advisers have a primary duty to act in the best interests of their respective shareholders, they must accept that there are limitations in connection with take-over and merger transactions on the manner in which the pursuit of those interests can be carried out. Inevitably therefore these General Principles and the ensuing Rules will impinge on the freedom of action of boards and persons involved in such transactions.

3. Shareholders shall have in their possession sufficient evidence, facts and opinions upon which an adequate judgement and decision can be reached and shall have sufficient time to make an assessment and decision. No relevant information shall be withheld from them.

4. At no time after a *bona fide* offer has been communicated to the board of an offeree company or after the board of an offeree company has reason to believe that a *bona fide* offer might be imminent shall any action be taken by the board of the offeree company in relation to the affairs of the company, without the approval in general meeting of the shareholders of the offeree company, which could effectively result in any *bona fide* offer being frustrated or in the shareholders of the offeree company being denied an opportunity to decide on its merits.

5. It must be the object of all parties to a take-over or merger transaction to use every endeavour to prevent the creation of a false market in the shares of an offeror or offeree company.

6. A board which receives an offer or is approached with a view to an offer being made should in the interests of its shareholders seek competent advice.

7. Rights of control must be exercised in good faith and the oppression of a minority is wholly unacceptable.

8. All shareholders of the same class of an offeree company shall be treated similarly by an offeror.

9. If, after a take-over or merger transaction is reasonably in contemplation, an offer has been made to one or more shareholders of an offeree company, any subsequent general offer made by or on behalf of the same offeror, or any person acting in concert with it, to the shareholders of the same class shall not be on less favourable terms.

10. During the course of a take-over or merger transaction, or when such is in contemplation, neither the offeror, the offeree company nor any of their respective advisers shall furnish information to some shareholders which is not made available to all shareholders. This principle shall not apply to the furnishing of information in confidence by an offeree company to a *bona fide* potential offeror or *vice versa*, nor to the issue of circulars by members of The Stock Exchange (who are brokers to any party to the transaction) to their own investment clients provided such issue shall previously have been approved by the Panel.

11. Directors of an offeror or an offeree company shall always, in advising their shareholders, act only in their capacity as directors and not have regard to their personal or family shareholdings or their personal relationships with the companies. It is the shareholders' interests taken as a whole, together with those of employees and creditors, which should be considered.

Shareholders in companies which are effectively controlled by their directors must accept that in respect of any offer the attitude of their board will be decisive. There may be good reasons for such a board rejecting an offer or preferring the lower of two offers. The board must carefully examine its reasons for doing so and be prepared to explain its decision to its shareholders.

12. Any document or advertisement addressed to shareholders containing information, opinions or recommendations from the board of an offeror or offeree company or their respective advisers shall be treated with the same standards of care as if it were a prospectus within the meaning of the Companies Act 1948. Especial care shall be taken over profit forecasts.

13. Where control of a company is acquired by a person, or persons acting in concert, a general offer to all other shareholders is normally required; a similar obligation may arise if control is consolidated. Where shares are being acquired as a result of which a person incurs such an obligation, he should, before making such an acquisition, ensure that he can and will continue to be able to implement the offer.

14. An offeror should only announce an offer after the most careful and responsible consideration. Such an announcement should be made only when an offeror has every reason to believe that it can and will continue to be able to implement the offer. Responsibility in this connection also rests on the financial advisers to an offeror.

Rules

1. The offer should be put forward in the first instance to the board of the offeree company or to its advisers.

2. If the offer or an approach with a view to an offer being made is not made by a principal, the identity of the principal must be disclosed at the outset.

3. A board so approached is entitled to be satisfied that the offeror is or will be in a position to implement the offer in full.

4. The board of the offeree company must obtain competent independent advice on any offer and the substance of such advice must be made known to its shareholders. The Panel would not normally regard as an appropriate person to give such advice a person who has a substantial financial connection with the offeror or offeree company of such a kind as to create a conflict of interest for that person.

5. When any firm intention to make an offer is notified to a board from a serious source (irrespective of whether the board views the offer favourably or otherwise), shareholders must be informed without delay by press notice. A copy of the press notice, or a circular informing shareholders of the offer, should, on the occasion of the first such press notice, normally be sent to shareholders promptly after the announcement.

Where there have been approaches which may or may not lead to an offer, the duty of a board in relation to shareholders is less clearly defined.

There are obvious dangers in announcing prematurely an approach which may not lead to an offer. By way of guidance it can be said that an announcement that talks are taking place which may lead to an offer should be made as soon as two companies are reasonably confident of a successful outcome to negotiations.

In any situation which might lead to an offer being made, whether welcome or not, a close watch should be kept on the share market; in the event of any untoward movement in share prices an immediate announcement, accompanied by such comment as may be appropriate, should be made.

6. Joint statements are desirable whenever possible, provided that agreement thereon does not lead to undue delay. The obligation to make announcements lies no less with the potential offeror than with the offeree company.

7. The vital importance of absolute secrecy before an announcement must be emphasised.

8. When an offer is announced, the terms of the offer and the identity of the offeror must be disclosed. The offeror must also disclose any existing holding in the offeree company which it owns or over which it has control or which is owned or controlled by any person acting in concert with it.

All conditions (including normal conditions relating to acceptances, listing and increase of capital) to which an offer or the posting of it is subject must be stated in the formal announcement.

9. Where an offer comes within the statutory provisions for possible reference to the Monopolies and Mergers Commission, it should be a term of the offer that it shall lapse if there is a reference before the first closing date or the date when the offer becomes or is declared unconditional as to acceptances, whichever is the later.

Except in the case of an offer under Rule 34, the offeror may, in addition, make the offer conditional on a statement being issued that there will not be a reference.

Where the law requires any proposed offer to be given prior clearance before it may be implemented, by for example the European Commission under the Treaty of Paris, the offer document should not be despatched until such necessary clearance has been obtained.

10. The offer document should normally be posted within 28 days of the announcement of the terms of the offer and at the same time, or as soon as practicable thereafter, the board of the offeree company should circulate its views on the offer, including any alternative forms of consideration offered. The Panel should be consulted if the offer document is not to be posted within this period.

Where there has been an announcement of an offer (as opposed to an announcement that talks are taking place which may lead to an offer) the offer cannot be withdrawn without the consent of the Panel.

11. Where directors (and their close relatives and related trusts) sell shares to a purchaser, as a result of which the purchaser is required to make an offer under Rule 34, the directors must ensure that as a condition of the sale the purchaser undertakes to fulfil his obligations under Rule 34. In addition, except with the consent of the Panel, such directors should not resign from the board until the first closing date of the offer or the date when the offer becomes or is declared unconditional as to acceptances, whichever is the later.

12. Any information, including particulars of shareholders, given to a preferred suitor should on request be furnished equally and as promptly to a less welcome but *bona fide* potential offeror.

13. There must be included in every offer document:

(1) a statement as to whether or not any agreement, arrangement or understanding exists between the offeror or any person acting in concert with it and any of the directors, or recent directors, shareholders or recent shareholders of the offeree company having any connection with or dependence upon the offer, and full particulars of any such agreement, arrangement or understanding; and

(2) a statement as to whether or not any securities acquired in pursuance of the offer will be transferred to any other person, together with the names of the parties to any such agreement, arrangement or understanding and particulars of all securities in the offeree company held by such persons, or a statement that no such securities are held.

14. Any document or advertisement addressed to shareholders in connection with an offer must be treated with the same standards of care with regard to the statements made therein as if it were a prospectus within the meaning of the Companies Act 1948. This applies whether the document or advertisement is issued by the company direct or by an adviser on its behalf. Each document or advertisement addressed to shareholders of the offeree company must state that the directors of the offeror and/or, where appropriate, the offeree company (including any who may have delegated detailed supervision of the document or advertisement) have taken all reasonable care to ensure that the facts stated and opinions expressed therein are fair and accurate and, where appropriate, no material facts have been omitted and also state that they jointly and severally accept responsibility accordingly. If it is proposed that any director should be excluded from such a statement, the Panel's consent is required. Such consent is only given in exceptional circumstances and in such cases the omission and the reasons for it must be stated in the document or advertisement.
A copy of the authority on behalf of the board of the company for the issue of such document or advertisement must be lodged with the Panel.

15. Shareholders must be put in possession of all the facts necessary for the formation of an informed judgement as to the merits or demerits of an offer. Such facts must be accurately and fairly presented and be available to the shareholder early enough to enable him to make a decision in good time. The obligation of the offeror in these respects towards the shareholders of the offeree company is no less than the offeror's obligation towards its own shareholders. In particular, whether or not the consideration in an offer is cash, information should be given about the offeror (including the names of its directors).
The offeror will normally be expected to cover the following points in the offer document and the board of the offeree company should, in so far as relevant, comment upon such statements in a letter to its shareholders:

(1) its intentions regarding the continuation of the business of the offeree company;

(2) its intentions regarding any major changes to be introduced in the business, including any re-deployment of the fixed assets of the offeree company;

(3) the long-term commercial justification for the proposed offer; and

(4) its intentions with regard to the continued employment of the employees of the offeree company.

16. Without in any way detracting from the necessity of maintaining the highest standards of accuracy and fair presentation in all communications to shareholders in a take-over or merger transaction, attention is particularly drawn in this connection to profit forecasts and asset valuations.

(1) Notwithstanding the obvious hazard attached to the forecasting of profits, any profit forecasts must be compiled with the greatest possible care by the directors whose sole responsibility they are.

When profit forecasts appear in any document addressed to shareholders in connection with an offer, the assumptions, including the commercial assumptions, upon which the directors have based their profit forecasts, must be stated in the document.

The accounting bases and calculations for the forecasts must be examined and reported on by the auditors or consultant accountants. Any financial adviser mentioned in the document must also report on the forecasts. The accountants' report and, if there is an adviser, his report, must be contained in such document and be accompanied by a statement that the accountants and, where relevant, the adviser have given and not withdrawn their consent to publication.

Wherever profit forecasts appear in relation to a period in which trading has already commenced, the latest unaudited profit figures which are available in respect of the expired portion of that trading period together with comparable figures for the preceding year must be stated. Alternatively, if no figures are available, that fact must be stated.

(2) When valuations of assets are given in connection with an offer the board should be supported by the opinion of a named independent valuer and the basis of valuation clearly stated. The document should also state that the valuer has given and not withdrawn his consent to the publication of his name therein.

17. (1) The offer document must state:

(a) the shareholdings of the offeror in the offeree company;

(b) the shareholdings in the offeror (in the case of a share exchange offer only) and in the offeree company in which directors of the offeror are interested;

(c) the shareholdings in the offeror (in the case of a share exchange offer only) and in the offeree company which any person acting in concert with the offeror owns or controls (with the names of such persons acting in concert);

(d) the shareholdings in the offeror (in the case of a share exchange offer only) and in the offeree company owned or controlled by any persons who, prior to the posting of the offer document, have irrevocably committed themselves to accept the offer together with the names of such persons.

(2) The document of the offeree company advising its shareholders on an offer (whether recommending acceptance or rejection of the offer) must state:

(a) the shareholdings of the offeree company in the offeror;

(*b*) the shareholdings in the offeree company and in the offeror in which directors of the offeree company are interested;

(*c*) whether the directors of the offeree company intend, in respect of their own beneficial shareholdings, to accept or reject the offer.

(3) If in any of the above categories there are no shareholdings then this fact should be stated.

(4) If any party referred to above has dealt for value in the shares in question during the period commencing 12 months prior to the beginning of the offer period and ending with the latest practicable date prior to the posting of the offer document, the details, including dates and prices, must be stated. If no such deals have been made this fact should be stated.

References in this Rule to shareholdings include, where appropriate, holdings of securities convertible into equity share capital and any rights to subscribe for such capital.

18. Where the offer is for cash or includes an element of cash, the offer document must include confirmation by the financial adviser or by another appropriate independent party that resources are available to the offeror sufficient to satisfy full acceptance of the offer.

19. Documents sent to shareholders of the offeree company recommending acceptance or rejection of offers must contain particulars of all service contracts of any director or proposed director with the offeree company or any of its subsidiaries (unless expiring, or determinable by the employing company without payment of compensation, other than statutory compensation, within 12 months); if there are none, this fact should be stated. If such contracts have been entered into or have been amended within 6 months of the date of the document, the particulars of the contracts amended or replaced should be given; if there have been no new contracts or amendments, this should be stated.

Offer documents on behalf of the offeror should state, except in the case of a cash offer, whether its directors' emoluments will be affected by the acquisition of the offeree company.

20. In order to facilitate the work of the Panel, copies of all public announcements made and all documents bearing on a take-over or merger transaction must be lodged with the Panel at the same time as they are made or despatched.

21. No offer, which, if accepted in full, would result in the offeror having voting control of the offeree company, shall be made unless it is a condition of such offer that the offer will not become or be declared unconditional as to acceptances unless the offeror has acquired or agreed to acquire (either pursuant to the offer or by shares acquired or agreed to be acquired before or during the offer) by the close of the offer shares carrying over 50% of the votes attributable to the equity share capital.

No offer for equity share capital may be declared unconditional as to acceptances unless, in addition to complying with the foregoing, the offeror has acquired the right to exercise over 50% of the voting rights of the offeree company. Classes of non-equity capital need not be the subject of an offer.

Where a company has more than one class of equity share capital, a comparable offer must be made for each class; the Panel should be consulted in advance if more than one class carries votes. An offer for non-voting equity capital should not be made conditional on any particular level of acceptances in respect of that class unless the offer for the voting capital is also conditional on the success of the offer for the non-voting equity capital.

This Rule does not apply to offers required to be made under Rule 34 which are subject to the special provisions set out therein.

22. An offer must initially be open for at least 21 days after the posting of the offer and, if revised, it must be kept open for at least 14 days from the date of posting written notification of the revision to shareholders; an acceptor shall be entitled to withdraw his acceptance in any case after the expiry of 21 days from the first closing date of the initial offer, if the offer has not by such expiry become or been declared unconditional as to acceptances; such entitlement to withdraw shall be exercisable until such time as the offer becomes or is declared unconditional as to acceptances. If an offer is revised, all shareholders who accepted the original offer must receive the revised consideration.

No offer (whether revised or not) shall be capable of becoming or being declared unconditional as to acceptances after 3.30 p.m. on the 60th day after the date the offer is initially posted nor of being kept open after the expiry of such period unless it has previously so become or been declared unconditional. An offer may be extended beyond that period of 60 days with the permission of the Panel, which will normally only be granted if a competing offer has been announced.

If any announcement of an extension of an offer the next expiry date must be stated.

Except with the consent of the Panel, all conditions must be fulfilled or the offer must lapse within 21 days of the first closing date or of the date the offer becomes or is declared unconditional as to acceptances, whichever is the later.

23. (1) After an offer has become or is declared unconditional as to acceptances, the offer must remain open for acceptance for not less than 14 days after the date on which it would otherwise have expired, except in the event that the offer becomes or is declared unconditional as to acceptances on or by an expiry date and the offeror has given at least 14 days' notice in writing to the shareholders of the offeree company that the offer will not be open for acceptance beyond that date. Such notice shall not be capable of being enforced in a competitive situation.

(2) If, once an offer is unconditional as to acceptances, it is stated that the offer will remain open until further notice, 14 days' notice should be given before it is closed.

24. By 9.30 a.m. at the latest on the dealing day next following the day on which an offer is due to expire, or becomes or is declared unconditional as to acceptances, or is revised or extended, the offeror shall announce and simultaneously inform The Stock Exchange of the position and shall also state the total number of shares (as nearly as practicable):

(1) for which acceptances of the offer have been received;

(2) held before the offer period; and

(3) acquired or agreed to be acquired during the offer period.

25. (1) If the offeror is unable within the time limit to comply with any of the requirements of Rule 24, The Stock Exchange will consider suspension of dealings in the offeree company's shares and, where appropriate, in the offeror's shares until the relevant information is given.

(2) If the offeror, having announced the offer to be unconditional as to acceptances, fails by 3.30 p.m. on the relevant day to comply with any of the requirements of Rule 24, then immediately thereafter any acceptor shall be entitled to withdraw his acceptance. Subject to the second paragraph of Rule 22, this right of withdrawal may be terminated not less than 8 days after the relevant day by the offeror confirming (if that be the case) that the offer is still unconditional as to acceptances and complying with Rule 24.

(3) For the purpose of Rule 23 (1) the period of 14 days referred to therein will run from the date of such confirmation.

26. The obligations of the offeror and the rights of the offeree company shareholders under Rules 21–25 must be specifically incorporated in the offer document. Where an offer is unconditional as to acceptances from the outset, Rule 21 is inappropriate and Rules 22–25 should be applied as necessary.

27. The Panel's consent is required for any partial offer.

In the case of an offer which would result in the offeror holding shares carrying over 50% but less than 100% of the voting rights of a company, such consent will not normally be granted if an offer for the whole of the equity share capital of the offeree company has already been announced or if the offeror or persons acting in concert with it have acquired, selectively or in significant numbers, shares in the offeree company during the 12 months preceding the application for consent. Any such offer must be conditional upon approval of the offer by shareholders in respect of over 50% of the voting rights not held by the offeror or persons acting in concert with it.

In the case of an offer which would result in the offeror holding shares carrying not less than 30% and not more than 50% of the voting rights of a company, such consent will be granted only in exceptional circumstances and in any event not unless the board of the offeree company recommends the offer. Any such offer must be conditional upon approval of the offer by shareholders in respect of over 50% of the voting rights not held by the offeror or persons acting in concert with it. Where such an offer is made the precise number of shares offered for must be stated and the offer may not be declared unconditional as to acceptances unless acceptances are received for not less than that number.

In the case of an offer which would result in the offeror holding shares carrying less than 30% of the voting rights of a company, consent will normally be granted.

Partial offers must be made to all shareholders of the class and arrangements must be made for those shareholders who wish to do so to accept in full for the relevant percentage of their holdings.

Where a company has more than one class of equity share capital a comparable offer must be made for each class.

In the case of a partial offer the offeror and persons acting in concert with it may not purchase shares in the offeree company during the offer period nor, in the case of a successful partial offer, may the offeror or persons acting in concert, except with the consent of the Panel, purchase such shares during a period of 12 months after the end of the offer period.

28. Where an offer is made for more than one class of share, separate offers must be made for each class and the offeror should state, if it intends to resort to compulsory acquisition powers under section 209 of the Companies Act 1948, that the section will be used only in respect of each class separately.

29. (1) Where an offer is made for equity share capital and the offeree company has convertible securities outstanding, the offeror must make appropriate arrangements to ensure that the interests of the holders of the stock are safeguarded and in particular that the existence of a conversion option over a period of time is adequately recognised. Taking this into account, the offeror should make an appropriate offer or proposal to the stockholders.

(2) The board of the offeree company must obtain competent independent advice on any offer or proposal to the stockholders and the substance of such advice must be made known to its stockholders.

(3) Whenever practicable the offer or proposal should be despatched to stockholders at the same time that the offer document is posted to shareholders, but if this is not practicable the Panel should be consulted and the offer or proposal should be despatched as soon as possible thereafter.

(4) The offer or proposal to stockholders required by this Rule may be carried out by way of a scheme to be considered by a stockholders' meeting.

(5) If an offeree company has warrants, options or subscription rights outstanding the provisions of this Rule apply *mutatis mutandis.*

30. All persons concerned with the consideration and discussion of any proposed offer must treat the information related to the potential offer as secret and must not pass it to any other person unless it is necessary to do so. Furthermore, such persons must conduct themselves so as to minimise the chances of an accidental leak of information.

No dealings of any kind (including option business) in the securities of the offeree company by any person, not being the offeror, who is privy to the preliminary take-over or merger discussions or to an intention to make an offer may take place between the time when there is reason to suppose that an approach or an offer is contemplated and the announcement of the approach or offer or the termination of the discussions.

No such dealings shall take place in the securities of the offeror except where the proposed offer is not deemed price sensitive in relation to such securities.

Without prejudice to the generality of the foregoing, a person shall be regarded as 'privy to the preliminary take-over or merger discussions or to an intention to make an offer' if, assuming he has received relevant information, either

(1) he is a director or employee of one of the companies involved in the proposed offer; or

(2) he is a professional adviser either to one of the companies involved in the proposed offer or to any director or employee of such a company; or

(3) that information was received in the context of a confidential relationship and it was necessary that he received such information.

The spouse and the close relatives and related trusts of such a person would be deemed to be in the same position as such person.

31. Save in so far as appears from the Code, it is considered undesirable to fetter the market. Accordingly, all parties to a take-over or merger transaction (other than to a partial offer) and associates are free to deal subject to daily disclosure to The Stock Exchange, the Panel and the press

(not later than 12 noon on the dealing day following the date of the relevant transaction) of the total of all shares of any offeror or the offeree company purchased or sold by them or their respective associates for their own account on any day during the offer period in the market or otherwise and at what price.

In addition all purchases and sales of shares of any offeror or the offeree company made by associates for account of investment clients who are not themselves associates must be similarly reported to The Stock Exchange and to the Panel, but need not be disclosed to the press.

32. If the offeror or any person acting in concert with it purchases securities during the offer period at above the offer price (being the then current value of the offer) then it shall increase its offer to not less than the highest price (excluding stamp duty and commission) paid for the securities so acquired. An announcement of any such purchase and the consequent increased offer must be made immediately.

If the offer involves a further issue of already listed securities, the current value of the offer should normally be established by reference to the means of the prices quoted by all those jobbers dealing in such securities at the time the purchase is effected. The same method should normally be used to calculate the value of such securities for the purpose of ascertaining what minimum increased consideration should be offered.

If the offer involves the issue of securities which are not already listed, the value shall be based on a reasonable estimate of what the price would have been had they been listed.

If there is a restricted market in the securities of the offerör, or if the amount of already listed securities to be issued is large in relation to the amount already listed, the Panel may require justification of prices used to determine the value of the offer.

Shareholders of the offeree company must be notified in writing of the increased price payable under this Rule at least 14 days before the offer closes.

33. If (1) the shares of any class under offer in the offeree company pur-
chased for cash by the offeror and any person acting in concert with it during the offer period and within 12 months prior to its commencement carry 15 % or more of the voting rights of that class,

   or

   (2) in the view of the Panel there are circumstances which render such a course necessary in order to give effect to General Principle 8,

then, except with the consent of the Panel in cases falling under (1) above, the offer for that class shall be in cash or accompanied by a cash alternative at not less than the highest price (excluding stamp duty and commission) paid for shares of that class purchased during the offer period and within 12 months prior to its commencement.

If the offeror considers that the highest price (as defined above) should not apply to a particular case, the offeror should consult the Panel which will have discretion to agree an adjusted price.

34. (1) Except with the consent of the Panel, where

   (a) any person acquires, whether by a series of transactions over a period of time or not, shares which (together with shares acquired by persons acting in concert with him) carry 30 % or more of the voting rights of a company, or

(b) any person who, together with persons acting in concert, holds not less than 30% but not more than 50% of the voting rights and such person, together with persons acting in concert, acquires in any period of 12 months additional shares increasing such percentage of the voting rights by more than 2%,

such person shall extend an offer on the basis set out below to the holders of any class of share capital which carries votes and in which such person or persons acting in concert hold shares. In addition to such person, each of the principal members of the group of persons acting in concert may, according to the circumstances of the case, have the obligation to extend an offer. A comparable offer shall be extended to the holders of any other class of equity share capital whether such capital carries voting rights or not.

(2) Any offer under this Rule must, if appropriate, contain the provision as to reference to the Monopolies and Mergers Commission required under Rule 9. Apart from the foregoing and the provisions of paragraph (3) below, except with the consent of the Panel, any acquisition of shares which might give rise to a requirement for an offer under the provisions of this Rule must not be made if the implementation of such offer would or might be dependent on the passing of a resolution at any meeting of shareholders of the offeror or upon any other conditions, consents or arrangements.

(3) Offers made under this Rule shall be conditional upon the offeror having received acceptances in respect of shares which, together with shares acquired or agreed to be acquired before or during the offer, will result in the offeror and persons acting in concert holding shares carrying more than 50% of the voting rights but shall be subject to no other conditions, except as required by paragraph (2) above. It follows that the offer shall be unconditional as to acceptances where the offeror and persons acting in concert hold shares carrying more than 50% of the voting rights before such offer is made.

(4) The offer required to be made under the provisions of this Rule shall, in respect of each class of share capital involved, be in cash or be accompanied by a cash alternative at not less than the highest price (excluding stamp duty and commission) paid by the offeror and persons acting in concert for shares of that class within the preceding 12 months; where any such shares have been acquired for a consideration other than cash General Principle 8 may be relevant and the Panel should be consulted. The Panel should also be consulted as to the offer to be made for any class of share capital in respect of which no acquisitions have taken place within the preceding 12 months or where there is more than one class of share capital involved.

If the offeror considers that the highest price (as defined above) should not apply to a particular case, the offeror should consult the Panel which will have discretion to agree an adjusted price.

(5) Immediately upon an acquisition of shares which gives rise to an obligation to make an offer under this Rule, the offeror shall make an announcement of his offer giving the information required by the Code.

The announcement of an offer under this Rule should include confirmation by the financial adviser or by another appropriate independent party that resources are available to the offeror sufficient to satisfy full acceptance of the offer.

(6) Except with the consent of the Panel, no nominee of the offeror or persons acting in concert shall be appointed to the board of the offeree company, nor shall the offeror and persons acting in concert transfer, or exercise the votes attaching to, any shares held in the offeree company, until the offer document has been posted.

35. Except with the consent of the Panel, where an offer has been announced or posted but has not become unconditional in all respects the offeror and persons acting in concert with it may not within 12 months from the date on which such offer is withdrawn or lapses either

(1) make an offer for the offeree company,

or

(2) acquire any shares of the offeree company if the offeror or persons acting in concert with it would thereby become obliged under Rule 34 to make an offer.

36. Except with the consent of the Panel, the offeror or persons acting in concert with it may not enter into arrangements to deal or make purchases or sales of shares of the offeree company, either during an offer or when one is reasonably in contemplation, if such arrangements to deal, purchases or sales have attached thereto favourable conditions which are not being extended to all shareholders.

37. Since dealings in the market or otherwise by a person with a commercial interest in the outcome of an offer may result in a *bona fide* offer being frustrated or may affect the outcome of an offer, such person must consult the Panel in advance and be prepared to justify his proposed action as not being prejudicial to the interests of the shareholders as a whole.

38. During the course of an offer, or even before the date of the offer if the board of the offeree company has reason to believe that a *bona fide* offer might be imminent, the board must not, except in pursuance of a contract entered into earlier, without the approval of the shareholders in general meeting, issue any authorised but unissued shares, or issue or grant options in respect of any unissued shares, create or issue or permit the creation or issue of any securities carrying rights of conversion into or subscription for shares of the company, or sell, dispose of or acquire or agree to sell, dispose of or acquire assets of material amount or enter into contracts otherwise than in the ordinary course of business. Where it is felt that an obligation or other special circumstance exists, although a formal contract has not been entered into, the Panel must be consulted and its consent obtained.

39. The board and officials of an offeree company should take action to ensure during a take-over or merger transaction the prompt registration of transfers so that shareholders can freely exercise their voting and other rights. Provisions in Articles of Association which lay down a qualifying period after registration during which the registered holder cannot exercise his vote are highly undesirable.

APPENDIX IV

Major Acquisitions
1968/69

Acquiring company	Acquired company	Value of consideration for equity			
		Total £000s	Cash £000s	Equity £000s	Other £000s
General Electric	English Electric Co	280,728	—	206,620	73,658
Thorn Electrical Industries	Radio Rentals	210,113	—	210,113	—
Allied Breweries	Showerings, Vine Prod. and Whiteways	103,229	—	98,909	4,320
American Tobacco International	Gallaher	76,050	76,050	—	—
Ranks Hovis McDougall	Cerebos	56,686	—	40,947	15,739
Tarmac Derby	Derbyshire Stone	40,744	—	40,744	—
Boots Pure Drug Co	Timothy Whites & Taylors	38,639	—	32,747	5,892
Brooke Bond Liebig	Liebig's Extract of Meat Co	35,989	—	28,898	7,091
Dunlop Co	George Angus & Co	29,480	—	29,480	—
English Calico	Calico Printers' Association	23,415	—	18,167	5,248
Courtaulds	International Paints (Holdings)	19,788	—	14,908	4,880
Initial Services	Allied Industrial Services	19,023	—	14,460	4,563
Reyrolle Parsons	C. A. Parsons & Co	14,460	—	—	14,460
Unilever	Reichold Chemicals	13,026	13,026	—	—
Tarmac	William Briggs & Sons	11,631	—	11,631	—
Great Universal Stores	Times Furnishing	11,575	6,119	5,456	—
Imperial Tobacco	National Canning	8,493	8,493	—	—
Slater Walker Securities	TWW	7,870	1,298	—	6,572
Associated Engineering	Edmunds, Walker	7,350	7,350	—	—
General Electric Co	Walsall Conduits	7,004	—	7,004	—
Clarkson (Engineers)	Tap & Die	6,346	—	6,346	—
Lindustries	William Warne	5,963	1,702	2,904	1,357
Rank Organisation	Strand Electrical Holdings	5,519	—	—	5,519

Extracted from 'The Times 500', 1969/70, covering the fiscal year 1968/69

Major Acquisitions
1969/70

Acquiring company	Acquired company	Value of consolidation for equity			
		Total £000s	Cash £000s	Equity £000s	Other £000s
Imperial Tobacco Group	Ross Group	39,816	—	20,792	19,022
Grand Metropolitan Hotels	Express Dairy Co	31,193	—	22,200	8,993
Hepworth Ceramic Holdings	Hepworth Iron Co	29,876	—	29,876	—
Hoechst U.K.	Berger, Jenson & Nicholson	26,144	26,144	—	—
Hepworth Ceramic Holdings	General Refractories	23,315	—	20,790	2,525
Nicholas Australia	Aspro-Nicholas	22,262	—	22,262	—
Glynwed	Allied Ironfounders	21,862	—	8,830	13,032
Burmah Oil	Halfords	14,180	—	14,180	—
Distillers Co	United Glass	12,949	12,949	—	—
Mecca	Clubman's Club	11,270	—	11,270	—
Hawker Siddeley	Brook Motors	11,110	11,110	—	—
Philips Brocklehurst	Anglo Portuguese Telephone Co	10,988	—	10,802	186
British Petroleum	Alexander Duckham & Co	10,916	—	10,916	—
Electrical & Musical Inds	Associated Fire Alarms	10,066	—	10,066	—
Charter Consolidated	Cape Asbestos	10,022	—	3,549	6,473
Ransome & Marles Bearing	Pollard Ball & Roller Bearing Co	9,430	9,430	—	—
Monsanto Textiles	Monsanto Chemicals	9,396	—	—	9,396
Forte's Holdings	Skyway Hotels	9,192	—	7,909	1,283
Slater, Walker Securities	Philips Brocklehurst	9,025	—	—	9,025
Dupont	Slumberland Group	8,590	—	3,168	5,402

Extract from 'The Times 1000', Table 2—1970/71, covering the fiscal year 1969/70

Major Acquisitions
1970/71

Acquiring company	Acquired company	Value of consideration for equity			
		Total £000s	Cash £000s	Equity £000s	Other £000s
Reed Group	International Publishing Corpn	104,674	—	95,554	9,120
Sears Holdings	British Shoe Corpn	70,747	—	70,747	—
Trust Houses Group	Forte Holdings	60,222	—	60,222	—
British American Tobacco	Wiggins Teape	52,095	8,100	—	43,995
Imperial Chemical Industries	Carrington Viyella	44,316	—	44,316	—
Courage Barclay & Simonds	John Smith's Tadcaster Brewery	36,745	—	10,062	26,683
Rio Tinto-Zinc Corpn	R.T.Z. Pillar	35,543	—	35,543	—
Grand Metropolitan Hotels	Mecca	30,074	—	12,709	17,365
Grand Metropolitan Hotels	Berni Inns	14,178	—	14,178	—
Trafalgar House Invests	Cementation	13,889	—	8,744	5,145
Shipping Industrial Holdings	Dene Shipping	10,479	—	10,479	—
Steetley	Berk	10,342	—	6,482	3,860
P & O Steam Navigation	Coast Lines	9,310	—	9,310	—
Lex Service Group	Steels Garages	8,998	—	3,804	5,194
Consolidated Goldfields	Greenwoods (St. Ives)	8,213	1,009	7,204	—
Brown Brothers & Albany	Brown Brothers	8,175	—	3,706	4,468
G. N. Haden	Carrier Engineering	7,917	2,000	3,932	1,985
Courage	Plymouth Breweries	6,414	—	—	6,414
Intl Timber Corpn	Horseley Smith & Jewson	5,328	—	1,226	4,102
United Builders Merchants	Mercian Builders Merchants	4,735	—	4,735	—

Extract from 'The Times 1000', Table 2—1971/72, covering the fiscal year 1970/71

Major Acquisitions
1971/72

Acquiring company	Acquired company	Value of consideration for equity			
		Total £000s	Cash £000s	Equity £000s	Other £000s
Watney Mann	International Distillers & Vintners	76,758	5,549	71,209	—
Cavenham	Allied Suppliers	70,748	—	55,811	14,937
Grand Metropolitan Hotels	Truman	39,525	10,941	11,624	16,960
C. T. Bowering & Co	Singer & Friedlander	24,096		24,096	—
Trafalgar House Invests	Cunard Steam Ship Co	23,214	989	15,573	6,652
Sears Holdings	William Hill Orgn	23,079		—	23,079
British Electric Traction	United Transport Co	22,525		22,525	—
Watney Mann	Samuel Webster & Sons	20,447		20,447	—
Whitbread & Co	Brickwoods	18,939		14,522	4,417
Delta Metal	Midland Electric Mfg	18,563		13,268	5,295
Redland	Purle Brothers Holdings	15,869		11,953	3,916
Macowards	Maple & Co	14,756		12,893	1,863
S. Pearson & Sons	Doulton & Co	14,680		7,370	7,310
S. Pearson & Sons	Penguin Publishing Co.	14,079		10,178	3,901
Rank Organisation	City Wall Properties	13,987		13,987	—
Carlton Industries	Oldham Intl	13,037	13,037		—
Reed Intl	Twyfords Holdings	11,829		10,354	1,475
Imperial Chemical Industries	Qualitex	10,959		10,959	—
Slater, Walker Securities	Wigham-Richardson	10,244		5,168	5,076
Great Universal Stores	J & F Stone Lighting & Radio	9,990	3,600	6,390	—

Extract from 'The Times 1000', Table 2—1972/73, covering the fiscal year 1971/72

Major Acquisitions
1972/73

Acquiring company	Acquired company	Value of consideration for equity			
		Total £000s	Cash £000s	Equity £000s	Other £000s
Grand Metropolitan Hotels	Watney Mann	378,268	—	169,708	208,560
Imperial Group	Courage	257,723	—	123,121	134,602
Bowater Corpn	Ralli International	87,094	—	87,094	—
British-American Tobacco	International Stores	63,519	—	63,519	—
Consolidated Gold Fields	Amey Group	54,729	—	54,729	—
Ocean Steam Ship Co	Wm Cory & Son	53,166	13,757	39,409	—
Burmah Oil Co	Quinton Hazell (Holdings)	48,706	1,277	33,680	13,749
Unigate	Scot Bowyers	41,687	—	22,591	19,096
Rank Orgn	Butlin's	38,196	—	19,600	18,596
Guest, Keen & Nettlefolds	Firth Cleveland	27,243	—	—	27,243
Richard Johnson & Nephew	Thos Firth & John Brown	26,945	—	14,153	12,792
United Drapery Stores	William Timpson	25,433	25,433	—	—
Lewis & Peat	Guiness Mahon	23,325	2,428	9,602	11,295
Acrow (Engineers)	Steel Group	22,417	—	15,371	7,046
Mathews Wrightson Group	Mathews Wrightson Hldgs	22,192	—	22,192	—
Bowyers (Wiltshire)	Scot Meat Products	20,263	—	20,263	—
Mathews Wrightson Group	Mercury Insurance Hldgs	19,740	—	15,120	4,620
Dalgety	Ass. British Maltsters	18,498	—	14,029	4,469
Glynwed	John Cashmore	16,038	724	15,314	—
J. H. Vavasseur & Co	Barclay Securities	15,697	975	6,195	8,527

Extract from 'The Times 1000', Table 2—1973/74, covering the fiscal year 1972/73

Major Acquisitions
1973/74

Acquiring company	Acquired company	Value of consideration for equity			
		Total £000s	Cash £000s	Equity £000s	Other £000s
Navcot Shipping (Holdings)	Shipping Industrial Holdings	90,437	90,437	—	—
House of Fraser	Army & Navy Stores	40,263	27,747	12,516	—
Champion International Corpn	AW (Securities)	40,026	40,026	—	—
Rank Organisation	Oddenino's Property and Investment Co	22,410	6,675	15,735	—
Peninsular & Oriental Steam Navigation Co	Bovis	21,810	—	21,810	—
Argyle Securities	Cornwall Property (Holdings)	16,950	—	8,851	8,099
Inchcape & Co	Mann Egerton & Co	16,813	—	12,565	4,248
British Match Corpn	Wilkinson Sword	16,795	—	6,384	10,411
British Land Co	Dorothy Perkins	16,302	16,302	—	—
Thomas Tilling	F. J. Reeves	13,879	—	8,737	5,142
International Stores	Pricerite	12,000	12,000	—	—
Bristol Street Group	Griffiths Bentley & Co	11,536	—	6,912	4,624
Gallaher	Forbuoys	10,939	10,939	—	—
Nottingham Manfg	Lancaster Carpets & Eng	10,704	—	—	10,704
Unilever	Kennedy's (Builders Merchants)	10,703	10,703	—	—
Norcros	Crittall-Hope Eng	10,601	—	10,601	—
Thorn Electrical Inds	Clarkson International Tools	10,251	10,251	—	—

Extract from 'The Times 1000', 1974/75, covering the fiscal year 1973/74

Major Acquisitions
1974/75

Acquiring company	Acquired company	Value of consideration for Equity			
		Total £000s	Cash £000s	Equity £000s	Other £000s
Town & City Properties	Sterling Guarantee Trust	27,309	7,523	8,689	11,097
C.S.R.	Australian Estates Co	24,606	24,606	—	—
American Tobacco Intl	Gallaher	23,322	23,322	—	—
Eagle Star Insurance Co	Grovewood Securities	13,857	—	13,857	—
Guest, Keen & Nettlefolds	Miles Druce & Co	11,688	11,688	—	—
Interlake Inc	Dexion-Comino Intl	9,065	9,065	—	—
Dawson International	Joseph Dawson (Holdings)	9,063	—	9,063	—
Charterhouse Group	Charterhouse Invest Trust	9,016	5,600	3,416	—
RCA Intl	Morris & David Jones	8,473	8,473	—	—
Bowater Corpn	Peter Dixon & Son (Holdings)	7,500	—	—	7,500
London Brick Co	Banbury Buildings	7,139	—	—	7,139
Brooke Bond Liebig	Baxters (Butchers)	7,010	—	7,010	—

Extract from 'The Times 1000', 1975/76, covering the fiscal year 1974/75

APPENDIX V

TYPICAL EXAMINATION QUESTIONS

1. Outline the origins and subsequent history of the City Code and the Panel on Take-overs and Mergers – their structure, spirit and sanctions.

2. In a take-over bid the bidder may propose to offer either wholly cash or an issue of its own securities in exchange for the ordinary share capital of the offeree company.

What are the advantages and disadvantages of each form of consideration so far as (*a*) the bidding company and (*b*) the shareholders of the offeree company are concerned?

3. A take-over bid may be vigorously opposed by the board of directors of the defending company. What are the usual grounds for opposing a bid and what means of defence are open to the board in such circumstances?

4. In presenting the 1969/70 Report of the Panel on Take-overs and Mergers, the chairman, Lord Shawcross said '. . . in a few years' time self-regulation in the take-over field will be taken for granted even by those who today are its sternest critics.'

How did the regulations referred to above come into being and what criticisms have been levelled at them?

5. How has public policy towards mergers in the U.K. developed since 1965? What safeguards have been introduced in order to curb the growth of monopolies?

6. (*a*) What are the usual bases adopted for the valuation of commercial goodwill?

(*b*) The net tangible assets of a company are valued at £80,000. Earnings for the past five years have been as follows:

						£
Year 1	..	..	..	..	..	13,000
,, 2	..	..	..	..	..	16,000
,, 3	..	..	..	..	..	19,000
,, 4	..	..	..	..	..	25,000
,, 5	..	..	..	..	..	27,000

Quoted public companies engaged in a similar industry show a return of $17\frac{1}{2}\%$ p.a. What values might be placed on goodwill in this case, using different methods of computation? Ignore taxation.

7. Stretchtwist Ltd. is a public company engaged in the plastics industry and it is proposing to make a bid for the whole of the issued share capital of Pliable Pins Ltd. which is a private company operating in a similar line of business. The ordinary shareholdings in Pliable Pins Ltd. are evenly distributed between twelve members. The preference shares are held by one other person.

In the event of liquidation the preference shareholders are entitled only to a repayment of the nominal value of their shares. There is no right to share in any profits after the 7% has been paid.

The expected market return on similar preference shares is 6%.

From the following information draft a concise and informative report to the Preference and Ordinary shareholders of Pliable Pins Ltd. setting out your recommendations as to what you would consider to be a reasonable price for each class of shares.

BALANCE SHEET

	£		£
Share Capital:		*Fixed Assets:*	
7% Preference Shares	20,000	Buildings	95,000
£1 Ordinary Shares ..	200,000	Plant & Machinery ..	105,000
	220,000		200,000
Revenue Reserve ..	70,000	*Current Assets:*	
Future Tax	10,000	Govt. Securities ..	60,000
	300,000	(market value £52,000)..	
Trade Creditors ..	25,000	Stock	20,000
		Debtors	40,000
		Cash	5,000
	£325,000		£325,000

PROFIT RECORD – YEARS ENDING DECEMBER 31ST

				Trading profit (before tax)	Investment Income	Directors' remuneration
				£	£	£
1964	..	..	..	24,000	—	2,500
1965	..	..	..	25,000	2,500	4,000
1966	..	..	..	23,000	3,000	7,000
1967	..	..	..	20,000	3,000	9,000

Notes: (a) It is considered that had outside Directors been employed the cost of Directors' remuneration would have been 4/5th of that actually charged.

(b) Trading profits are before charging Directors' remuneration, any appropriations or crediting Investment Income.

8. Meredew has owned 500 ordinary shares in Purbeck Ltd. for many years. He had regarded them as valueless until last month (March, 1975) when the company paid a dividend for the first time in 16 years.

The balance sheet of Purbeck Ltd. at 31st December, 1974, was:

	£		£
Issued share capital ..	50,000	Fixed assets	63,500
(£1 Ordinary Shares)		Current assets	70,000
Profit and loss account ..	45,000		
Proposed dividend ..	5,000		
Current liabilities	33,500		
	£133,500		£133,500

The company's profit for the year ended 31st December, 1974, was appropriated as follows:

				£
Net profit for the year				14,000
Dividend				5,000
Retained profit				£9,000

Remuneration of £13,000 for the company's three directors was charged in the calculation of profit.

The company's accounts reveal that the fixed assets were professionally valued as having a realisable value of £90,000 at 30th November, 1974.

There is no evidence to suggest that the current assets would realise any figure different from that shown in the accounts.

Purbeck Ltd. is a private company, and Meredew has heard that similar private companies in the area have recently been sold at values giving an earnings yield of 12½ per cent.

On the London Stock Exchange ordinary shares of public companies in the same industry as Purbeck Ltd. currently have a dividend yield of 5 per cent.

Ignore taxation.

(a) You are required to value the £1 ordinary shares of Purbeck Ltd on:
   (i) Book value basis (balance sheet net assets per share);
   (ii) Liquidation basis (break-up value);
   (iii) Dividend yield basis;
   (iv) Earnings yield basis.

(b) Brief statements expressing one limitation that could apply to each valuation.

9. A few years ago, a relative of yours bought 640 ordinary shares of 25p each in Public Eye Ltd, publishers of magazines and newspapers.

On 24th January, 1975, it was announced in the daily press that an offer had been made for the whole of the ordinary share capital of the company by the Pirate Paper Group Ltd, on the following terms:

Five 'A' non-voting ordinary shares of £1 each and £1·12 nominal of 10 per cent Unsecured Loan Stock, 1997/2002 of the Pirate Paper Group in exchange for every 16 ordinary shares of 25p each in Public Eye Ltd.

Both boards of directors consider that a full merger will be of benefit to both companies and their shareholders.

The relative seeks your advice on this matter. Draft a report to him, indicating whether you recommend acceptance or rejection of the offer, giving reasons for the course of action recommended.

Notes: (1) The 10% Loan Stock is to be valued at par.

(2) Middle market quotations for the ordinary shares of the two companies over the previous six months have been as follows:

		Public Eye Ltd	Pirate Paper Group
August 23rd, 1974	.. ..	70p	£2·60
September 23rd, 1974	..	70p	£2·45
October 23rd, 1974	.. ..	65p	£2·42
November 24th, 1974..	..	70p x.d.	£2·70 x.d.
December 23rd, 1974	..	62p x.d.	£2·64 x.d.
January 23rd, 1975*	.. ..	67p	£2·65
February 23rd, 1975†	..	77p	£2·40

* Last dealing day before the announcement of the proposed merger.
† Last practical date before the posting of the offer document.

(3) Ordinary dividends paid and proposed for each company are as follows:

Public Eye Ltd		%	Pirate Paper Group			%
Year ended			Year ended			
February 28th, 1970	..	20	March 31st 1970			12½
,, ,, 1971	..	21	,, ,, 1971		..	12½
,, ,, 1972	..	21	,, ,, 1972		..	12½
,, ,, 1973	..	18	,, ,, 1973		..	12½
,, ,, 1974	..	18	,, ,, 1974		..	12½
,, ,, 1975	..	18	,, ,, 1975		..	12½
		(forecast)				(forecast)

10. You are the holder of the following shares in Disco Ltd:

(a) 666 Ordinary Shares of 15p each;

(b) 100 £1 8 per cent Cum. Preference Shares;

(c) 400 5 per cent non-cumulative second preference shares of 25p each.

An offer is made by Stereo Ltd to acquire the whole of the issued Share Capital of Disco Ltd on the following terms:

Present Holding in Disco Ltd	Consideration offered:
(a) For every six ordinary shares of 15p each	One ordinary share of 50p each in Stereo Ltd, *plus* 75p, nominal of 8½% unsecured loan stock, 1989–94.
(b) For each 8% Cum. Preference share of £1	110p nominal of the above loan stock
(c) For every four 5% non-cum. Second Preference shares of 25p each	67½p nominal of the above loan stock

In the offer document both companies forecast increases in profits and ordinary dividends for the current year:

Disco proposes to pay 12 per cent (against 11⅜ per cent paid in previous year) while Stereo propose to raise the dividend to 16 (against 15½ per cent paid in previous year).

The day before the announcement of the bid, Disco shares were quoted as follows:

15p Ordinary at 48p;

8 per cent Cum. Preference at 100p;

5 per cent Non-cum. Preference at 14p.

According to the offer document, Stereo Ordinary Shares were last quoted at 286p and it is anticipated that the unsecured loan stock will be worth par.

Prepare a statement showing the expected increase in market value and gross income which might be obtainable upon acceptance of the offer.

11. You are the holder of 200 ordinary shares of 50p each in Switchgear Ltd, bought ten years ago at £1·25 each.

The profits and dividends of Switchgear Limited for the past three years have been as follows:

	Profits before tax	Div. Rate
	£	%
Year to 31st July 1973	806,000	18½
,, ,, ,, ,, 1974	846,000	18½
,, ,, ,, ,, 1975	609,000	18½

The quoted market price of the 50p ordinary shares on the 14th June, 1976 was 252½p.

The very next day, Electrical Components announced that an offer was to be made for the whole of the ordinary share capital of Switchgear Ltd and the terms were subsequently given in the offer document issued three weeks later, viz.

Switchgear Limited
for each 50p Ordinary Share in
Switchgear

Electrical Components
to be exchanged for:
One ordinary share of 25p each
(then quoted at 175p each, the
current dividend rate being 16% p.a.)
plus
£2·55p nominal of 6% Convertible
Unsecured Loan Stock 1993–8
(valued at £110 per cent)

Initially, the offer was rejected by the directors of Switchgear Ltd, who then mounted a spirited defence by forecasting pretax profits of £980,000 for the year ending July 31st, 1976 and promising to pay a final dividend of 23·5 per cent which, together with the interim dividend of 8·5 per cent already paid, would increase the total dividend for 1975/76 to 32 per cent.

This defence led to a higher offer from Electrical Components who increased the proportion of 6 per cent convertible unsecured loan stock in the total offer, from £2·55 nominal to £3·10 nominal (now valued at £111 per cent).

At that point, the merchant bankers advising Switchgear Ltd expressed the opinion that the revised offer was fair and reasonable. The directors therefore left the question of acceptance or rejection of the offer to be decided by the individual shareholders.

State: (a) the expected increase in capital value and income upon acceptance of the revised offer.

(b) your comments about the content and terms of the revised offer, and

(c) whether you would have preferred a cash offer of £5 per share if such an alternative had been available.

12. You are the holder of 100 £1 ordinary shares in Hugon Limited whose shares are officially quoted on the London Stock Exchange. The company has paid dividends on the ordinary share capital as follows:

1972–73=20 per cent   – paid 11th September, 1973
1973–74=22½ per cent – paid 9th September, 1974
1974–75=25 per cent – paid 16th September, 1975

The company anticipates being able to maintain the same rate of dividend as for 1974/75 in the current year according to the directors' report. The ordinary shares were quoted at 525p each on 1st February, 1976.

The very next day, the company unexpectedly received a take-over bid from Convenience Foods Ltd, on the following terms:

For every four Ordinary share of
£1 each in Hugon Ltd

*Consideration offered
in exchange*
Ten Ordinary shares of 25p each
in Convenience Foods Ltd, credited,
as fully paid *plus*
£15 nominal of 5¾% Debenture
Stock, 1993–98 of Convenience
Foods Ltd

Convenience Foods Ltd has previously paid an ordinary dividend of 17½ per cent but forecasts an increase to 18½ per cent for the current year. According to the official offer document dated 23rd February, 1976, their ordinary shares were last quoted at 127½p each. You can assume that the Debenture Stock (yet to be issued) will justify a price of £97·50 per £100 nominal. Before deciding whether or not to accept the offer, you require to know the likely increase in capital value and gross income which might be obtainable. Calculate the required information and also show the percentage increase in capital value and income.

13. In 1970, a public company announced proposals for substituting an equal nominal amount of unsecured loan stock, 1990–1995 bearing interest at the rate of 9·1 per cent, per annum for the existing 1,444,268 7 per cent Cumulative Preference Shares of £1 each.

The company earned profits of £183,816 before charging corporation tax.

Show (1) the annual saving to the company of substituting debt for preference share capital, and

(2) the benefits accruing to the ex-preference shareholders assuming that they accepted and voted for the proposal.

Note: The rate of Corporation Tax applicable to the year 1970 was 45 per cent.

INDEX